CHRISTIANITY THROUGH JEWISH EYES

The Quest for Common Ground

Walter Jacob

HEBREW UNION COLLEGE PRESS

Library of Congress Cataloging in Publication Data

Jacob, Walter, 1930-
   Christianity through Jewish eyes.

   Bibliography: p.
   1. Judaism—Relations—Christianity—History. 2. Chris-
tianity and other religions—Judaism—History. 3. Reform
Judaism—History—Addresses, essays, lectures. I. Title.
BM535.J25   296.3'87'2   74-23451
ISBN 0-87068-257-1

Manufactured In The United States of America

To My Parents ז"ל
With Love and Admiration

Contents

Foreword

The Alumni Association is committed to the publication of works which reflect sound scholarship and are likely to be of special value to colleagues in the congregational rabbinate.

Dr. Jacob's book eminently meets these criteria. He has thoughtfully selected some of the major contributors to a developing dialogue between Judaism and Christianity during the past two centuries. To anyone reflecting on the relation of these two traditions Dr. Jacob's work will prove genuinely helpful.

By this publication we salute a colleague who has managed to combine an active congregational ministry with a fruitful commitment to scholarship. Dr. Jacob is the Rabbi of Rodef Sholom Congregation in Pittsburgh. In addition to sermonic publications, he is the author of "Our Biblical Heritage" and has edited a volume titled "Paths of Faithfulness", and "Essays in Honor of Solomon B. Freehof". He is also the translator and editor of "The First Book of the Bible: Genesis" by Benno Jacob, his learned grandfather.

Dr. Jacob is an active alumnus of Hebrew Union College-Jewish Institute of Religion serving as a Trustee of the Alumni Association, a member of the Board of Governors of the College-Institute, and a member of the Rabbinic Board of Overseers. The Association presents this volume with great pride in a worthy colleague.

Rabbinic Alumni Association
of Hebrew Union College-
Jewish Institute of Religion

Samuel E. Karff
Chairman, Publications Committee

VII

Preface

The Judeo-Christian dialogue is a phenomenon of the last two centuries. Although Judaism and Christianity have existed side by side for nineteen centuries, during much of that time polemic was the only acknowledgment of coexistence. The secularization of modern man and the emancipation of the Jew from his medieval ghetto have brought Judaism and Christianity face to face under new circumstances. Christianity is weaker than ever before, while Judaism and the Jewish people feel a new confidence. As a result, it may now be possible to find a new ground for a common understanding. Both Judaism and Christianity have moved hesitatingly toward this point; this study will discuss the development of the new relationship.

This volume is selective. Many writers of monographs on Christianity have been omitted because it is concerned with the thinkers who have made a major contribution and with that contribution alone; it is not meant as a broad introduction to modern Jewish thought. One could easily assemble a hundred occasional pieces by writers and rabbis, as well as many novels dealing with Christianity, but that was not our purpose.[1] Also omitted are Jewish historians from Jost to Baron who have summarized various Jewish approaches to Christianity.

---

1. For a partial description of these writings, see Gsta Lindeskog, *Die Jesusfrage im Neuzeitlichen Judentum* (Uppsala, 1938); also Sanford Seltzer, "Reactions to Jesus in the Reform Rabbinate" (unpublished thesis, Hebrew Union College, 1959), and Chaim Lieberman, *The Christianity of Scholem Asch* (New York, 1949).

The writers treated in this book have been allowed to speak for themselves through quotations. To a large extent they worked independently without recognizing the labors of their predecessors; few, except the most recent ones among them, cite the writings of any other Jewish scholar in the field. The translations of the quotations are by the author unless otherwise indicated. Other writers have dealt with this subject in a briefer fashion; among them are Lindeskog, Klausner, Schoeps, and Sandmel.

I wish to acknowledge my gratitude to my father, Dr. Ernest I. Jacob, for his suggestions, and to my wife, who has always taken an interest in the progress of this book. Special thanks are also due to my devoted secretary, Mrs. Louise Dickman Marcovsky and to my son Kenny Jacob.

The library of the Hebrew Union College, especially Mr. Herbert C. Zafren, and the library of the Pittsburgh Theological Seminary have been most helpful. The author is grateful to the editors of the *Journal of the Central Conference of American Rabbis,* the *Jewish Quarterly Review,* and *Judaism* for permission to use essays which appeared in those publications in a different form.

1

Introduction

In modern times Jews have broken their silence about Christianity. We need not speculate in this study about the earlier long period of silence. During the Talmudic period, lengthy discussion of Christianity and other religions was consciously avoided. During the Middle Ages, there was some interest in Christianity, but it was dangerous to speak freely about the faith of the persecutor. Recent research by Simon, Blumenkranz, and Katz has shown this literature to be larger than previously thought.[1] For many centuries, the Karaites carried on a polemic discussion on Christianity; perhaps this was because they were more dependent on Scripture than the rabbinic Jews, who were guided by tradition. Despite the new material now assembled, it remains clear that from the time of Jesus to the end of the eighteenth century, there was relatively little interest in Christianity among Jewish thinkers, and that the main expressions of such interest were public disputations and legal statements which classified Christianity as a monotheistic, not a pagan, religion.

This study concerns itself with the Jewish quest in modern times for a common ground with Christianity. Not all Jewish thinkers who concerned themselves with Christianity considered it a friendly spiritual partner; for many it was an irreconcilable rival. Both paths developed within the last two centuries, and while one group sought a genuine relationship with Christianity, even if that would necessitate some changes in Jewish thought, the second group felt that Christianity was a religion of the past. Its historic weaknesses were clear, they believed, and became continually more manifest in modern times. It had no future, especially when compared to the strengths of Judaism, which they saw as much better suited to the needs of modern man.

1

Major thinkers, and a host of minor writers, preachers, and essayists, used the new found freedom from the ghetto as an opportunity to vent their feelings against the religion of the oppressor. This was still dangerous in many lands, but in Western Europe, after Voltaire, almost anything could be said with impunity. Even the reluctant Moses Mendelssohn did not hesitate to express himself frankly once he had begun. The beginnings of this Jewish study of Christianity were rather angry, as if polemic were necessary to arouse interest in the problem and the air had to be cleared before a true discussion could begin.

We must also recognize the Jewish discussion of Christianity as part of the general Jewish struggle to gain equality. The complacency of the Christian majority had to be shaken and Judaism shown to be an equal, if not superior, form of religion. As the rejected religion of the distant past, which had given birth to Christianity, it was viewed as an ancient relic. Aggressiveness was necessary to show that fossilization had not occurred. This effort was directed at both the Christian community and the half-assimilated Jew, who needed proof of the value of his own religion. Nineteenth-century Jewish apologetic was also a reaction against the Hegelian stress on Christianity; Samuel Hirsch used Hegel's methods to demonstrate that Judaism, not Christianity, was the superior religion.

Aside from these general considerations, which played a major role in the Jewish study of Christianity, scholars were attracted by the nineteenth-century excitement about New Testament studies and the life of Jesus. Joseph Salvador and Abraham Geiger were Jewish pioneers in this area. They, and others, could offer unique insights through Jewish literature, which had been ignored by Christian scholarship. Not until this century did the Christian world awaken to the need for studies of first-century Judaism.

Some churchmen, like some Jewish leaders, were anxious to begin a Judeo-Christian dialogue, while many sought practical cooperation outside the field of theology. In joint projects cooperation has been achieved between the liberal wings of both groups. The goal of dialogue and a measure of understanding may seem distant in matters of doctrine, but many churchmen find it useful to work together with Jews on social projects and practical concerns. As the major barriers between the dominant Christian groupings have declined, liberal Christians have sought a reconciliation with Judaism.

In matters of dialogue there has also been considerable hesitation among Jews. They have looked upon such efforts with justified suspicion, remembering that the medieval public debates between Judaism and Christianity had disastrous results for most of the Jewish participants and their communities. Many Jews considered studies of Christianity to be outside the scope of legitimate scholarly effort, and as a result Montefiore and Klausner were vigorously criticized for their writings in this field. It was pleasant for a rabbi to address church groups or good to invite the bishop for a dinner at the synagogue, but steps beyond this were considered taboo.

As we begin our study, we must ask whether it is a fruitful avenue of inquiry. The basic natures of Judaism and Christianity make a mutual appraisal difficult. Both religions are exclusive and proclaim a universal mission. If there is one true revelation, then anyone who holds a different tradition must be wrong, although the nature of his error can be viewed as due to a variety of causes: ignorance, willful stubbornness, and so forth. Much religious thought of the Middle Ages followed this pattern of seeking out the opponent's shortcomings.

Any group that holds such exclusive views can follow two paths in its attitude to the remainder of the world; it can condemn or it can ignore. Until modern times Christianity chose to condemn other religions, attacking them vigorously. Tolerance was impossible, for it would have permitted error to thrive in a world regarded as destined to become Christian. It was Christianity's task to convert all men to the only road to salvation. All methods, from the pen to the sword, were devoted to this task. Many religions succumbed to the assault of Christianity, and with Constantine it became the official religion of the Roman Empire. His successors succeeded in winning much of the world except the Jews. Attempts to convert the Jews through philosophical persuasion and physical force continued through the centuries, but the onslaught was resisted; many died, few converted. Christianity remained intolerant, manifesting this tendency through violence toward the

Jews. The doctrine of exclusiveness was a Jewish heritage, for Judaism, from the earliest times, has considered itself the only true religion. Adopting this doctrine, Christianity expressed it militantly through its strength in the Roman Empire and subsequently in the European states. Christianity's loss of power in modern times has been a major factor in its development of tolerance.

Judaism, on the other hand, expressed its exclusiveness by silently ignoring the new religion through much of the last two millennia. This represented a radical change from the Biblical period, during which erroneous forms of religious life were vigorously attacked through word and deed. The Jewish attitude changed when pagan religions ceased to endanger Judaism. Early Christianity was ignored because it represented no threat to Judaism; in any case, it was a form of monotheism. Later it was dangerous for Jews to express opposition to the powerful official religion.

Despite long periods of persecution, Jewish thought has never surrendered the doctrine that all men will eventually become Jews or at least pure monotheists. Although proselytizing was prohibited in the Christian lands, the goal of the universal conversion remained. Silence continued as the apologetic Jewish attitude till the medieval disputations made it necessary to defend Judaism. If Judaism is right and all other religions wrong, there is nothing to be discussed. This continues to be the modern Orthodox position.

In the last two centuries, however, the Jewish attitude to other religions has changed. This development is almost as revolutionary as the post-Biblical silence, which came after centuries of prophetic attack. The new attitude reflects the altered condition of the Jew in the modern world. Jews have become full participants in Western society. Considerable social and intellectual interchange existed between Jews and Christians throughout the centuries, but it did not often involve serious religious discussion, nor did it touch the masses of Jews and Christians. The two religions influenced each other subtly, but Judaism did not feel challenged by this type of contact.

When Jews began to enter the mainstream of European life at the conclusion of the eighteenth century, Christianity loomed not as a threat but as a temptation; conversion guaranteed economic and social success in areas otherwise closed. Jews faced a Christian society and—like Mendelssohn, for instance—were plainly asked to convert. Thus, they were forced to concern themselves with Christianity and to provide answers for the new way of life. Each generation grappled with both the practical and theoretical implications of the new relationship. Even moderate Orthodox leaders, like Benamozegh, became engaged in open encounter with Christianity.

The Jewish scholars engaged in this area were rarely interested in dialogue; they wished to defend Judaism against the new missionary threat of Christianity, which had appeal as a path, not to heaven, but to economic and social advantage. For Jews on the periphery of Judaism it was convenient to adopt Christianity. Such cynical conversions typify numerous proselytes of the last two centuries, including the great Heine. Scholars arose to defend Judaism from this kind of defection.

Other Jews read the liberal studies of Jesus and noted the caricature of first-century Judaism. Ignorance and academic anti-Semitism led to such imbalanced writing. Beginning with Geiger, Jewish scholars labored to correct such misconceptions. Academic anti-Semitism played a major role, whether cloaked in the philosophy of Hegel and Schelling or in the historical approach of Treitschke. In the United States, Isaac Mayer Wise found a cruder type of prejudice and answered in kind. Only recently have Jews been able to devote themselves to pure scholarship without apologetics. They may not have attained absolute objectivity—indeed, that may be impossible—but at least the effort has been made.

When the Jewish study of Christianity began in the nineteenth century, it was the work of isolated individuals. No school of thought developed. Moreover, most of the scholars involved devoted only a portion of their effort to this field. With the exception of Montefiore, Schoeps, and Sandmel among those discussed in this book, it was not their principal area of study. The influence of the earlier Jewish writers on Christian thought was almost nonexistent; only the more recent writers have aroused some interest and a response from the Christian community. Buber, Baeck, and Rosenzweig attained great stature within the

Jewish community, but this was not achieved by their writings about Christianity, which were usually ignored as an eccentricity that had to be tolerated. Montefiore and Klausner, who wrote at length on Christianity and expressed friendly sentiments, were often suspected of going too far. Montefiore's approach to Christianity was not understood until the end of his life.

Although Jewish interest in the study of Christianity has increased in this century, one cannot speak of a tradition or school in either America or Europe. Sandmel has brought a deeper understanding of early Christianity to the rabbinical students of the Hebrew Union College, but none of them has entered this field of study.

In the early part of the twentieth century, Jewish studies of Christianity in America and Europe demonstrated optimism. Many individuals felt the time had arrived for a genuine relationship between the two religions on both the practical and theoretical levels. Even the beginnings of Nazism did not deter Montefiore, Buber, Rosenzweig, or Schoeps from pursuing this goal. Each continued to seek a deeper appreciation of Christianity, and to introduce Jews to the inner world of Christianity, as far as it can be entered by an outsider. Their efforts at understanding were genuine, yet the Christian reaction was weak. Some belated response and critique came after the Second World War.

Not all Jewish scholars followed this approach; Leo Baeck sought to attain an understanding of Christianity in Jewish terms through reclaiming the Jewish portions of the New Testament for Judaism. This effort led to distortion, but it was an original approach to understanding through the recognition of basic similarities in another religion. This effort, as well as Baeck's more polemic works, was also ignored by most Christian scholars.

More recent Jewish students of Christianity have tried to be objective. One must acknowledge their fairness, but it is doubtful whether they will encourage meaningful dialogue. Though they may succeed in clearing the air, the new atmosphere they create is too aseptic. Their studies are akin to autopsies, which may be useful but tell us little about the living being. Emotion is necessary in dialogue; one must have strong commitment, otherwise the enterprise loses its value.

As we pause to survey the entire field we must wonder why

studies of Christianity have remained peripheral to Jewish life. One must remember that recent history has cast much doubt on all interfaith ventures. The destruction of European Jewry, especially German Jewry, among whom the dialogue had gone farthest, led many to reconsider. If such a catastrophe was possible despite the work of great minds, then the whole venture might be hopeless. More recently, the lack of Christian sympathy for Israel during the crisis of June, 1967, has caused American-Jewish leaders to reevaluate the dialogue on these shores. Perhaps too much energy has been expended in an area that will not lead us forward despite good intentions on the part of a few.

These reservations, now commonly voiced, mean that genuine dialogue will be delayed. Old fears and hesitations among Jews have been reawakened rather than dispelled. The future course of this path has become more uncertain.

Despite these reservations, however, we must realize that dialogue will continue. It will gather momentum as it finds stimulation through the development of the common ecumenical interests of Protestants and Catholics. Some of the feelings so engendered will certainly affect Jewish life whether we wish it or not. Furthermore, we Jews have become assimilated in America; since there are no signs of withdrawal from the general cultural scene on the part of American Jews, the problem of our relationship with non-Jewish neighbors and the nature of that relationship will continue. Even if the older generation feels disillusioned and doubtful, the next will try this path again. Dialogue will remain important for all of us who live in the United States and Western Europe. In other lands it may remain outside the realm of possibility for a considerable length of time.

Most of the writers discussed in this book would have welcomed a response from the Christian community, but it was not forthcoming. Therefore, in their writings we see a series of monologues; even Buber and Baeck witnessed reactions to their writings in this area only toward the end of their lives.

As we look forward to continued and increased dialogue, we must ask about its nature. The writers presented here have shown us a number of possible avenues; none of them has yet been fully explored, and it is hoped that this book will make that task easier.

2

Background of Conflict

For many centuries Jewish discussion of Christianity remained minimal. The comments on Christianity found in Jewish literature may appear impressive when summarized in a brief chapter or assembled in a book, but such excerpts represent material collected from thousands of volumes. It is clear that Christianity did not initially loom large in Jewish thought, and in the early centuries the few discussions were concerned with the definition of the distinction between Judaism and Christianity. Later, when Jewish animosity toward Christianity grew, it was expressed in legends, but even this was never widespread. Persecution and enforced disputations in the Middle Ages made it necessary to discuss and refute Christian doctrine. Finally, the daily relationship between Jews and Gentiles had to be defined in every era for the sake of social and economic intercourse. Relatively little literary effort was expended on these tasks. Interest in the essential differences between Judaism and Christianity did not awaken until emancipation in the eighteenth century forced Judaism to adopt a new approach toward Christianity. Some Jewish concern with Christianity can be traced back to the earliest period of Christian history. The first debates and earliest conflicts are recorded in the Gospels. When allowance for all editorial and theological changes has been made, it remains certain that some Pharisees opposed Jesus both for his method of interpreting Scripture and for his actions. It is also clear that some Sadducees were incensed by Jesus' incursion into the Temple and his arousal of the people against them, and that a Sadducean High Priest tried Jesus on a charge unknown to us. The early sources were colored by later historical developments, but some of the reaction there reflected must have existed, although its true tone was probably mild. These disagreements were part of a general struggle at the time between many divergent Jewish opinions. This was not a conflict between two different religions, but between opinions within Judaism. The bitter terminology of the Gospels reflects the vigorous debate and animosity that stemmed from later Christian disappointment at the Jewish refusal to accept Jesus. Jesus was a Jew, and his views represented one tendency among a people divided into many divergent groups during this period immediately prior to the destruction of the Temple.

Paul's transformation of a small Jewish sect into a new religion met strong Jewish opposition, as is evidenced in the later sections of the New Testament. The theology of Paul was vigorously rejected by Judaism, and Paul was not welcome in the synagogues of the Diaspora. The Jews of the period agreed almost universally that Jesus was not the Messiah; they rejected the concept of Original Sin, upheld the election of Israel, and continued to regard the Law as valid. Thus, Paul's success among the Gentiles was offset by failure among the Jews, and Judeo-Christianity remained a tiny sect destined to vanish without a trace. The Jewish rejection of Jesus and the new religion did not come through his official pronouncements. Rather, the new movement was simply ignored. The first- and second-century Jewish sources did not deem it worthy of mention. Jews rejected early Christianity by remaining Jews and not through vocal opposition to the new path of the disciples of Jesus.

Thus, Josephus and Philo did not mention Jesus—the Jesus passages of Josephus were interpolated by pious Christian scribes during the Middle Ages. Similarly, the Mishnah, which was completed at the beginning of the third century, contains much first-century material but no allusions to Jesus. Several possibly relevant passages in the Tosefta, some Baraitas of the Talmud, and a few Midrashim may stem from the first or second century. However, these passages contain no clear reference to Jesus or Christianity. They speak of "that person" or use other vague terms, which makes it uncertain whether they actually refer to Christianity or to a group within Judaism. The paucity of statements about Jesus and his followers should not surprise us, for many significant events of Jewish history were omitted by the Talmud. The influence of Jesus and his teachings on first-century Judaism was too weak to be noticed. In those centuries of rapid religious, social, and political change, many movements and individuals were soon forgotten.

Both the Palestinean (400 C.E.) and Babylonian (600 C.E.) Talmuds contain stronger reactions to Christianity. The occasional references to Jesus in the later sections of the Talmud indicate that the rabbis knew little about him; they were more concerned with certain aspects of Christian doctrine. Generally, one might state that "the teachers retired into their schools after the destruction of Jerusalem and devoted themselves entirely to the development of the law, . . . and did not concern themselves with movements outside their own sphere."[1] There were, however, some allusions to Christianity, especially in the Midrashic literature, for Jewish exegesis of Scripture denied the foundations of Christian doctrine and rejected the special exegeses of the New Testament, Paul, and the early Church Fathers. The Midrashim gave a Jewish interpretation to the destruction of the Temple, Israel's Exile, the validity of the Covenant, the eternity of the Law, and Israel's mission, as well as various Messianic verses of Scripture. At times it is clear that the writers were seeking to refute Christian doctrine; in other cases the veiled allusions may have been aimed at sectarian tendencies within Judaism rather than at Christianity.

The Jewish reaction to Christianity slowly became stronger, but it was still mild in comparison to the polemics of the Church Fathers or the edicts of early Church councils against Jews. Though Jews were beginning to suffer from Christian persecution, their view of Christianity remained reasonable.

The first bitter attack on Christianity was the *Toledot Yeshu,* compiled in the sixth or seventh century by a member of the dissident Karaite sect. This polemic account of the life of Jesus denied the historical foundations of the Gospels and attacked the basis of Christian theology. Virgin Birth, Messianic claims, the Resurrection, miracles, and other matters were rejected in a spirit of mockery. The *Toledot Yeshu* was the first outspoken Jewish refutation of Christianity, and its hostile tone shows that there was strong animosity between the two religions. Although it was not mentioned by any medieval scholar or philosopher, it enjoyed wide circulation among the general Jewish population. Several other Karaite authors wrote critically of Christianity, but their influence was limited.

In the main Jewish tradition, the Babylonian Saadia Gaon (882–942) was the first to concern himself seriously with Christianity. Saadia, a systematic thinker, dealt with the sectarian Karaites, with Christianity, and also with several contemporary Messianic claimants. He rejected the Trinity, Jesus' claim to be Messiah, the abrogation of the Law, and all anthropomorphic views of God. His rejection of Christianity was logical and used both Scriptural and historical arguments. His defence of Judaism was vigorous and without apologetics.

Later Jewish philosophers also discussed Christianity from the Jewish point of view. The Spaniard Judah Halevi (1080–1145) wrote his *Kuzari* in the form of a dialogue built around the framework of a pagan king's search for the true religion. Halevi presented the Christian views fairly, but stated that the Jews continued to be the chosen people and that God's special revelation to them had not been superseded. He held that Christianity and Islam were preliminary steps designed to prepare mankind for the acceptance of Judaism.

Moses Maimonides, (1135–1204), the greatest Jewish philosopher and legal scholar of the Middle Ages, dealt with Christianity only peripherally. He also felt that Christianity, although contaminated by idolatry, would prepare the world for Judaism, since it acknowledged the Torah even if wrongly interpreting it. "The teachings of the Nazarene and the Ishmaelite serve the divine purpose of preparing the way for the Messiah, who is sent to make the whole world perfect by worshipping God with one spirit, for they have spread the words of the Scriptures and the law of truth over the wide globe" (*Hilkhot Melakhim*). Maimonides' thirteen principles of faith, which constitute a popular summary of Judaism, may have been partially directed against Christianity.

Other Spanish and Near Eastern Jewish thinkers also dealt with Christianity but not at length. The most significant among them was Joseph Albo, who was forced into a disputation before Pope Benedict XIII in 1413. Albo's *Ikkarim* gave a clear philosophical statement of the principles of Judaism, and he often refuted Christian ideas indirectly. In an entire chapter devoted to Christianity, Albo rejected the Virgin Birth, the Trinity, and the Davidic descent of Jesus.

A less systematic approach to Christianity was provided by various Jewish Biblical and Talmudic commentators of the Middle Ages. Rashi, the eleventh-century French exegete, rarely referred to Christianity directly, but he criticized it obliquely by stressing the unity of God and Israel's Messianic expectations. A similar pattern may be found among his followers, the Tosafists, and in the work of the Spaniard Ibn Ezra. Joseph Kimchi (1105–70) of Provence composed a polemic against Christianity in the form of a dialogue. In this work he forcefully rejected the deification of Jesus, as well as the Messianic claims and the miracles of Jesus. Kimchi's son continued the polemic through debate with young Christian scholars. Several medieval authors wrote specifically for Jews who had to defend themselves in public disputations; their books contain numerous references that could be used to deny a Christian interpretation of Scripture. Jewish medieval chroniclers mention many disputations in which Jews acquitted themselves well.

A systematic critique of Christianity by Isaac Troki, a Karaite scholar, appeared in the sixteenth century; at the same time a number of polemic pamphlets also appeared. Troki's *Hizzuk Emunah* remained popular and was widely read till modern times. Troki was well informed about Christianity; he did not mock it, but sought to present a clearly reasoned Jewish position. Jesus was rejected because he was not of Davidic descent, his deeds had not brought peace to the world, and his efforts had not resulted in a universal kingdom—his time was not the "latter days" of the Bible and sin had continued in the world. Troki examined the Biblical verses commonly used by Christians, presenting a Jewish exegesis in opposition, and he offered a powerful critique of the New Testament. His book was the best Jewish presentation of Christianity made during the Middle Ages. It was remarkably free from bitterness, especially when considered in the light of the uninterrupted Christian persecution of Jews; it led to a number of Christian attempts to refute it after a Latin translation was made by Johann Wagenseil in 1665.

Alongside these views the Jewish moral and legal literature also expressed an attitude toward Christianity. These books were not primarily concerned with theology, but with the personal and business relationships between Jews and Christians. The popular moral guide *Sefer Hasidim*, written in the Rhineland communities devastated by the Crusades, advised strict separation between Jew and Christian. Christian doctrine, thought, and custom were despised, and all personal contact was to be avoided. On the other hand, Moses of Coucy, writing in the thirteenth century, felt that Jews should treat Christians as equals. It was the duty of Jews to set a standard of moral excellence for Christians so as to attract them to the true religion. As Jacob Katz pointed out, a change occurred with Menahem Ha-Me'iri, a fourteenth-century Provençal, who gave Christians a positive religious status in Jewish thought. Prior to him Christians had been considered above the level of idolaters but below Jews. Ha-Me'iri felt that Christianity was close to the heights of Judaism, for, despite some misconceptions, it recognized the basic unity of God. Ha-Me'iri was tolerant, and his "positive evaluation of Christianity stemmed in the main from his esteem for the maintenance of legal institutions and moral standards in society."[2] This type of thought continued, becoming a part of all Judaism through Joseph Karo's *Shulhan Arukh*, which has served as the basic guide for Judaism from the sixteenth century to the present day. The *Shulhan Arukh* and its commentaries considered Christianity and Islam monotheistic, as did Maimonides with some reservations earlier.

At the end of the Jewish Middle Ages, friendlier contact between Jews and Christians began in Western Europe, and consequently the animosity between the two religions decreased. In the eighteenth century it was possible for two outstanding representatives of Orthodoxy, Ya'ir Hayyim Bacharach and Jacob Emden, to minimize the distinctions between Judaism and Christianity. Emden "even went so far as to state that Jesus had never intended to abrogate the Torah so far as Jews were concerned, but had wished merely to spread Jewish tenets and the seven Noachide Commandments among non-Jews."[3] These men were interested in establishing a friendlier view of Christianity, but social segregation and the ritual distinctions between Jews and Christians remained untouched. Although they lived at the beginning of the modern era, they did not envision any widespread contact between Jews and Christians. The next century brought Jews and Christians together; this led to new appraisals of Christianity by Jews.

The Jewish reaction to Christianity passed through three stages during the first eighteen centuries. For hundreds of years Christianity was virtually ignored or was only mentioned incidentally. Eventually its history and doctrines were subjected to intense and systematic criticism. Finally it was given some status and recognized as a monotheistic religious path that would prepare the world for Judaism. Jewish interest in Christianity remained peripheral; a paragraph or chapter here and there might be devoted to Christianity, but in the enormous Talmudic and Midrashic literature Christianity was hardly mentioned. The greatest works of later ages also ignored it. Jews have always been a small minority in a vast Gentile world, but Judaism, secure within itself, felt no need to define its relationship with the outer religious world.

Jews lived autonomously during most of these centuries. Consequently, their daily contacts with Gentiles did not touch their religious life in a deep way. The modern world has changed this aspect of Jewish life along with many others, so a new stage in our relationship with Christianity has been reached.

3

Moses Mendelssohn

The Pioneer

Moses Mendelssohn (1729–1786) broke the silence of the medieval period and renewed the possibility of dialogue with Christianity. It was natural that he should do so, for he was the first modern Jew; he stepped forth from the ghetto, but continued to live a thoroughly Orthodox Jewish life in the general society of his age. His emancipation was made possible by the era of enlightenment and by his own gifts of mind and spirit, which forced some recognition from the court and the intelligentsia of Berlin. The path upward had not been easy and he was never free of disability. He knew the suffering of his coreligionists. It was natural that a portion of his life should be spent in fighting for the rights of his oppressed people. He succeeded to a considerable degree both through his literary and personal efforts as well as through his influence upon Lessing, Dohm, and other intellectual leaders who took upon themselves the task of struggling for the Jew.

The non-Jewish world knew Mendelssohn mainly as a leading philosopher of the Enlightenment. His scholarly interests were those of the period—principally aesthetics, psychology, and ethics. There was little specifically Jewish in his writings until his exchange of letters with Lavater and his book *Jerusalem*. *Jerusalem* might never have been written had not Mendelssohn, in 1769, been challenged to convert by a Swiss theologian, Johann Casper Lavater. The strict dichotomy between Mendelssohn's philosophical writings as well as those intended for Christians and those directed toward Jews becomes clear when it is realized that

the former were composed in German while many of the latter were
in Hebrew. A good portion of his work was an apologia for
Judaism and a plea for tolerance; in this way he began the modern
dialogue. Yet he remained cautious in approach, and he was wary
of "tolerance" that only veiled a new missionary effort to convert
the Jews.[1]

The famous challenge from Lavater formed an introduction to a
translation of portions of Bonnet's *Palingenesie,* a popular defense
and justification of Christianity. Lavater asked that Mendelssohn
read the piece, and "publicly refute the fundamental arguments
upon which the basis of Christianity rests if he were not in
agreement with it. However, if he found them right, then he ought
to do what wisdom, love of truth, and sincerity demanded";[2] in
other words, convert. Mendelssohn had no alternative but to
defend himself. In so doing he worked out a philosophy of Judaism
appropriate to his system of thought; he also began his critical
dialogue with Christianity.

Mendelssohn was loath to enter this type of public discussion.
He reminded Lavater of previous conversations: "You could
hardly have forgotten how often I sought to shift the conversation
from religious themes to more casual ones."[3] Furthermore, it had
been agreed that such conversations would never be quoted and
would remain absolutely private. The remainder of his first
response was an attempt politely to extricate himself from entering
into dialogue and from commenting on Christianity. He had
thought about his own religion critically for many years, he said,
and would have abandoned it long before had he not been
convinced of its validity and spiritual strength.

The whole affair might have ended there, but Lavater printed
portions of Mendelssohn's reply, with significant omissions. This
forced Mendelssohn to continue the debate, which he did in an
essay eventually printed together with one by Lavater. Finally
Mendelssohn wrote the notes for a thorough critique of
Christianity in *Gegenbetrachtungen über Bonnet's Palingenesie,* but
he did not publish or complete this work for reasons of health and
because he did not wish to awaken the storm it might have caused.
He did correspond extensively with Bonnet. The controversy was
continued to some extent in *Jerusalem.* Other thoughts on

Christianity were expressed in a long epistle to Crown Prince von Braunschweig-Wolfenbüttel and in a number of additional letters and essays. The total number of pieces concerned with Christianity remained small, and the discussion of Christianity never touched more than a few elements of that religion.

There is little doubt that part of Mendelssohn's hesitancy was brought about by fear for the uncertain political situation of his fellow Jews. He did not wish to arouse new opposition; at the same time he wanted to remove an old Christian fear that the Jews had some secret knowledge of Jesus and his age which they kept to themselves: "I am very well provided with formidable weapons, wherewith to combat that religion, if I were so inclined; . . . I herewith affirm before the public, that I have, at least, nothing new to bring forward against the faith of the Christians; that, for ought I know, we are acquainted with no other accounts of the historical facts, and can produce no other records than those which are universally known."[4] Mendelssohn admitted willingly enough that certain slanders about Christianity were widespread among Jews, though they were not as frequent as those among the Christian majority about Judaism. It could hardly be otherwise. "As long as those who were powerful still spilled blood in behalf of religion, those who were weak had no alternative but . . . to snap their fingers in their pockets, that is, to slander the religion of their opponents behind closed doors. As the mood of persecution has weakened on the one side, so has hatred given way to gratitude on the other; now it is the duty of all *good* people to consign the old discords to oblivion."[5]

He reiterated his high respect for Christianity and for those who followed its teachings, and he berated Lavater for being astonished at this. "Let the Almighty Creator, to whom all of us pray, be my witness that I do not wish to make any statements which might trouble some innocent soul, even if they were to burn on my tongue like glowing coals. Let Him be my witness that I have the greatest respect for the numerous great and honorable men who acknowledge these teachings as divine."[6] Naturally, he continued, the words and thoughts of men whom he respected could not keep him from reaching quite different conclusions on religious matters.

The newspapers of the day make it clear that a majority found

Mendelssohn's reluctance praiseworthy; some rather openly attacked Lavater for having begun the controversy. A good many followed it closely.[7]

Mendelssohn quite often dealt with the figure of Jesus. He was willing to recognize him as a special person, but when Lavater published this fact without Mendelssohn's qualifying remarks, Lavater was reminded that such statements had been made with strong reservations, which he had chosen to omit. If Christians believe this man was a prophet, so be it, said Mendelssohn. Nothing in such a belief contradicts Judaism as long as Jesus did not teach contrary to the words of God or common sense. The only question remaining concerns Jesus' status when compared to Moses. "Whether he was greater than Moses or not, is certainly not a matter of dogma on either side."[8] Naturally, the Christian claim that Jesus was the Messiah was discussed and denied. Mendelssohn was unable to understand how any Christian could believe that Jesus had come to abrogate the laws of Moses. "This founder of the faith never declares in any specific statement made in the name of God that he intended to abrogate any portion of the laws. We are supposed to conclude this from vague phrases and acts. This God who proclaimed His laws, with numerous public preparations, to an entire people through an extraordinary emissary, shall this God now quietly abrogate these same laws without any specific declaration, but so to speak by tacit agreement? That is inconceivable!"[9]

As far as the death of Jesus was concerned, Mendelssohn attempted no defense of the Jews of that era nor did he try to lay the blame elsewhere. "How should I know what my ancestors in Jerusalem seventeen or eighteen hundred years ago, considered just or unjust verdicts? I would be very hardpressed if I felt obliged to vouch for all the verdicts which for example are handed down by the royal high court here, during my own time. Moreover, on our part we possess no reliable account, no official document, and no reports of that great event which we can set against yours. . . . How can we form such definite judgments upon a question about which we know so little?"[10] He did not deal with the person of Jesus or his disciples further and felt no need to treat the early or late figures of Christianity in detail; he concerned himself primarily with certain basic Christian doctrines, which Judaism forced him to reject.

Much of Christianity rests upon miracles. Mendelssohn did not see how miracles could prove any faith. All religions possess miracle tales. They convince the believer and have no meaning for those outside the fold. "The Jewish, Christian, and Mohammedan miracles oppose one another. . . . By what criteria are we to distinguish truth from error, in a matter of such importance."[11] He took a similar position on proof from revelation. "So far as every revelation supposes an historical fact, the force of that revelation can be substantiated no otherwise than by Tradition, Testimonies, and Monuments. There we agree. But you, Sir, with other apologists of Christianity, receive miracles as an infallable criterion of truth, and believe that when there appears to be credible evidence of a prophet's having performed miracles, there can be no longer any doubt of the divineness of this mission; whence you demonstrate, indeed, by very sound logic, that there is nothing impossible in miracles; and that the testimony of miracles may also deserve belief. It was of that argument that I said, one may defend with it any religion one pleases. Do you think, Sir, that we can produce no testimonies of amazing miracles wrought by extraordinary men of our nation, long after the times of Jesus of Nazareth? Those testimonies are held, at least by us, as authentic and venerable as you hold yours. Here, then, are testimonies against testimonies."[12] On the basis of miracles there is little choice among religions. However, Mendelssohn credited Judaism with an additional distinction: "I believe that Judaism knows nothing of a revealed religion, in the sense in which it is taken by Christians. The Israelites have a divine legislation: laws, judgments, statutes, rules of life, information of the will of God, and lessons how to conduct themselves in order to attain both temporal and spiritual happiness: those laws, commandments, etc., were revealed to them through Moses, in a miraculous and supernatural manner; but no dogmas, no saving truths, no general self-evident positions. Those the Lord always reveals to us, the same as to the rest of mankind, by *nature and by events*, but never in *words* or *written characters*."[13] Mendelssohn drew the logical conclusion: "I, therefore, do not believe that the resources of human reason are inadequate to the persuading of mankind of the eternal truths requisite for their happiness; and that God has need to reveal them to them in a preternatural manner. They who maintain this, deny the omnipotence or the goodness of God. . . . He was, in their opinion, good enough to reveal to mankind the truths on which their happiness depends; but He was neither omnipotent nor good enough to grant to them the faculties of discovering them themselves. . . . According to the notions of true Judaism, all the inhabitants of the earth are called to happiness; and the means thereof are as extensive as the human race itself; as liberally dispensed as the means of preventing hunger and other natural wants."[14] Of course, there are also false prophets in the Bible who managed to produce great miracles, so the notion of the miraculous must be rejected as religious proof. Even if someone came along and performed miracles directly before us, it would prove nothing about the validity of his teachings. This discussion was of importance to Mendelssohn, and he emphasized it again in his long letter to von Braunschweig-Wolfenbüttel. Judaism is based on natural law and revealed ceremonies, so it is superfluous to associate miracles with it.

Mendelssohn also dealt with the supposed Biblical proof texts for the New Testament. He found that they proved nothing. "How insufferably wretched would the fate of man be if the eternal solution of all mankind were dependent upon the exegesis of obscure passages in a book written in Asia in times long gone by, in a strange and now dead language, and for a specific people!"[15] He found the exegesis of theologians generally forced or incorrect. If one granted the possibility of some of this exegesis and let it serve as the basis for discussion: "God have mercy on my soul! I cannot possibly decipher the basis of my eternal salvation out of the questionable dreams of Daniel nor can I derive it from the lofty poetry of a prophet. These texts are intended to awaken the heart and were not composed for the instruction of the mind."[16] Nor could he understand a theory of salvation that excluded the largest portion of mankind for so long; the people of India, for example, had to wait until someone sent them a priest with the proper revelation in order to attain it.[17] Mendelssohn felt that all people can attain salvation through their own ethics and religion. Israel's unique possession is a specially revealed Law, which is valid only for them and is meant to lead them to their salvation. In short the entire thought pattern of Christianity may be convincing and believable to a Christian; it may be utilized by Christian thinkers as the basis for complete systems of philosophy; but it remains unconvincing to a Jew.

This attitude explains Judaism's reluctance to missionize. There are many ways to salvation. The especially revealed Law of Judaism is meant for Jews; it is their ceremonial law. Efforts at conversion and religious controversy only bring increased hatred and misunderstanding. "As I have now been publicly challenged it is incumbent upon me to express myself publicly, but I call upon God as witness that I do so most reluctantly and that I would never have taken such liberties on my own account. I hate all religious disputes and especially those which are conducted in public. Experience has taught me that they are useless; they engender more hate than enlightenment."[18]

Mendelssohn resented the continual attacks upon Judaism and constantly reminded his world: "Now Christianity, you know, is built on Judaism, and when it falls down, the former must necessarily become a heap of ruins with it. You say, my conclusions undermine the foundations of Judaism, and you proffer me, for safety, your upper story. Must I suppose that you are mocking me? When there is the appearance of a contradiction between one truth and another, between Scripture and reason, a Christian, in earnest about 'right and light,' will not challenge a Jew to a controversy, but conjointly, with him, seek to discover the groundlessness of the discrepancy. Both their causes are concerned in it. Whatever else they have to settle between themselves may be deferred to another time. For the present, they must use their joint endeavors to avert the danger, and either discover the false conclusions, or show that it was nothing but a paradox which frightened them."[19]

Despite the strong arguments he advanced and his strong desire to defend Judaism adequately, Mendelssohn felt it appropriate to stress the common ground. Quarrels between Judaism and Christianity merely lead to the general weakening of religion: "It is unbecoming for one of us, openly to defy one another, and thereby furnish diversion to the idle, scandal to the simple, and malicious exultation to the revilers of truth and virtue. Were we to analyze our aggregate stock of knowledge, we certainly shall concur in so many important truths, that I venture to say few individuals of one and the same religious persuasion would more harmonize in thinking. A point here and there, on which perhaps, we still divide, might be adjourned for some ages longer, without detriment to the welfare of the human race. The truths which we jointly admit have not yet been preached so widely that we may expect any material benefit will arise to the good cause, from the final decision of those debatable questions. . . . What a world of bliss we should live in, did all men adopt the true principles, which the best amongst the Christians and the best amongst the Jews have in common! You will easily imagine, that with such sentiments, my talents as a polemicist cannot be of the first order."[20]

The external forms of religion are for a given age and a certain set of circumstances, Mendelssohn maintained. Thus he always held that "no external religion can be universal; and that by making proselytes, I am extending the religion of my forefathers, beyond the boundaries originally prescribed to it."[21]

Mendelssohn himself had been understanding all his life, as shown by a much earlier letter to Lavater. "I readily and most cordially concur in what you say of the morality of the New Testament. I fully believe that Jesus himself did not teach, by a good deal, what Christian Rabbins have been preaching in his name for so many ages; for the sake of which they so frequently butchered people, and, now and then, were butchered themselves.

"Christianity like yours, Sir, if universally adopted would transform our earth into a Paradise. And in so important a business, who would carp at a name? Shall the purest system of Ethics be called Christianity? Why not, if that answer any good purpose? But this Christianity is actually an invisible church consisting of Jews, Mohammedans, and Chinese, in which Greeks and Romans must principally be counted."[22]

Although it was the letter of Lavater that set in motion Mendelssohn's response to Christianity, there were other attempts to convert this leading Jewish thinker. *Jerusalem* was a reply to such an effort in an anonymous pamphlet. Though Mendelssohn probably did not know the identity of the author (Sonnefels of Vienna), he felt obliged to answer it.[23] The major focus of *Jerusalem* was not the nature of Christianity but the respective functions of Church and State and an attempt to show how Judaism fits within these limits.

The long correspondence with Lavater attracted much public attention and was eagerly followed by Christian intellectuals. Many joined the side of Mendelssohn. The immediate effect was a heightened interest in the emancipation of the Jews. The long-range effect was the beginning of the Jewish-Christian dialogue.

4

Joseph Salvador

The First Modern Jewish Life of Jesus

Pioneers are often forgotten; those who begin new avenues of study in Jewish areas are no exception. Thus few today remember Joseph Salvador (1796–1873), who was one of the first to undertake a serious evaluation of Christianity from a Jewish point of view. Salvador, professionally trained as a doctor, was a French Jew of Sephardic ancestry. He had a Catholic mother and one brother who was married to a Huguenot, but he remained loyal to Judaism and devoted himself to interpreting Judaism and Jewish history in the spirit of nineteenth-century rationalism.

Salvador's interest in Judaism was aroused by the anti-Semitic riots in Germany in 1819, which were motivated by the desire to reimpose medieval disabilities on the Jews. In his two earliest works,[1] he depicted Moses as the founder of the first republic and of a perfect social order in ancient Israel, claiming that these achievements entitled Jews, not only to rights, but to a place of honor in democratic societies. Subsequently Salvador was a center of controversy in the French political struggle between the constitutionalists and the clerics. His works, once influential, have been largely neglected in this century.

Salvador sought to interpret Judaism historically, rationally, and as adaptable to modern times; he applied the same standards to Christianity and was remarkably successful so long as his efforts were limited to the beginning stages of the Christian religion. He is especially noteworthy as being one of the earliest scholars, Jewish or Christian, to portray Jesus in a first-century Jewish setting. His pioneering effort in this vein, a lengthy life of Jesus, appeared in France and was soon translated into German.[2] With this volume one may date the beginning of the systematic modern Jewish study of Christianity.

In this book Salvador emphasized the historical background of the Gospels, thus opposing the romanticism of mid-nineteenth-century Christian studies of Jesus. Even those who agreed with his point of view, however, felt he would have been more successful if he were better acquainted with the sources and able to analyze the texts thoroughly. Renan, who described Salvador's later *Paris, Rome, Jerusalem* as "one of the most original books about religious questions to appear in years," and lauded him as "the first critic of the legendary Jesus in France," called attention to his lack of deeper knowledge.[3] Isidore Cohen, editor of the *Archives Israélites,* noted Salvador's similar weakness in Talmud and later Jewish sources, as did others.[4]

Salvador realized that his studies would arouse controversy, as had his earlier chapter on the trial of Jesus, which had been vigorously attacked in 1828. Never reluctant about public controversy, he can be regarded as a French counterpart of Isaac Mayer Wise, the pioneer American Reform rabbi, who somewhat later in the United States expressed himself even more forcefully on the subject of Christianity, and remained undaunted when attacked by both the non-Jewish and Jewish communities in Albany, where he held a pulpit for several years.

In the preface to his book on Jesus, Salvador stated his desire to be impartial, asserting that he only wished to show early Christianity in the light of historical research. "The first book shall be dedicated to an exposition of the favorable circumstances which led to the formation of Christianity; it is an introduction which shall concern itself with these questions in its three chapters: the earliest historical origin and respective position of various nations at the time of the arrival of the son of Mary; . . . to discover the nature of the pattern whose most significant result was Christianity. Further to determine the condition of the intellectual and spiritual position of the upper and lower classes of the Oriental and Greek people. Finally to discover all the indispensable details of the land which was the cradle of Christianity, to which it owes its first plans, its early apostles, and its first language; and to ascertain as well the difference among the various Hebrew schools of thought which were diffused in Judea as well as the Diaspora." After the elements of Christianity had been clearly portrayed, their combination in the life and teachings of Jesus was to be shown. Finally Salvador intended to demonstrate that the struggle among the apostles eventually led to the development of Christian doctrine and the Church.[5] In the book, Salvador divided early Christian ideas in a way that was to become classic in Jewish studies. He traced the ethical elements to Judaism and the impurities to pagan sources. The twentieth-century scholar Leo Baeck developed this theme to the ultimate degree in his essay "Romantic Religion" and in his reconstruction of the original Gospel.

Salvador's method and conclusions were vehemently attacked, especially by the Catholic conservative press. He was accused of atheism, pantheism, and humanism. An exchange of letters with the editor of the *Gazette de France* in 1838 was followed by many similar conflicts.[6] Yet many critics, including de Sacy and Gruzat, acknowledged his efforts despite their disagreement with the results.[7]

Salvador considered the Gospel of Matthew to be the best and earliest source, and held that John represented the third and last stage in the development of early Christianity.[8] He did not undertake a detached analysis of the New Testament texts, as did his German contemporary, Strauss. Rather, he began by asking whether Jesus had ever existed or was a creation of fantasy. He concluded that a real figure was revealed by the Gospels despite their contradictions and that the theory of a fictitious Jesus contained too many improbabilities. The silence of Jewish tradition and the fact that none of our sources is contemporary should not be regarded as an obstacle; the oral tradition of Christianity can be considered reliable, just as the Jewish oral tradition of that age seems accurate. Jesus should be accepted as a historical figure. The legendary material enshrouding accounts of his life parallels that of other folk heroes and can be readily removed.[9]

One might claim that Salvador stood between Strauss and Renan in the nineteenth-century study of Jesus. He did not follow the precise analysis of Strauss, which almost eliminated any picture of Jesus. On the other hand, unlike Renan, he did not present a romantic Jesus. Salvador wished to look at Jesus rationally and see him as a part of first-century Jewish life. His position influenced Renan, and his early works about Moses and Jewish institutions provided material that Renan used.[10]

Salvador began by questioning the doctrine of Immaculate Conception. Was there any foundation to the rumors of illegitimacy? Here Salvador discussed the few facts known about Joseph, the relationship of Jesus with his mother, Mary, as well as the circumstances of their early visit to Egypt.[11] Whatever may have occurred, Salvador felt, the couple left for Egypt to escape the rumors. He eliminated all Messianic elements of the story as obvious additions, also peeling away the legendary layer with its adoring kings and star of Bethlehem.[12] In this way he sought to reconstruct a simple, rational life.

Salvador was also concerned with determining the elements of Christianity to be ascribed to Jesus and those marking an earlier contribution by John the Baptist. He felt that John had successfully combined some of the best elements of the divergent Jewish schools and saw him as functioning entirely within the Jewish community: "So the foundation of a new Jewish school was undertaken; it developed from the union of the genuine, but diffident Essene morality with the keen missionary zeal of the Pharisees." Similar to the other teachings of that period it sought to lead toward the perfection of the Messianic Age.[13] The simple teachings of John the Baptist were later invested with a new spirit by Jesus. "In the person of Jesus a new combination was formed; it joined the moral elements of the land of Israel with the highest form of the Oriental doctrine of resurrection, which the captive tribes had brought with them from Babylonia and Persia." Jesus personified the prophecies and hopes of Scripture and through resurrection transferred them to the next world.[14] This meant that he borrowed much from the Pharisees and made it his own. With this mixture he soon won some converts away from them.[15] "The peculiarity of these thoughts lies in the extreme expression given this amalgam of the holy records of the Jews and the new beliefs brought from Babylon and Persia; this amalgamation had continued through several centuries. It was the new method which, when joined to the moral law for a long or short period of time, should enable it to reach its goal more speedily. This also explains the Platonic and other modifications of thought which the promoters of Christianity felt they had to bring into the doctrine of their founder. Finally, the peculiarity of the thought required the death of Jesus. From the beginning the son of Mary was obsessed by the need to die; he eagerly sought death and calmly accepted it."[16] Contrary to other Jewish scholars, Salvador traced the separation of Christianity and Judaism to the lifetime of Jesus. It began with Jesus; his disciples merely widened the breach.

Salvador considered the antagonism between Jesus and the Pharisees to be historical, not a later addition. The Pharisees deserve applause for the freedom they permitted Jesus. "Despite the unfavorable family situation of Jesus when seen in the light of morality or prejudice, Jesus was permitted three long years of absolutely undisturbed freedom. According to the testimony of his own chroniclers, he wandered freely through the land, spoke, preached, and sought to defeat his opponents everywhere—in the cities, in the countryside, in the Pharisaic synagogues, and even in the very precincts of the Temple. This has been so reported although the Pharisees have been portrayed in the darkest colors, although their hatred, scorn, and desire for the death of the new teacher have been vastly exaggerated." Subsequently, when Jesus extended his teachings and committed blasphemy, as this was defined by Pharisaic doctrine, he must have understood the dangers involved and realized that the penalty might be death.[17] Yet his death must be viewed as a part of his destiny from the very beginning; later it was the fundamental pillar of the new religion. "The historic and continuing guiding principle of the activities and statements of Mary's son remains his death. He had contemplated it far in advance. . . . It led to the quick success of his promises among the foreign masses."[18] Death was not an incidental aspect of the life of Jesus, but the main event in the existence of this man who considered himself the Messiah.

The trial of Jesus was twice discussed thoroughly by Salvador. He described the events and the Jewish involvement, concluding that the verdict of the tribunal was justified since Jesus had been guilty of blasphemy.[19] The details of the trial had become confused in the Gospel tradition, he felt, but in essence the trial and the sentence were proper; the execution, of course, was left to the Romans, who alone had the legal power to do so. Moreover, they had their own suspicions about Jesus.[20] The political implications of Jesus' activities were recognized by the Roman governor, who found execution an easy solution.[21] In contrast to many other Jewish writers from Mendelssohn to the present, Salvador did not gloss over the final episode of Jesus' life, nor did he seek to excuse the Jewish court, for he felt that justice had been done. Jesus' life demanded such a death; otherwise it would have been meaningless. Jesus had failed in his original intention. "It is certain that the personal plan of the son of Mary failed; he wished through his words to unite the different schools of the Hebrew people. He sought to articulate their hopes in the dogma expressed by him, but neither before nor after his death was this realized. His struggle with Pharisaism was never crowned by a decisive victory."[22] As a result, the apostles of Jesus concentrated on spreading his teachings outside the realm of Judaism. The death of Jesus and his resurrection marked the final separation from Judaism.[23] As the figure of Jesus developed and was changed from a historical personality to a symbol, it drifted farther from Judaism and began to appeal more to the pagan mind.[24] "It could then be readily predicted how the person of Jesus would assume the characteristics of mythology; it could happen through a sudden twist of the poetic and symbolic expression of the Hebrews when influenced by the mysticism and the dogma of resurrection brought from the Orient."[25] This change had not occurred during the lifetime of Jesus, but the tendency already existed.

The new teachings sought to combine the most appealing aspects of Judaism with certain pagan elements that would interest the population of the Near East. Jesus' heavy borrowing from Judaism was made clear in Salvador's analysis of the Sermon on the Mount, the earliest by a Jewish scholar. Later Claude Montefiore and others were to continue with much more detailed analyses. Hardly a single commandment has been attributed to the individual inspiration of Jesus which does not stem from Jewish ethical

teachings; this is true both in idea and form.''[26] The distinction in
the ethics lies in Judaism's emphasis on society and Jesus' stress
on the individual. This, too, is a distinction frequently emphasized
by later Jewish students of Christianity. Salvador did not agree
with those who sought to mark the distinction by characterizing
only the strengths of one system and the weaknesses of the other;
such attacks had come only from Christian quarters—this was a
defense of Judaism.

Jesus' emphasis on the next world and his rejection of this world
reflect one aspect of first-century Judaism, but Jesus carried it to
an extreme. "The concern of his effect, his life, and his soul did
not rest upon the freedom or the positive, happy aspects of this
world; in his eyes those remained the special realm of Satan. This
world was an old, vanishing phantom, which would have to be
replaced by a new creation.''[27] Salvador pointed to the effect these
teachings had on Christianity's role in the world. "In this spirit the
life of man was removed from the natural realities of this world and
it concentrated upon the most glowing fantasies of the imagination
and the heart. They were to provide complete nourishment for
everything, especially for personal anxieties and hopes.''[28]
Christianity remained forever weak as a social and ethical force. It
never recovered from its emphasis on the individual and its
negation of this world, and it was also ineffective in the
nineteenth-century world despite its influence in the political
upheavals which had occurred. This was discussed at some length
in Salvador's last book, *Paris, Rome, Jerusalem*, which dealt with
the problem of contemporary Christianity; in the title *Paris*
represented the Revolution (1789–1815), *Rome* the Reaction
(1815–1848), and—since both had failed modern man—*Jerusalem*
the future, with the entrance of Judaism into world history.
Through the fusion of the spirituality of Rome, the civilization of
Paris, and the spirit of Biblical Judaism, a new culture would be
produced. Judaism would decisively influence history; it would be
the climax of world religious life. Though he shared the dream of
Jerusalem reborn with Moses Hess, with whom he corresponded,
Salvador gave the nationalistic impulse universal meaning. In this
he was more akin to Formstecher, Hirsch, Steinheim, and Wise,
who all considered Judaism the religion of the future.

Continuing the analysis of the evolution of Christianity, Salvador demonstrated that the apostles added many pagan elements to the teachings of Jesus in an effort to adapt the religion to the Oriental environment. This second phase of Christianity owed part of its development to Peter, but was primarily formed by Paul. "The convictions of this last apostle immediately attained such distinctive features that all the following events must be reckoned as part of his own life-story."[29] Salvador agreed with many scholars in assigning Paul paramount influence in the development of Christianity. "Paul was a many-sided, cultured man who became the leader of the second phase, or the second school, of Christianity. The symbol of Jesus Christ left the national sphere to serve broader society through its personification. This was done at his command. After a long struggle with the Christians of the first school and with practically all the apostles, including Peter, he forced them to abandon the point of view of the Synagogue and the Jewish schools. He induced them to establish a separate entity, the Church. In this way the division of the Jewish people into two parts occurred; they became Jews and Christians. So Paul, who possessed the greatest amount of energy, guaranteed the means by which the Eastern nations would be offered the new belief. Who knows whether in the light of historical reality his influence upon the success of Christianity was not proportionally greater than that of its original founder?"[30] Salvador traced the travels of Paul with some thoroughness. Describing in detail the innovations that Paul made in Christian doctrine, he discussed the Pauline attitude to the Law, the idea of Original Sin, and other matters, concluding that all these changes served to attract pagans. The old Jewish effort to gain converts had been reemphasized by the Pharisees, but despite their successes they were unable to overcome some obstacles.[31] Through Paul's work, however, Christianity became a missionary religion.

The last phase of the early Church was represented by the apostle John, in whom Salvador saw the final poetic form of the new Christianity. "Paul made a new Adam of Jesus. . . . The apostle John evoked another figure . . . that of the heavenly. Adam, a figure through which the doctrine of the Trinity would be further enhanced. . . . From that moment on the apostle saw

something completely different from a moral force or a moral type
in his teacher. He was more than a living instrument of wisdom
through which society would be improved, or who would provide
specific laws to improve the discernment of the conscience. His
Gospel recognized in the son of Mary the immediate cause and
creator of the world."[32] This third stage led to the final division
between Judaism and Christianity.

Salvador recognized and appreciated the strength of Christianity
and its successful introduction of Jewish ideas into the world.
Therein lay its power and incidentally also the power of Islam;[33]
yet each religion, through conquests and the amalgamation of
foreign ideas, had lost many of the positive characteristics of
Judaism. Salvador criticized this aspect of Christianity severely.
"With regard to the unity of God, which his teaching proclaims, all
the errors of polytheism are hallowed by it. In respect to religious
equality, of which it has been very proud, one must point out that
the inequality of castes has been vastly increased. Poverty, which
is no less terrible for the moral than for the physical man, has had
innumerable apologists who have spoken from its altars heaped
with gold and riches. The right of the personal will of the people
has disappeared." Its power to influence mankind was gone. In the
future Christianity would, however, help to bring about a new
philosophical religion which would refuse to forsake purity for
mass appeal. It would not precisely be Judaism, but would closely
resemble Judaism.[34] As previously indicated, this thought was
shared by many contemporary Jewish thinkers.

Joseph Salvador has been largely forgotten in this century, but
his influence in the mid-nineteenth century must not be underestimated. His works were widely read in France, Italy, Germany,
and England; they were the center of stormy religious discussions.
The second and third editions of this work, the translations of
his main works into German, and the critical acclaim he received
in England, show his influence in the world of Christian
scholarship.[35] His views were analyzed in numerous essays.
Moreover, the very fact that an entire book was devoted to an
examination of the ideas of Salvador, Gibbon, and Strauss,[36]
setting Salvador on a par with these two well-known giants of the
period, gives an idea of how he was regarded in his own time.

Thus, although Salvador played a minor part in the nineteenth-century reconstruction of the life of Jesus, it was considerably more important than attributed to him by Schweitzer, who cited him only once (and then erroneously as Salvator) in a footnote.[37]

Salvador's lasting contribution was his clear and detailed account of the life of Jesus as seen through the eyes of a modern Jewish writer. He was the first modern Jew to concern himself with a historical investigation of early Christianity, but he was to be followed by other Jewish writers who shared his analysis of Christianity as the religion of the past and also saw some form of Judaism as the religion of the future.

Salvador had a sympathetic understanding of the early form of Christianity but not of its later development as a world religion. By nature aggressive, he forced recognition from the scholarly world and did not pass unnoticed, as did so many of his German contemporaries.

5

Elijah Benamozegh

Orthodox Critic

In the nineteenth century, the largest European Jewish communities were in Central and Eastern Europe, so most scholarly endeavor came from those areas. However, the Jews of France, Italy, and England also made contributions to Jewish learning and to a Jewish understanding of Christianity. Elijah Benamozegh (1823–1900), an Italian rabbi and director of the rabbinical seminary in Leghorn, was the Italian spokesman for Judaism. In contrast to most Jewish scholars who concerned themselves with Christianity, he was Orthodox and an energetic opponent of Liberal Judaism.

Since Benamozegh's principal works dealt with a reinterpretation of ethics, he sought to compare Christian and Jewish ethics, rather than concerning himself, like most other Jewish scholars, with the early development of Christianity. In this he was a pioneer. He set the stage for modern Jewish encounters with Christian thinkers. His main work may be considered a mild polemic, for he wished in it to show the superiority of Jewish ethics and demonstrate Christianity's debt to Judaism. Nonetheless, he recognized the achievements of Christianity and attempted a fair appraisal.

The strength and appeal of Christianity, according to Benamozegh, rests on its ethical system, which he considered the most important factor in its success in ancient and modern times.[1] Naturally Christianity should pride itself on this contribution to mankind, but it had turned pride to conceit. After all, numerous passages in the classical philosophers and the sacred writings of the pagan East matched the most sublime passages of the Gospels. In these instances, however, Christianity might still claim the superiority of sustained power and purity, for it has exercised greater influence over men than any other philosophy or religion. Benamozegh limited himself to a defense against Christianity's assertion of superiority over Judaism. "Without justice and fairness, even without logic, its morality has been declared to excel that of Judaism. Christianity itself, with a lack of consistency which will soon become apparent and with considerable prejudice, has given free rein to its prejudice and has allowed itself to become affected by these intoxicating perfumes."[2] Benamozegh's book, without underestimating Christianity's contribution to civilization, was a response to claims of Christian superiority.

Benamozegh sought through analysis to discover the basis for Christianity's feeling of superiority. This feeling, he asserted, cannot be established on the basis of divine revelation since the Mosaic Law is divine; nor is it conceivable that God should reject one form of morality for another. Also, we cannot accept Marcion's idea of two divine systems conflicting with each other. If God were to reject one system for the other, then God would not be perfect. Rather, unless one revelation is based upon its predecessor, the entire concept of revelation becomes senseless. Benamozegh countered the argument that the second revelation demonstrated the slow evolution of man toward perfection by the need for an eternally perfect standard by which he can measure himself. "Otherwise we would labor with motion, which has neither beginning nor end; we would possess aspiration without a goal. We would work without a plan, a model, or an ideal."[3] Benamozegh continued with the thought that if one revelation replaced another, it would be equally possible for a third to replace the second. Once the process had begun, it could reasonably be expected to continue. This would justify Protestantism or any other movement within or outside Christianity.[4] In other words, the Christian argument is fraught with danger for Christianity itself.

Benamozegh discussed the different interpretations of revelation in the two religions, criticizing Christianity sharply for its emphasis on gradual revelation, which depends on man's readiness to accept and understand. This would mean that God adapts Himself to human weaknesses. Such a religion does not lead, but follows the path of human nature. Benamozegh stated that such revelation lacks all meaning, for the God who provides it is created in the image of man; such revelation could equally well have been discovered by man through reason.[5] Judaism, on the other hand, believes in the eternal God and in the immutability of His word; this must remain as the basis and the measure of man through all the ages.

The theoretical distinctions between the two religions interested Benamozegh, but he principally wished to compare the more practical aspects. "Let us descend from these speculative heights where truth, though it may shine with great brilliance, is not readily reached by the common man. Let us try to compare and to determine its conditions and limitations. Finally let us examine in detail whether Christianity is really the author of this morality, or whether its principles and elements, too soon forgotten, were not furnished by the milieu in which it grew up, by the doctrines which surrounded it and by its mother religion." He made it his task to lay bare Christianity's debt to Judaism. Similarly he wished to discuss the original elements of Christianity.[6] He found little in the practical ethics of Christianity that was not rooted in Judaism.

In his discussion of Christian ethics, Benamozegh was especially critical of Christianity's emphasis on the individual, as were his French-Jewish contemporary, Joseph Salvador, and other Jewish scholars later on. The Pentateuch does not neglect the individual, he said, but in contrast to the New Testament, it stresses the group, the nation. "Can the duties of a nation be treated like those of an individual, and can international right ever be replaced by the Imitatio Christi?"[7] Benamozegh considered this a crucial defect in Christian morality, seeing it as especially wrong because he was a fervent Italian nationalist. Nor can the idea of universal brotherhood overcome the fault. Christianity neglects many aspects of human life in its ethical system. "For the benefit of universal brotherhood Christianity sacrificed sometimes the individual to the family, by exaggerating the rights of parents, sometimes the family to the all-embracing State. Christianity went so far as to abolish the nations within mankind."[8] Benamozegh conceded that this might be a noble ideal, but the course of human history had proven it utterly unrealistic. In ancient times this outlook kept Christianity from understanding the Jewish struggle against Rome; as a result, Christians sided with the Romans and brought about the final split between Judaism and Christianity. Christianity simply could not understand the need for political as well as spiritual liberty.[9] The subsequent consequences of this were far more significant. As Christianity spread and became the dominant religion of many lands, Christians became interested in affairs of state, and adapted the emphasis on the individual to the new situation. Christianity became a State religion in which the State set itself to be the conscience of the individual. "Faith was surrounded by penalties and hangmen; violence, injustice, and tyranny served a religion of charity. Christianity was condemned to become violent, just because it had only charity and not justice, because it preached only love and not respect as well, because it attempted to cultivate the most sublime virtue at the expense of an equally holy but even more necessary one."[10] When this system of individual ethics was elevated to the national level, its defects became obvious. Benamozegh contrasted this with the dual approach of Judaism—the tradition for the individual, and the Mosaic Code for the nation.[11] This defect in Christian ethics is the chief distinction between Judaism and Christianity.

Benamozegh continued with a detailed analysis of Jewish and Christian ethics, following the traditional paths of earlier centuries. He emphasized Pauline Christianity's stress on faith over works, describing the historical consequences of this doctrine and showing the major role it had played in Catholicism and Protestantism.[12] This idea was the rejection of the Law, also the work of Paul. In the Pauline view, the Law was not a path to salvation, but demonstrated the human weakness deriving from man's Original Sin; it had to be replaced by another road to salvation.[13] Christianity rejected this world and its pleasures; its sharp distinction between the body and the spirit had led to many aberrations, according to Benamozegh. These tendencies constantly led to a refusal to become involved in the world and to struggle against social evils. Thus, social justice has never been a major goal of Christianity.[14] In its attempts to reach lofty heights,

Christianity overlooks some essential components of ethics. Justice as an ideal is almost entirely absent, while charity and love, which are also present in Judaism, are excessively stressed.[15] Judaism provides a balanced and more thorough approach to ethics, according to Benamozegh's critique.

An entire chapter of his work was devoted to the repentant sinner who comes to accept a new way of life. He felt that Jesus made too much of such individuals. Jesus had been motivated by the hope of gathering disaffected individuals around himself. Even if these practical elements are discounted, there are ethical dangers in this emphasis. These dangers do not exist in Judaism. The Jewish religion welcomes the sinner, but does not single him out unless he distinguishes himself in life after repenting. The Christian attitude finds its origin among the Pharisees, but the excesses are a Christian addition.[16] Benamozegh felt that Christianity's emphasis on loving one's enemy represented an exaggeration of Judaism's "Love your neighbor as yourself." In contrast to the professed emphasis on love, Christianity increases the scope of enmity: for Jews the political enemy has always existed, but Christians add the religious enemy. Judaism has learned tolerance and has long expressed it through the Noachide laws; it can feel no religious enmity.[17]

In his entire comparison of Jewish and Christian ethics Benamozegh rigorously defended the Pharisees, who were so often attacked by the New Testament. Christian morality, he pointed out, had been derived from them or from other first-century Jewish groups. Christianity had borrowed extensively, but was unwilling to acknowledge the debt.

In his discussion of the idea of the Messiah, Benamozegh dealt with the role of Jesus as Messiah. He compared Jesus and the Jewish Messianic pretender Sabbatai Zevi, including this in a larger appreciation of Jewish mysticism.[18]

Benamozegh wished to present a balanced view of Judaism and Christianity, but his apologetic approach did not allow him to succeed. He objected to the views of his contemporary, Joseph Salvador, who stressed the historical, political, and institutional factors to the exclusion of ethical and religious elements. To Benamozegh, Salvador's interpretation of Judaism and Christianity was unbalanced, and he sought in his book to compensate for this defect in the Frenchman's writings.[19]

Although Benamozegh's critique of Christian ethics was severe, he did not overlook the contributions of Christianity to human development. Christianity "had greatly assisted the progress of human morality. It had destroyed altars smoking with innocent blood and places where prostitution had been elevated to the rank of a religious duty. It had proclaimed the common origin and the universal brotherhood of man. . . . These good deeds and many more will always be recognized by mankind. Judaism happily did so as well. We admire these children of ours . . . although they have not yet introduced the Messianic Era into the world, but they have prepared the road for its advent. Yes, the Synagogue does admire them, and though gravely injured at the hand of the Church, it has never stopped proclaiming this . . . "[20]

Benamozegh, like Joseph Salvador and Isaac Mayer Wise, dreamed of a new religion; he believed that pure Judaism would be accepted into the structure of Christianity and that a religion capable of appealing to all men would evolve. He expressed these thoughts in a later book entitled *Israël et l'Humanité*. This volume was marked by a quieter tone. It contained none of the polemics of his earlier work and was imbued with the optimistic spirit of late-nineteenth-century thought.

Benamozegh sought to defend Judaism and, above all, Jewish ethics against Christian disparagement. His work is primarily an apologia demonstrating Christianity's debt to Judaism. With Benamozegh began a series of Jewish endeavors to deal with Christian thought rather than the history of Christianity. This Italian rabbinical scholar confronted Christianity as an Orthodox pioneer in this field.

6

Abraham Geiger

A Liberal Jewish View

Abraham Geiger (1810–1874) was one of the most aggressive fighters for Reform Judaism in Germany. In a long, bitter struggle he forced his opponents to recognize the Reform rabbinate. This battle was to cost him dearly, but it and his scholarship made him a recognized leader of German Jewry. Geiger was more than a Reform rabbi; he was a pioneer in scientific Jewish studies. The influence of his life, personality and his numerous works was felt for a generation.

Geiger wrote no books about Christianity, but in essays and letters he concerned himself with a reinterpretation of early Christian history, Christianity's influence upon Western civilization, and its contemporary confrontation with Judaism. The controversial nineteenth-century studies of the New Testament by Christian scholars like Strauss and Renan aroused his interest and critical appraisal, and he was the first to emphasize the need for a thorough study of the Jewish background of Christianity. He was equally concerned with fighting the intellectual anti-Semitism of New Testament scholarship, which had neglected the Jewish aspect of Jesus, directly and indirectly expressing disdain for ancient and modern Judaism.

Geiger thought well of Strauss's *Life of Jesus.* "Fortunately a book has been found, which is sufficiently significant that one may look to it for support and a man toward whom one may be predisposed. The book is Strauss's *Life of Jesus*, which is excellent; it must be read by all who wish to be in step with the times. It is a work of greatest importance for scholarship, but can be no less influential on Christian theology."[1] He amusedly noted that one reviewer of Strauss's work was frightened by the light of reason shown there. Geiger's own work was appreciated and acknowledged by Renan in the introduction to his *Life of Jesus.*

Three decades later Geiger wrote a longer opinion of Strauss and Renan which was less enthusiastic and more critical. He criticized Renan for his new fictitious Jesus while Strauss was blamed for neglecting Jewish studies. "How does this man appear in both of these works? There is the hidden rock upon which the little tossing boat is ruined after it has ventured from the channels of historical criticism into biography. Every biographical venture contains a danger. When an individual is lifted as a fixed point out of the fluid movement of the total history, he is given additional significance. Then one is continually tempted to justify his special importance in the portrayal." As little is known about Jesus, it is tempting to fill the gaps; Geiger was very critical of this method: "This happened to both scholars, to each in his own way, but one was no better than the other. The Jesus of Renan appears basically as an eccentric dreamer vacillating back and forth between a national Jew and a world citizen, now introduced to asceticism by John the Baptist, then rising above outer forms . . . eventually a glorified Jesus is attained who represents the ideal of religious and ethical perfection for all time, an ideal which is still not fully recognized and even less realized." Even if this figure was not a deity he had been elevated to a universal ideal. "However, when we close the book, quietly ponder its contents, translate its poetry into dispassionate prose, then through this necessary analytic process of thought the hero evaporates completely into thin air." Geiger approved the method of investigation used by Renan, but not the fictitious Jesus that resulted from it. He criticized Strauss for vacillating under the attack of his coreligionists. "Nor is it better with Strauss, since he preserves the reader from all tensions and inner struggle and leaves 'Jesus standing there in great dignity.' Even in the introduction he is presented to the reader as a special individual, which makes it impossible to treat him in the proper historical manner. He is portrayed as the individual in whom the deeper consciousness of mankind first arose to true life." Such statements were considered by Geiger to rest on false assumptions. "Should we inquire for the facts upon which this portrayal is based, Strauss refuses to provide specific evidence as such accounts cannot be acknowledged as historical." Any evidence came from a later period and so reflected legendary elements, which can tell us little about the real Jesus; they were certainly insufficient for Strauss's claims.[2] Geiger had made a thorough study of this period from Jewish sources in his *Urschrift und Übersetzung der Bibel* (1857).

Geiger expressed his views on the life and nature of Jesus most clearly in his lectures on history. Jesus "was a Jew, a Pharisaic Jew with some Galilean coloration; he was an individual who shared the hopes of his time and believed that this hope had been fulfilled in him. He uttered no new thoughts nor did he break through the boundaries of nationalism." As a Pharisee he followed the school of Hillel and fitted well into the framework of Jewish history, which had been ignored by Strauss, Bruno Bauer, and other Christian scholars. Geiger felt that Jesus had considered himself the Messiah, but this was not unusual, for other Jews had made similar assertions during various oppressive periods of Jewish history.[3] He agreed with those nineteenth-century scholars who had relegated a detailed life of Jesus to the realm of legend; such efforts represented a gallant attempt to supplement the limited existing material.[4] Despite these reservations, Geiger tried to characterize Jesus. "He represented a strange mixture of clear-headedness, a troubled spirit, and reverie as is often the case with men of this kind; it depends entirely upon circumstances whether the appearance of such men leads to a passing sect or an enduring religious group." His life and thought were absolutely Jewish except perhaps for his belief in demons and his conception of the resurrection; his appearance might have led only to the creation of another Jewish sect, but for the catastrophic destruction of Jerusalem in 70 c.e., shortly after his death. In this way Geiger sought to account for the division between Judaism and Christianity and for the success of Christianity in the Roman Empire. It represents a rather casual answer to a difficult problem which required far more attention. Geiger also acknowledged the role played by Paul in the transformation of the sect into a new religion. He judged Paul to have been deeply influenced by Hellenistic Judaism and its idea of the Logos as developed by

Philo. Through this thought Paul changed the original Messianic sect into a religion in which Jesus serves as intermediary between God and man.[5] Once again we are treated to a simple analysis of a difficult problem; however, Geiger elaborated on this later.

In Geiger's view, Jesus lacked the originality necessary to establish a new religion, but he possessed deep inner conviction and spirituality. "We cannot deny him a deep introspective nature, but there is no trace of a decisive stand that promised lasting results . . . there was no great work of reform nor any new thoughts that left the usual paths. He did oppose abuses, perhaps occasionally more forcefully than the Pharisees, yet on the whole it was done in their manner." Similar protests were mentioned by Josephus and the Talmud.[6] Jesus felt that a new period of world history would begin, perhaps even before he died. His followers continued to believe in him after his death and anxiously awaited the new age. Jesus himself had already been resurrected in anticipation of this new period. According to Geiger these were the basic elements of early Christianity and all else represented later accretions. "We may not dilute or cast doubt upon this historical fact, but we may also not make other improper additions if new confusion shall not thus arise." Jesus as son of God or as Logos was not part of this early period and it was "mockery" to read Hegelian concepts into those times. "Also, all that denies national or legal elements of Judaism must be rejected and be attributed to its later evolution. Moreover the noble religious and ethical concepts and teachings which are put into his heart and mouth, even if we only provisionally and with reservations attribute them to him, must not be taken as his own. He was not their creator nor the first to conceive or state them; rather at best he took them from those who preceded his work and then made them his own."[7] By viewing Jesus as a Jew living in a definite period of Jewish history, Geiger virtually eliminated all his special characteristics, thus making his magnetism and influence unintelligible. This overstatement and apologetic approach posed new questions to which Geiger did not address himself.

Maintaining that the original little Christian sect appealed only to Jews prior to its transformation by Paul, Geiger put forward a series of admittedly speculative working hypotheses as an aid in the reconstruction of early Christianity. He tried to show the similarities between the early Christian sect and other Jewish groups of the time. Regarding Jesus as a member of the Pharisees, the dominant religious party of the era, Geiger held that he represented the Pharisaic hope for the Messiah and the future, pointing out that resurrection was, after all, a Pharisaic doctrine. The Law was important to the Pharisees, so Jesus' emphasis on the Law fitted into this pattern. Jesus and early Judeo-Christianity were also influenced somewhat by Sadducean thought and so could be attractive to Sadducees: "The High Priesthood of Jesus, his death as a sacrifice, the participation in the Eucharist with his blood and body became a new priesthood endowed with the sacredness and holiness of the old." Because the new sect could offer asceticism to the Essenes, while Zealots would be attracted by its dissatisfaction with the world and its doctrine of the end, it "remained rooted in Judaism even if much was dropped or displaced."[8]

The little Judeo-Christian group soon ceased to be a Jewish sect and began to address itself to the pagan world. Geiger divided this period into two stages, tracing the beginning of the change to Paul's predecessors and its culmination to Paul. During the first stage the sect remained Jewish while adding some special thoughts about the Messiah and the Messianic Age. This period was represented by the original version of the Gospel of Mark, which Geiger considered the earliest of the Gospels. The later version of Mark contained the phrase "Son of God," which was also used by the other Gospels; this marked the second stage in the development of Christianity. "In the second stage of its development and through it, Christianity almost ceased to be a path within Judaism despite all efforts to maintain itself within Judaism." It stood on the periphery till Paul undertook the final separation.[9] In Geiger's judgment, Paul had been deeply influenced by Hellenistic Judaism with its different concept of the Messiah and its emphasis on the Logos. Paul's radical thought gained impetus through the destruction of the Temple and the revolt of Bar Kokhba, "which wiped out all practical hopes and uprooted the entire previous system of thought."[10] These steps led to the development of Christianity as a separate religion. Geiger did not concern himself with the later stages of Christian evolution.

Although Geiger undertook no thorough study of the Gospels, he did comment upon them in his writings. He felt that Mark was composed nearest the time of Jesus and thus was the most reliable, though it too contained much legendary material. Geiger saw little that was new in the Gospels. "We either find nothing new in them or new material presented in the pathological manner evoked by these pathological times."[11] He often mentioned the influence of Philo and Hellenistic thought on the Gospels, and he saw them as a combination of Palestinian and Greek Judaism.[12]

Geiger discussed the influence of Christianity on civilization in his "Introduction to Jewish Theology."[13] He recognized the strength of Christianity; the essence of its mission was to struggle against the natural elements within man and to unite mankind. He admired these concepts and the men who had dedicated themselves to their fulfillment and who attempted to bring about some unity among the nations of the world. "Therein lies the strength of Christianity; however, what was and is its strength also represents its weakness." Geiger, like many others, was appalled by the destructive aspect of Christianity. Upon encountering the noble civilizations of the ancient world it destroyed them; its vision of the new world left no room for the old, which had to be eliminated for "all legitimately only begins with him [Jesus] and after this event it [Christianity] did not tolerate any other force in the development of world history, as long as it possessed the power to do so."[14] Geiger admitted there was much to be said about the culture and art of the Middle Ages but emphasized that "the restoration of science and art only began when one again began to create from the Greek-pagan antiquity."[15] The long pagan struggle against Christianity was not primarily concerned with theology since the old gods had lost their appeal, but originated in the realization by pagans that Christianity would annihilate their culture. Christianity eventually succeeded in destroying the old world by force of arms, but for many centuries it failed to penetrate "those segments of mankind which still contained a healthy nucleus capable of producing a healthy growth."[16] The new humanism, the invention of printing, and the fall of the Byzantine Empire, with its concomitant scattering of Greek scholars, revived the old learning; this occurred despite the opposition of major elements within the Church.[17] "This pretense, which constituted the strength of Christianity, also represented its weakness, for it was unwilling to work as a spiritual force within mankind, but sought to stand above mankind and denied mankind any other legitimate relationships. It would be foolish and also blasphemous if we did not acknowledge the divine mission of a religion which has exercised such power for eighteen hundred years. On the other hand, it would be an equal mockery of history if we denied or renounced the mission of the religion that was the mother and source of the new religion and maintained itself through the entire period when the other was developing its full power, even maintaining itself in the face of oppression."[18] The tendency toward exclusiveness has been essential to Christianity for almost two thousand years and remained strong in the nineteenth century; this led Geiger severely to criticize contemporary Catholicism: "Progress and development are its enemies," he said. Hopefully this type of Catholicism would soon fall, but he did not believe it would occur.[19] Still, he hoped for a liberal Catholicism,[20] and he thought it necessary to criticize the reactionary elements of the Church, feeling that such outspoken opinions would help Jews on the periphery of Judaism to more fully appreciate their own religion.[21]

Geiger understood the modern forces that had weakened the hold of the Church on general culture. Among them nationalism was very important,[22] but it was not sufficiently powerful since State and Church often had common interests. Opposition to change was strong in Catholic lands but also existed among Protestants. Only revolution could bring a decisive change and a real break with the past. "A hierarchy artfully constructed and become mighty through the influences of centuries obstructed all independent development initiated by the community itself; although this is most true of Catholicism, Protestantism is also not free of restrictive spiritual authority. Finally, Christianity as the ruling Church is so involved with affairs of state that its interests and the influence of its power lie deeply rooted there. Therefore, both the civil and the ecclesiastical authorities are interested in maintaining this power structure." A complete break with the past is necessary.[23] Judaism is not troubled by such problems.

Christianity had also been opposed to reason and philosophy until they became subordinate to it.[24] Christianity sought to subdue reason and succeeded, although reason eventually arose anew. Geiger contrasted this with Judaism, which is not disturbed by the tension between religion and reason.[25]

Geiger adjudged Christianity's basic understanding of history to be defective since it holds that a single point in the past represents the totality of experience. This leads Christians to a peculiar view of the formative period of their faith and forces Christianity into a strange bond with the particular forms of first-century Judaism. "Judaism is self-sufficient, develops out of its own resources and may abandon the outer garb of a particular period without surrendering anything of its essence; Christianity, on the other hand, rests upon the configuration of the Judaism of a particular period and must eternally cling to what appeared at that particular time in the historical flow of life; for it these elements must remain eternally complete."[26] More important is the Christian view that the final page of world history was written long ago and that, as a result, no progress is possible. All has "already been realized eighteen hundred years ago; the final stone was laid. It was the final stone of one world and the cornerstone of the other world. No truth remains to be added."[27]

Christianity became an otherworldly religion, Geiger explained, because no other path had been possible. Due to the serious weakening of both the Jewish and the Greek worlds, "it was innoculated with the germ of that diseased state and has carried it ever since." The search for power led Christianity to Rome and to the Latin language and culture, rather than to weaker Byzantium. However, the transplantation of the young Oriental religion to Rome was not wholly successful; in the realm of ideas it led to mysticism and romanticism, which have remained dominant. "Christianity is the true mother of the mystical and the romantic; on the contrary, Judaism is clear, concrete, vigorous, happy with life, and intellectual; it does not deny the mortal world but seeks to illuminate it."[28] This criticism was later developed much more thoroughly by Baeck.

Emphasizing Christianity's often unacknowledged debt to Judaism,[29] Geiger remained a constant critic of Christianity's influence on the world, which he regarded as negative. "I would not care to investigate whether Christianity's stigmatization of reason, its restriction of free will, and its theory of Original Sin are or were not obstacles to a free ethical life."[30]

Geiger's discussion of Christian doctrine was not thorough or systematic. His comments usually appeared in works dealing with Judaism, where they were often used for contrast, as well as in letters to friends. He began a work on Christianity, but it remained in his literary estate not ready for publication.[31]

So far as contemporary Christianity was concerned, Geiger saw dangers to Judaism in its strong missionary drive. Two Berlin converts, Stahl and Runtel, constantly harassed the Jewish community.[32] Conversion was tempting, an easy path to economic, cultural, and social recognition, especially since the Jewish struggle for equal rights had faltered. Geiger wrote two public letters to dissuade prospective converts who were motivated by such considerations.[33] In these letters he expressed a greater sensitivity toward Christianity, on one occasion stating that he was not interested in the distinctions between the two religions and did not want it to appear that he "wished to fight, debase, and shame Christianity." He wrote appreciatively of the "religion in which millions had found comfort and salvation for eighteen hundred years." Nevertheless, he felt, it was his duty to defend Judaism and to restrain those tempted to convert.[34] After these preliminary remarks, however, he continued in his customary frank manner. He did not care for soft-toned apologetics and mocked the way in which some "enlightened" Jews imitated Christianity and its pattern of thought. He was scornful of their unwillingness to criticize Christianity even in matters which they considered wrong.[35] Because he preferred polemic, he appreciated Isaac Troki, the sixteenth-century Karaite critic of Christianity, and he analyzed Troki's work as part of a broader study of the Karaites.[36]

Geiger was saddened by the shortcomings of modern Christian scholarship, which displayed much erudition of classical antiquity, but little knowledge of ancient Judaism. Many Christian scholars, he pointed out, had not even mastered Hebrew or Aramaic.[37]

"Everyone who views the birth of Christianity historically should admit to himself that he must properly treat the three contributing factors—contemporary Palestinian Judaism, Greek Judaism, and the Greco-Roman Culture."[38]

Late in life Geiger returned to criticism of Strauss and Renan. "This phenomenon, that men who are admired for their religious liberalism by one side and damned for it by the other, are so unfamiliar with this area of which precise knowledge is absolutely essential to a scientific treatment of the subject, is deplorable. The fact that they stubbornly hold on to old prejudices is most unfortunate from many points of view."[39] Moreover, Geiger asserted, there were no accurate Christian studies of New Testament times, and Jewish studies of this period, including his own, were ignored. The few exceptions were noteworthy and Geiger mentioned them in his correspondence. He himself was acknowledged by Renan and Delitzsch.[40] He felt that the real danger of inadequate Christian scholarship was its wide acceptance by the half-educated public; it led many astray precisely when they considered themselves enlightened.[41]

Judaism had suffered from Christian hatred since its earliest days. "Troubled times like those of civil war or a struggle among brothers came to Judaism with its [Christianity's] dominance, but along with it came some recognition in a world where it was attacked." Another path might have been followed. Christianity "could have led to the salvation of the world as an inwardly freer and outwardly expanded Judaism; however, it became the scourge of intellectual freedom and a promoter of spiritual oppression." The bitter hostility had diminished in the nineteenth century, but Geiger, contrary to many of his contemporaries, was not blindly optimistic. He had begun with high hopes, but eventually recognized that the old antagonism had been only partially replaced by a more enlightened attitude.[42] Deeply disappointed, he was well aware of the new racial anti-Semitism awakening toward the end of the century. Despite this he believed that Christianity had enough in common with Judaism to bring about a better era. "If we agree on the historical foundation, then it must be admitted that Christianity was a natural development from Judaism and paganism. Both had deteriorated at that time; this led to an easier

Christian victory, but also to the introduction of many weak elements. A healthy new development can bring us nearer each other, but only without haughtiness or stubbornness on either side."[43]

7

Hirsch, Formstecher, and Steinheim

The Philosophical Counterattack

In the mid-nineteenth century, German-Jewish thinkers were faced by the challenge of the philosophy of Kant, Schelling, and Hegel. Each of these men was concerned with the place of religion and specifically the role of Christianity in the world, and gave Judaism only a secondary role in the scheme of things. Samuel Hirsch, Salomon Formstecher, and Salomon Steinheim sought to defend Judaism against them. All three tried to reverse the roles of Judaism and Christianity and to demonstrate how much Judaism towered over Christianity. In their picture of the world they assigned Christianity an honorable but lesser place. Their efforts led them to study early Christianity and to comment upon it in detail. These three German-Jewish thinkers differed considerably in their underlying philosophical approaches and were hostile to each other, but they agreed in their opinion of Christianity and in many specific attitudes toward it.

Samuel Hirsch (1815–1889) was a modern German rabbi who had taken part in the development of Liberal Judaism and its struggle with Orthodoxy. He spent much of his life in Germany and Luxembourg but in 1869 accepted a pulpit in Philadelphia; his most significant literary works were written before he came to the United States. He was deeply influenced by Hegel and accepted his view of religion as the intuitive apprehension of the Whole; the religious man identifies himself with the Absolute, Who is free and slowly unfolds Himself in time. Man's religious experience, therefore, is one of freedom. Hirsch did not identify nature with God, as Hegel did, but saw it as subject to unchangeable laws. Man

51

is closer to God than to nature, or at least has that potential within him; therefore, he has been given the gift of freedom. Hirsch interpreted human freedom in an ethical sense. Freedom provides man with the means of conquering his natural impulses—this may be accomplished by striving to attain the ideals of ethics, which are provided by God.

Hirsch also disagreed with Hegel's interpretation of Christianity, presenting a lengthy critique of it, and he similarly criticized Strauss, whom he regarded as a disciple of Hegel.[1]

In Hirsch's view, Judaism and Christianity could be discussed in a spirit different from the prevailing animosity of the day. Mutual hatred and failure to understand each other could be overcome. "If the widely held prejudice that Judaism and Christianity must necessarily oppose each other with enmity . . . that neither religion can believe itself to attain its goal and vocation as long as the other continues to exist beside it, then we would only reluctantly proceed to deal with Christianity and its relationship to Judaism. . . . Judaism does not oppose Christianity with enmity, and it never has."[2] Jewish enmity for Christianity, he continued, has only been a response to the vilification of Judaism by Christians. Such libels had continued from ancient times to Hirsch's contemporaries, among them the Christian theologian Bruno Bauer, who argued on theological grounds that Jews should not be emancipated or obtain political rights since the inferiority of Judaism as a religion made this impossible.[3] Along with Geiger, Phillipson, Holdheim, Steinheim, and others, Hirsch engaged in a long and fiery polemic against Bauer, vigorously defending Judaism and stressing the affinity between Judaism and Protestant Christianity, which has a greater "this worldly" orientation than Catholicism. Because of the similarities between the Jewish and Protestant conceptions of the State, it was not possible on theological grounds to deny Jews the right to participate in the modern state.[4]

Hirsch discussed Jesus at length, and, like many other scholars, he drew a sharp distinction between the Jesus of the Synoptic Gospels and the Jesus of John. Although Christianity favored the abstract Jesus of John, Hirsch thought it would be better for modern Christianity to emphasize the historical Jesus of the

Synoptic Gospels. In this way Jesus could become a real person, not an abstract ideal.[5] Hirsch's studies led him to conclude that Matthew is the best historical account of Jesus.[6] The figure of Jesus uncovered in Matthew, after the removal of later accretions, is a Jew who attempted in his own life to exemplify the ideals by which every Jewish life should be guided. "Every Jew, for that matter every man, should be what Jesus was; that was the summons of every prophet. Every Jew and every man will become so; that is the promise of the Messianic hope."[7] Jews, however, can strive for this noble goal equally well without the example of Jesus. The mission of Jesus, according to Hirsch, was the guidance of others along his path. Every man can become a son of God; Jesus wished to increase the number of Israelites devoted to their religion, for he was solely concerned with fellow Jews.[8] The message of Jesus sounded reasonable to the Jews of his time, even though it offered nothing new.[9] Hirsch considered its major contribution to have been the renewal of the prophetic voice in a silent age. "At the time of Jesus' appearance, Judaism had forgotten the source of its truth. The voices of living prophets had long faded away."[10] Jesus directed his efforts toward his fellow Israelites because he sought to make the goal of all Israel meaningful for the individual Israelite. Only after that task was completed might it become possible to win the heathens from idolatry.[11] Jesus certainly did not intend to establish a new religion, according to Hirsch's reading of Matthew; rather, "he wished to realize the total content of the old [religion]."[12]

Aside from evaluating Jesus as a Jew, Hirsch sought to show him as a first-century figure. No proper understanding can be achieved without acknowledging the Roman fear of political unrest; it is equally necessary to remember the numerous internal divisions among the Jews. Both Pharisiac and Saducean opposition to Jesus were natural. "When would they not have persecuted such an individual! What would our present-day Christian Saducees and Pharisees say about such a man if he did not remain absolutely silent?"[13] So far as the crucifixion of Jesus was concerned, Hirsch felt there was no need for evasion, although a good deal in the Gospel account remained shrouded in obscurity and reflected later interpolations and alterations. Certainly Pilate was not a gentle man; he had been a harsh ruler, and the change in his portrayal represents later additions. "We may even admit that there were irregularities at the trial or that it may have been intentional judicial murder . . . ," but due to the uncertainty of the sources it will remain problematic; Romans and Jews were mutually responsible for the deed.[14]

Samuel Hirsch had a high regard for Jesus as a person, but not as an original teacher. "All that he taught, as he himself admitted, had already been given by Moses and the prophets. He did not die for an idea; nor did he leave his disciples a legacy independent of his person. The unusual attainment of Jesus lay in something that was far more than an idea, it lay in his personality. He understood, realized, and fulfilled the idea of Judaism in its deepest truth—that was the greatness of Jesus."[15]

The change from Judaism to a new religion did not come through Jesus; it began with John and culminated in the words of Paul. The Gospel of John made Jesus an abstraction rather than a historical figure; furthermore, it ignored his Jewish roots in contrast to the other Gospels' more historical accounts. When viewed through the eyes of later Christianity the two accounts complement each other.[16] Yet it was not in John, but in the work of Paul, that the Church found its true roots. In particular, the first eleven chapters of his Epistle to the Romans "were a monument of his deep and rich spirit, which even more than the Gospel of John will eternally be an ornament and a source of comfort to mankind." In those chapters Paul began to present the ideas that were to become the foundation of the Church. Original Sin, the doctrine of Grace, and the divinity of Jesus finally separated the two religions.[17] Along with these doctrines came a sharp polemic against the Jews. Hirsch understood these attacks in an unusual way: "Paul carried on a sharp and violent polemic against Judaism, and he was correct about the Judaism which he attacked, but unfortunately, the Judaism he attacked was and is only the Judaism of Paul and his followers; it is not the Judaism of the Jews." Hirsch indicated that Paul had been a young and immature student of Judaism when he left it. Since his knowledge was limited and he did not grasp the essence of Judaism, he was attacking something he did not understand. Unfortunately, later Christian scholars and philosophers have seen him as an expert in Jewish matters.[18] Paul's limited grasp of Judaism led to an erroneous evaluation of the "Law" and to other misconceptions. Hirsch believed that much Christian enmity toward Judaism can be traced to Paul; here lie the roots of "Christianity's hatred of Jews and heretics, its fiery stake, its persecution mania, its missionary spirit—up to the slandering of Judaism by the Hegelians—all were the consequence of his statements. . . . Because Christ had appeared, Judaism forfeited its right to exist." This was equally true of the pagan world.[19]

The fiery and deeply religious nature of Paul was recognized by Hirsch, who felt that Paul had tried to limit the effect of his temperament on his doctrine in order to avoid the possibility of extreme interpretations. Hirsch judged the results of Paul's work negatively, but he recognized that all of later Christianity was an attempt to finish the structure which Paul had begun.[20]

The world had to wait until the Reformation for a new attitude to develop. Protestantism, which contains its own difficulties and contradictions, is a "negation of Pauline Christianity." Underneath it lies the thought that "every man is free before God, and each is made in the image of God." This attitude has survived despite Luther, who was deeply akin to Paul and wished to reestablish a purified Pauline religion. "The Protestant Church wishes to be Pauline, but that is impossible." Protestantism might be considered a step backward, but Hirsch welcomed it for the freedom and individualism to which it gave birth. Hirsch saw Protestantism in a better light than earlier Christianity because it had led to the hopeful era in which he lived.[21]

Samuel Hirsch found little merit in Christianity, aside from the Jewish pattern of Jesus' life. Nevertheless, he felt that Christianity had played a positive role in world history. It had brought ethics and monotheism to the pagan world. "The heathens shall arrive at these thoughts, and for that reason the Pauline form of Christianity was a necessity. . . . Therefore, the two supporting pillars [Original Sin and divine Grace] were necessary in order to bring the consciousness of the truth to the pagan world; that is the mission of the Catholic Church."[22]

The mission of Pauline Christianity was preparation for the true religion of Jesus—Judaism. Finally "all men will arrive at a full . . . belief in God through Jews like Jesus who make the mission of Israel their own."[23] When paganism has been conquered, a religion of tolerance and love will be established by a joint effort of Jewish and Protestant thinkers;[24] according to Hirsch, this religion will be Judaism. Moreover, like many other nineteenth-century Jews, including Isaac Mayer Wise, Hirsch felt that the universal acceptance of a purified Judaism would occur soon. Just as countless Christians have abandoned belief in Original Sin, so numerous Jews have laid aside the ceremonial aspects of the Law. "The purely human has on the whole been victorious; it is up to us, each of us, to let it become victorious in our individual lives. The religion of love and tolerance will surely be the religion of the future."[25] This profoundly optimistic statement appeared in the later of Hirsch's two books on Christianity. That volume was milder, although his basic judgments of Christianity remained as in the earlier, more detailed study.

Samuel Hirsch uncompromisingly felt that Judaism was superior to Christianity. He shared this frank appraisal with Formstecher and Steinheim. The need to defend Judaism from the attack of the Hegelians led him to undertake a strong counterattack. Judaism remained the only possible hope for the religious future of mankind.

Samuel Hirsch began a new pattern in the Jewish approach to Christianity. It was paralleled by Salomon Formstecher (1808–1889), lifelong rabbi of Offenbach, who sought to harmonize Judaism and modern civilization. Formstecher's efforts were given practical expression at the rabbinical gatherings of the nineteenth century, and received a philosophical foundation in his book *The Religion of the Spirit*. This volume sought to provide a modern philosophical basis for Judaism by building upon the thought of Schelling, who saw the world as a living organism in which each element has a definite function. Beneath changing phenomena there is a single unifying substance—the divine world soul. Religion, as defined by Formstecher, exists in two forms as knowledge of the ideals inherent in nature and in the spirit. Although this dualism may exist now, it is not the ultimate form, for nature in the end will be subordinated to the spirit; in this way Formstecher removed the danger of pantheism from his philosophy of Judaism.[26] He classified religions by their proximity to nature or to spirituality; paganism is natural religion, while Judaism is the ultimate spiritual religion; all others stand between. Formstecher foreshadowed Max Brod, who divided religious life into the pagan, Christian, and Jewish paths, but actually linked modern Christianity with paganism. Brod saw secularism in its Christian-pagan form as a major threat in the twentieth century. For Formstecher the struggle against paganism meant battling the rising influence of the deterministic scientific point of view as well as visions of a secular utopia. In contrast to Brod, he was hopeful and felt that man would develop beyond the pagan stages to the ultimate level of the pure religion, Judaism.

Formstecher did not consider Judaism perfect in its early stages, but maintained that it is continually progressing toward the goal of perfection. Because its development occurs within the boundaries of a spiritual religion, at each stage it remains opposed to the pagan religions. Its ultimate aim is the elevation of individual lives. "Judaism attains the stage of perfection only when its ideal is realized in the life of the individual."[27] In contrast, pagan religions develop within the limitation of their attachment to the objects of nature and thus cannot attain perfection. As soon as they free themselves from nature and recognize a monotheistic Being they cease to be pagan. Within history the two forms of religion must oppose each other. "Paganism and Judaism must continue throughout history to develop as opponents, and they must move on until each religion has recognized and attained the ideal set for it: When paganism has reached the culmination of its development, it will be convinced that in deifying the forces of nature it has only grasped one manifestation of God." It will then acknowledge the existence of spiritual religion and will acknowledge the world mission of the latter. "Judaism has the power to lead mankind up to the stage of its destiny . . . Judaism through its prophetic spirit hopes for a spiritual dominion of the world consisting of reverence for God, the Father of all mankind, and a loving bond of universal brotherhood. This ideal is so purely ethical that paganism would never have fashioned it."[28]

The unique element in this vivid description of religious life is the establishment of Judaism as the ultimate form of religious life. The world must come to Judaism, and this task has been aided by the two daughter religions of Judaism, Christianity and Islam. "Christianity and Islam are the northern and southern missions of Judaism to the pagan world; they are the means used by Providence to overthrow the deification of nature and to lead the generations of man to the apex of perfection. Both are an amalgamation of Judaism with paganism, and both consider themselves to possess the absolute truth and find their mission in the task of advancing this truth till it is the common property of all mankind."[29] Judaism cannot grant equality to these religions. They embody only a few of its own truths as a means of preparing mankind for Judaism. "In essence their mission is a movement of Judaism, which leads itself through paganism and then back to itself." Since paganism assumed different forms in the past and in the present, Islam and Christianity were forced to combat it in a variety of ways, which sometimes meant amalgamation with paganism—this was essential and unavoidable, especially during the earlier stages of the struggle.[30] Thus Formstecher, contrary to Brod, found virtue in the paganization of Christianity.

With mid-nineteenth-century confidence, Formstecher considered Judaism to be the apex of universal religious life. Early in history Judaism influenced the pagan world indirectly through Islam and Christianity; with their preparatory role now at an end, Judaism should begin to exert its proper influence. Hirsch was not encouraging proselytism, which he believed to be contrary to the spirit of Judaism, but hoped for the dominance of the Jewish over the pagan elements of Christianity and Islam. This is the second stage in the development of Judaism.[31]

Formstecher was less interested than Hirsch in the development of Christianity and more interested in its current role. Christianity has a mission, he asserted, but it is a transitory one. "Christianity recognizes salvation as its task and atonement as the goal for which it aspires. . . . The living symbol of this salvation and atonement is found by Christianity in the death of Jesus." Alongside the statement of Christianity's mission Formstecher offered his principal critique. "The relative and transitory nature of its truth is demonstrated by the fact that it celebrates the beginning of the solution of its mission as the end."[32] Formstecher found support for this thought in the Gospels.

"Christianity surrounded the ethics of Judaism with the metaphysics of paganism in order to find the structure to realize its task."[33] For the same reason it took the ethics of Judaism and removed all ceremonies and notions particular to Israel; thus it became universalized until replaced by pagan metaphysics and worship. Some of these forms have appeared in Judaism, especially in the Kabbalah, but they remained peripheral, while in Christianity they became central. Christianity, therefore, contains only elements of the truth, but it refuses to consider itself in this way: "Christianity pointed to its absolute truth in order to bring salvation and atonement to paganism according to its peculiar nature."[34] Therein lies the weakness of Christianity.

Christianity was sent into the world by Judaism at a critical juncture of history when Roman paganism was dying. In order to be successful, Christianity had to develop along both spiritual and political paths. In the latter, evidence of heathenism has remained dominant through the ages; the entire hierarchy was formed along pagan lines.[35] When the Church attained power, it strove to eliminate some pagan influences from its structure. There was a continuous battle between pagan and Jewish elements within Christianity. The struggle was difficult because paganism, in contrast to Judaism, is a powerful element in Christianity. "The heathen-Jewish element, which was tolerated in Judaism and which was always considered of secondary importance, became the living substratum of Christianity; it appeared as the primary Christian element, first with predominantly Jewish and then with predominantly pagan characteristics; finally it will lead back to the realm of Judaism."[36] Formstecher listed and discussed the pagan elements in Christianity: among them were Transubstantiation, the cult of relics, prayer for the dead, the elevation to the sainthood, and many customs.[37]

Because its mission was primarily to the northern lands, where freedom and individualism reigned, Christianity, more than Islam, was forced to adapt itself to the pagan world. It succeeded only through persuasion, philosophical discussion, and adaptation.

Islam, on the other hand, labored in the southern lands with their different climate and among people accustomed to tyranny, so it conquered and triumphed by seeking absolute submission. "In the objective process of the unfolding of the spirit, Christianity denotes the element that looses itself from the bonds of nature, demanding absolute freedom. Islam, likewise, possesses elements that extricate it from the realm of nature, but it achieves this transition not through freedom, but through unthinking submission."[38]

The Reformation prevented the Jewish element from being overwhelmed by paganism. In modern times, Protestantism has shifted the balance markedly toward the Jewish element; yet much remains to be done if Protestantism is to be victorious, especially as its influence is negligible in large parts of the world. Formstecher felt that the spirit of reason and the new development of philosophy would enable the task to be completed;[39] he was more optimistic than Samuel Hirsch.

Formstecher was hopeful especially for German Christianity, which he deemed close to Judaism. Judaism was ready to accept leadership; it had developed sufficiently and was prepared for this position.[40] The final day will come "when Christianity has recognized that it must reconcile men not with God, with whom they are already reconciled through His all-goodness, but rather with its own spirit, from which it has become estranged through its worship of nature; when it is realized that Christianity must be viewed only as a mission of Judaism to paganism, but not at all as one to Judaism itself." When this occurs, Christianity will have accomplished its mission.[41] All paths lead to Judaism, which represents the hope of mankind.[42]

In Formstecher's philosophy of history and God's plan for Judaism, Christianity played a significant but subservient role. This viewpoint was a response to the Gentile philosophers who excluded Judaism from their plan and placed Christianity in the center. Formstecher's judgement of Christianity was harsher than that of Samuel Hirsch. The tone was more argumentative, and the result was more a bitter response to the Christian world than an attempt to understand it.

Salomon Steinheim (1789–1866), a well-known physician of Altona, pursued Jewish studies as an avocation and was at times attacked for dilettantism by his contemporaries, including Formstecher.[43] He made numerous original contributions in the field of medicine, but always found time for Jewish studies and for participation in the struggle for political and religious rights for his coreligionists. Steinheim disagreed with the underlying premises of Hirsch and Formstecher; he accepted Kant's view of the limits of human reason but rejected his moral metaphysics. Only revelation can answer the ultimate questions which reason must ask. Steinheim's conclusions about Christianity were often akin to those of Formstecher and Hirsch, but they were built on a different foundation. He thought all attempts to formulate a philosophy of Judaism on rational grounds futile and considered both Formstecher and Hirsch wrong in their attempt to follow Hegel and Schelling.[44]

Steinheim began his theological writings with a direct response to an essay by Heinrich Ritter in 1833. It was published in the leading Lutheran journal, but when the Jewish identity of the author became known, no further pieces by him were accepted. Steinheim twice published in the *Zeitschrift für Philosophie und katolische Theologie* (1834 and 1847); both essays engaged in brief dialogue.

Jewish scholars criticized Steinheim for using Christian journals; however, nothing Jewish was available at that time. Later he published in all the Jewish periodicals, although they were more interested in history and archaeology than philosophy.[45]

In Steinheim's view, Christianity was a mixture of Jewish and pagan ideas. An entire volume of his philosophical work is devoted to the history of paganism within Christianity. In this book, *The Struggle of Revelation with Paganism: Synthesis and Analysis*, he was primarily concerned with doctrine and ethics and their historical development. Seeing himself in the role of watchman, he considered it his duty to warn Christianity against dangers that would lead it into the realm of paganism: "Let all of those who have counterfeited our pure concept of revelation, and have adulterated it with pagan philosophical elements, rebuke as an enemy of Christianity the individual who has accused them of neglect of duty and unfaithfulness in the stewardship of their precious talent. This will not cause him to shrink back; he will rather accept this title if they speak of their own mixture as a kind of Christianity. I cannot designate it so. A Christianity which is not as much based upon revelation pure and simple as upon myth and philosophy is not worthy of the name! It may be a good philosophy, a myth filled with significance, a pleasant emotional religion—I have nothing against these. Only let it not be called revelation and the teaching of Christ, but the very opposite, apostasy from it. It leads to the gods of Meru and Mt. Olympus, but not to God, who revealed Himself to Moses upon Sinai, the God who instructed Christ and the Apostle to the Gentiles. The criterion of revelation is that it led to Him and to the knowledge of His nature and will, as far as it has pleased Him to illuminate and correct our reason in these matters. That man would show himself a true friend and promoter of the religion of Christ whom these others would justifiably view, as the enemy of their Christian belief. Yet that is the doctrine of the unity of God, the freedom of man, and the creation of the world. Upon these three pillars, and upon them alone, every revealed religion, including the religion of Christ, does and must rest if it is to retain the name of revealed religion."[46] This expressed his feelings toward Christianity, which were developed in the following volume, an openly polemical work. He sought to separate the Jewish elements from the pagan accretions in Christianity and to show how the pagan elements had entered Christianity. Steinheim concentrated on a vivid portrayal of the eternal battle between these two elements within Christianity. To him the pagan aspects remained as threatening in the guise of Hegel as in the forms of the Middle Ages. Max Brod carried the scenario into the twentieth century with equally devastating results.

Steinheim's critique of pagan elements in religion was not limited to Christianity, for he showed that a similar process had taken place in Judaism. The conflict between true revelation and the systems created by myth, reason, and philosophy exists in all religions. True revelation, according to Steinheim, must be established on the criteria of "unity, creation, and freedom." The true revelation is always an auditory experience, he said, while all false variations are visible experiences; in Christianity and other religions the chief symbol is the visible incarnation. In early Judaism the primary pagan element was the sacrificial cult. Although purified in Leviticus and through the admonition of the prophets, it remained a barrier to the development of the true religion.[47]

In tracing the development of Christianity's true ideas and pagan notions from their origin to the present day, Steinheim was not interested in the life of Jesus as such and only wanted to discover whether he fitted into the category of true revelation. "We must always inquire: Does he stand within the belief in unity, creation, and freedom which form the harmonious trinity of the old canon? Or has he raised a doctrine in the manner of John, alien to them, but similar to the old theologies of paganism and the teachings of Plato?" He found that Jesus stood completely "within the sphere of true revelation,"[48] acknowledging his debt for this conclusion to the Christian theologian Sepp, whose careful analysis and comparison of the Gospels impressed him. On the other hand, he rejected the work of Strauss.

Steinheim sought to discover where precisely pagan elements had been introduced into the new religion. "These simple conclusions were opposed by the philosophical author, the platonic Christian, John with his doctrine of the Trinity. Here is the point at which the old and the new religious philosophers recognize and proclaim the nucleus of the new teaching, the Christian theology."[49] The change occurred chiefly through John rather than Paul. In the first century, according to Steinheim, the religion of Jesus and Christianity were separate entities. In the next generation the former found a representative in Peter and the latter Paul; the influence of both men can be seen in the various writings of the New Testament, as Steinheim demonstrated with some thoroughness.[50]

Naturally, as Christianity spread to other lands its pagan elements attracted philosophical minds. Throughout the ages philosophers have been closer to Paul and John than to the Jewish elements of Christianity. Thus Christianity degenerated from its original strength and purity, but this had advantages: "We have guarded ourselves categorically against the charge or the suspicion of harboring hostile feelings against the sublime founder of the new brotherhood, the man who unlocked the sanctuary for the pagans. However we distinguish sharply . . . but with all sharpness of the distinction and the discussion . . . we are completely and sincerely convinced of its providential character and value as a means of attracting and overcoming paganism and dogmatic rationalism in all its forms.''[51] Thus it is clear that Steinheim fully appreciated the role Christianity had played in the upward development and progress of mankind.

Among the elements in Christianity that encourage paganism, Steinheim noted the doctrines of the Trinity and Original Sin, which destroy man's freedom and God's justice.[52] He also mentioned the latent idolatry of Christian art, pointing out that the worship of images holds special dangers for simpler adherents of the new religion. Steinheim then proceeded to describe the centuries of Christian development—its philosophical and theological changes, which were in essence a losing battle against paganism. In this rambling, discursive volume, Steinheim also turned to philosophical questions and touched on the development of ideas in Judaism and other religions.

Outside the purely religious sphere, pagan ways had corrupted the nature of governments. Steinheim felt that the Christian state had failed to curb the hunger for power, the use of force, and such terrible institutions as slavery, even in democratic lands like the United States.[53] Like Formstecher, he also criticized the detrimental pagan influences within the structure and hierarchy of the Church.[54]

To Steinheim, all of Christianity, past and present, represents a compromise. He saw the history of Christianity as an extended struggle between its chief elements, with paganism almost always victorious. At times the paganism in Christianity virtually threatened the destruction of true revelation. Only the Reformation brought a change, although earlier movements had made similar attempts. The Reformation provided a new basis for progress, even though this was not Luther's intention. Steinheim included a critical analysis of the beginning portions of Luther's Genesis in the fourth volume of his book, a detailed attack on

Luther's Biblical exegesis. Steinheim understood Luther's weaknesses but considered his work so important that he wrote: "Blessed be the memory of Luther, despite every way in which he may have erred in word and deed! His memory shall also be holy for us!" Aside from theoretical freedom and return to revelation, Protestantism ended the Inquisition, though this was replaced by new persecutions instigated by Luther.[55] Steinheim knew that the wave of intense anti-Semitism unleashed by Luther continued to exercise influence in his own day, even on the more liberal Lutheran ministers.[56] Despite these reservations he judged the Reformation to have been a forward step. "What had been knocked together by force sought to separate itself again with the same force, only it worked more slowly."[57] The Reformation gave man freedom; it continued to restrain his powers of reason, but those were also eventually freed. It had done little for revelation, however. "In the midst of the circle of idolatry, which matched that of paganism in extent and intensity, amidst all the helpers, intercessors, and representatives of the miserable outcast, there suddenly arose a spark of revelation as an aid to man's salvation, which had been excluded by the Reformation."[58] The Reformation moved slowly; its conceptions of freedom and of reason were limited. It did not strike a clear blow in favor of true revelation, but it helped the compromise which we call Christianity to progress.

Steinheim felt doubts about his age and did not share the optimism that characterized other Jewish thinkers of the time. Like Brod a century later, he regarded the advances in natural science and the new schools of philosophy and theology as a return to paganism. For this he criticized Christian thinkers as well as Jewish ones like Mendelssohn.[59] Schelling and Hegel were especially singled out for long discussion,[60] and much of the last volume of his book was a critique of contemporary Christian and Jewish philosophers, theologians, and Biblical scholars.

Though fully aware that he and his idea of revelation represented a minority view, Steinheim was not disturbed. "What leads us into the struggle with these powers?—us who are weak into battle with men, into the struggle of the spirits? Let me be permitted to respond to this question with a thought of the great Reformer [Luther]: . . . 'Only when the day of universal redemption is at hand would it dawn on me to see whether I could possibly reinstate Moses again and to lead the little brooks to the right spring and river.'"[61] Steinheim chose not to wait until that distant time and wished to undertake the task in his own day, even though he realized that he would not be understood or appreciated.[62] Among the few evidences of Christian appreciation of Steinheim is his correspondence with his lifelong friend Detlev August Twesten, a theologian who lived in nearby Kiel. Only fragments of letters and a diary have survived. Among Jews, Geiger published some of Steinheim's essays as well as critiques of his work. Heinrich Graetz, the historian, understood Steinheim best and praised him as the German Philo; despite this, he was soon virtually forgotten.[63]

Hirsch, Formstecher, and Steinheim saw Christianity as an antagonist which could be challenged. Each established the superiority of Judaism. Their books were polemical; the foundations upon which they were based differed, but the results were very similar. Although Hirsch and Formstecher were optimistic about the early acceptance of Judaism as the universal religion, Steinheim considered that a distant vision. Yet the polemic was not an end in itself. As Steinheim said: "One does not fight a war for the sake of war, but for the sake of peace . . . so also those friends of peace who are victorious in this polemic must always aim at peace."[64] Each man wished to correct the inferior status given Judaism by contemporary philosophers and scholars. They all intended Judaism to be recognized as a superior form of religion by those who rejected and mocked it.

Despite Steinheim's occasional publication in Christian journals, none of these writers was widely read by the non-Jewish world. Samuel Hirsch and Salomon Formstecher were leaders at the rabbinical synods that sought to reform Judaism; Hirsch, Formstecher, and Steinheim were active in the struggle for Jewish emancipation. Their views of Christianity influenced the Jewish community, but hardly in the direction of better understanding, for in the final analysis, these three men, led to make vigorous counterattacks by Christian hostility to Judaism, continued the tradition of viewing Christianity in a sharply critical manner.

8

Isaac Mayer Wise

An American Approach

Isaac Mayer Wise arrived in the United States in 1846 from Bohemia, where many of the ancient restrictions on the Jewish population were still in force. Deeply imbued with the spirit of liberalism and strongly influenced by the optimism of the nineteenth century, he sought to impress these ideals on American Judaism. Indeed, his whole life was devoted to establishing Reform Judaism in the United States, a task for which his talents as organizer and publicist eminently qualified him. He remains venerated as the founder of the organizations of American Reform Judaism, although his theological speculations have been largely discarded. In his own lifetime, other reformers, such as Einhorn and Kohler, enjoyed perhaps greater sway among the more philosophically inclined, but Wise, through his popular writings and personal influence, was the leader of the mass of Reform Jews.

Wise was one of the first American rabbis to express himself publicly on Christianity. At first, the Jewish community was enraged at his boldness, but later it began to appreciate his efforts and even saw them produce a change in the outlook of American Jews toward Christianity. Wise's approach to Christianity was not entirely logical or consistent—the same fault that appears in his theological discussions of Judaism, where in some matters he held extremely radical views, while in others he clung to tradition. However, his views on Christianity were more consistently radical.

His concern with Christianity was not initially motivated by theology, but came about, rather, as the result of the proselytizing efforts of Christian missionaries, who constantly approached him and his congregation in Albany, where Wise had his first American pulpit, and later in Cincinnati, where he spent the rest of his life as a rabbi and as president of the Hebrew Union College. One such conversion invitation was contained in a pamphlet written by the secretary of the Presbyterian synod of New York. It elicited a strong counterstatement from Wise, published as a series of articles in the *Occident,* in which he "attacked Christianity critically from the nationalistic standpoint."[1] Wise continued unfailingly to respond to the crudity of what he called "the conversionist craze of American orthodox Christianity . . . more acute [in the United States] than even in England and Prussia."[2] The following passage is characteristic of his passion and vigor: "The volume hereby presented to the reader was written and published in response to those missionary chieftains of the city of Cincinnati who took a vulgar renegade from Judaism by his hand, and appointed him a missionary to the Jews; and notwithstanding the man's illiteracy, furnished him with a pulpit and invited the Jews week after week by pompous advertisements in the public press and handbills freely distributed in the streets to come and hear that renegade. The author, considering that uncalled-for action of church dignitaries an insult to Judaism, felt it his duty to resent it, and so he did."[3]

Such polemics evoked much unfriendly reaction from both Jews and Christians: "A host of pious souls prodded me with pens and pencils, as though Satan had let loose all the legions of hell against me. . . . The Christians were even more bitter than the Jews."[4] Many newspapers commented unfavorably on his *Occident* articles. Indignant preachers saw to it that he was removed from the state library committee. Jews felt his actions might serve to arouse anti-Semitism, though many were delighted that he was able to defend them and Judaism in so stirring a manner.

Because Wise undertook his initial discussion of Christianity in heat, it contained some rather strong statements devoid of scholarly foundation. These early efforts, however, were important, for they directed Wise's attention to the study of Christianity, which was to remain an enduring interest and was to produce a large number of books and essays on the subject.

Wise understood that if he was to proceed with an informed discussion of Christianity he must tread delicately. As he noted: "It is not right, perhaps, that I write a lecture on the Christianity of history, as I do not comprehend and understand Christianity as a Christian would; and I know, on the other hand, that Christians like Hitzig, Kuenen, Wellhausen, or Millman and that learned professor of Harvard College, writing on the Judaism of history, make very considerable mistakes, partly by their ignorance of the Jewish literature and the people that produced it. I will, therefore, be brief and cautious in my remarks on this important subject."[5] To be sure, Wise often disregarded his own injunction and wrote very bluntly, but this was due more to the shortcomings of his style than to any desire to criticize.

Wise was acutely aware that his was a pioneer effort in America—unlike Europe, where Mendelssohn, Jost, and Geiger had prepared the ground for such discussion—and he therefore took extreme pains to set forth his facts and their reasons: " . . . to the best of our knowledge no Jewish lecturer has yet ventured to discuss these topics publicly and under the light of free and independent thought. And why not? In the first place the Jews were not permitted to criticize Christianity or even to defend and expound publicly their own beliefs. Those who ventured to speak, like Rabbi Lipman, author of the *Sepher Nitzachon,* were slain or mistreated. The books were burned or stored away in some monastery where none could find them. Any passage found in any Jewish book in the least offensive to the priestly taste was eradicated by the censor, or even by the Jews themselves who feared the wrath of their neighbors. Nor were Christians permitted to speak. . . . No wonder, then, that the Jew kept silent when the Christian was not permitted to speak. Nor was it advisable for the Jew to speak overly loud of his opinions among Jews, if they were of the non-conforming kind . . . and so the Jew was silent, although his silence was misconstrued to the effect that Judaism had no apology for its doctrines and no arguments against its opponents. Thank Heaven we are in America, and in Cincinnati, where free thought and free speech are the birthright of every law-abiding person."[6]

Wise cautioned his readers, advising them that he would

approach both Judaism and Christianity through "the electric light of reason," and though some of them might feel hurt, this was the price of impartial investigation. Undoubtedly, he felt that current scholarship buttressed him far more than it actually did. Wise was an autodidact, and his reading had been scattered and uneven. So, with firm belief in his sources he warned: "Whoever is afraid of the two-edged sword of truth and the cold steel of logic is not expected to listen to these lectures. . . . We will have to cut into both Judaism and Christianity, as there are old sores in each system which must be cut now or later, and will be cut and healed by the world's steady progress, whether we recognize them or not. Whatever cannot stand the rigid application of reason is doomed to perish. Whatever is in the way of the unity and fraternity of the human family will be overthrown. Whatever is unkind, uncharitable, ungenerous, intolerant, illiberal or unfree cannot last much longer in our country. There can be no harm in exposing any elements of this kind at once and radically."[7]

In dealing with Christianity he felt that his training as a rabbi would never interfere with objectivity. "On numerous occasions he [Wise] has been told that people were anxious to read what he writes on subjects in the New Testament, because they wish to learn what is said about them from the Jewish standpoint. This is a mistake. The author who now speaks to you is a Jew of the nineteenth century, whose motto is, 'The world is my country and love is my religion'; whose people are all of God's children; and whose standpoint in philosophy, science and criticism is as purely objective and as free of every prejudice or bias as long years of reading, research, and travelling make a human being. He wears no sectarian shackles, stands under no local bias, and obeys no mandates of any particular school. Whatever he says or has said on subjects contained in the New Testament, in order to be understood correctly, must be examined from the only standpoint of reason."[8]

Wise then proceeded to deal with Jesus and the Gospels in the dispassionate light of nineteenth-century skepticism. Here he followed the lesser disciples of Bauer and Strauss; at times he seemed as skeptical as Bauer, though he was not consistent. His precise sources remain unknown, except for Wislicenus's *The*

Bible Considered for Thinking Readers (1864). Samuel Sandmel has shown that Wise annotated Wislicenus's essays and used them as a source for the unfinished "Jesus Himself," published in the *American Israelite* in 1869 and 1870.[9] Sandmel shows how in these essays Wise moved from extreme skepticism to an acceptance of the historicity of Jesus. Yet the earlier skepticism appeared again later. Be that as it may, Wise felt that his work not only led to a better understanding of Christianity, but also accrued to its benefit; thus he could state, rather innocently, that what he had to say about Jesus, the Last Supper, and other important Christian matters, "is made in defense not only of religion, but also of Christianity and the character of Jesus."[10]

Apart from his *Judaism and Christianity*, where he analyzed the Gospels, Wise did not deal with the life of Jesus systematically. In his other books he concerned himself primarily with a few aspects of Jesus' life and with the doctrines that were built upon it. Thus he wished to prove that "the crucifixion of Jesus was not decreed by the Almighty, his martyrdom was not necessary for the salvation of mankind, and the dogma of the vicarious atonement has no foundation in the Gospels . . . "[11] Naturally, a discussion of the crucifixion was important to Wise, since Jews have suffered so much as a result of this event. Aside from dogmatic considerations of the Church, which he considered foolish, Wise felt that the death of Jesus could be explained quite simply: "The martyrdom of Jesus of Nazareth has been gratefully acknowledged by his disciples whose lives he saved by the sacrifice of his own, and by their friends who would have fallen by the score had he not prevented the rebellion ripe at Jerusalem. . . . The simple fact has been made the foundation of a novel myth to suit the gross conceptions of ex-heathens. Modern theology, understanding well enough that the myth can not be saved, seeks refuge in the greatness and self-denial of the man who died for an idea, as though Jesus had been the only man who died for an idea. . . . But Jesus did not die for an idea. He never advanced anything new to die for. He was not accused of saying or teaching anything original. . . . He died to save lives of his friends, and this is much more meritorious in our estimation than if he had died for a questionable idea."[12] As for the Jewish role in this matter,

Wise thought that "the world has sinned more against the Jews than a hundred Christs could atone for on the cross."[13]

Wise neglected the life of Jesus because he regarded it as a fictitious account. He did not believe that Jesus had ever existed historically as the person described by the Gospels. "All so-called lives of Christ or biographies of Jesus are works of fiction, erected by imagination on the shifting foundation of meager and unreliable records. There are very few passages in the Gospels which can stand the rigid application of honest criticism."[14] Here he followed the patterns of scholarship of Strauss and Bauer rather than Renan. But this did not detract from the ethical and moral teachings of Christianity, which he considered independent of the life of Jesus. "The universal, religious, and ethical element of Christianity has no connection whatever with Jesus or his apostles, with the Gospel or the Gospel story; it exists independent of any person or story. Therefore, it needs neither the Gospel story nor its heroes. In the common acceptation of the terms, one can be a good Christian without the slightest belief in Jesus or the Gospels."[15]

It must be remembered that Wise spoke with a firm belief in the optimism of his age and sincerely felt that all of mankind was rapidly moving toward the millennium. "Like rabbinic Judaism, dogmatic Christianity was the product of ages without typography, telescopes. . . . These right arms of intelligence have fought the titanic battles, conquered and demolished the ancient castles, and remove now the debris, preparing the ground upon which there shall be reared the gorgeous temple of humanity, one universal religion, one universal religion of intelligence, and one great universal brotherhood. This is the new covenant, the gospel of humanity and reason."[16]

Wise had little ability to imagine Jews in a first-century environment, and he could not fit Jesus into the nineteenth century. He felt that the religions he was demolishing—Orthodox Judaism and Christianity—both stood in the way of the future; this led to radical statements about them. Without a strong Messianic inclination he might have expressed himself very differently.

At other times, Wise concerned himself more with the theological implications of the life of Jesus. Modern theology, he wrote, cannot get over the absurdity that the Almighty Lord of the universe, the infinite and eternal Cause of all causes, had to kill an innocent man in order to be reconciled to human beings. However abstractly the theologians speculate and subtilize, there is always an undigested bone of man-god, god-man, and vicarious atonement in the theological stomach, and it is for this reason that theology appears so ridiculous in the eyes of modern philosophy. However nicely the idea may be dressed up, the great God of the immense universe looks too small on the cross of Calvary; and the human family is too large, has too many virtues and vices, to be perfectly represented and dependent on one rabbi of Galilee.[17] He wondered aloud about the ritual of the Christian Churches: "The same Jesus, it is supposed, who objected to all the sanctimonious observances of the Pharisees and priests, and looked upon outward piety, the religion of performances, as conducive to no good and productive of hypocrisy; who opposed the entire Levitical laws and institutions; the same Jesus is supposed to have instituted a new outward observance, and made it a condition, *sine qua non*, to obtain salvation. We furthermore believe to have a good right for maintaining, that no words of Jesus were worse misrepresented and misconstrued than those spoken at his last supper."[18] Naturally, each of these statements was supported by numerous pages of documentation.

Wise was most disturbed by the miracles on which Christianity rested, for he thought that this basic irrationality prevented the spirit of the modern age from penetrating deeply into the Christian people. He dealt with this matter often and vehemently. "Again miracles must be believed, they can never appeal to reason. Each miracle requires a separate act of belief. Those who expect us to believe in revelation which is a miracle according to that supernatural standpoint, and then want us to believe another number of miracles in order to establish the fact of revelation, evidently ask too much of the reasoning man. We can more easily believe one than a dozen miracles, especially if any one suffices to prove the dominion of mind over matter, and the one, as is the case in the Sinaic revelation, conveys all the instruction to the human mind which it needs, to understand the relation between God and man, and affords him a valid standard of truth and right-eousness."[19] He felt that the Talmud suffered from the same weaknesses and shortcoming. "Neither the Christian nor the Jew can be willing to admit, that the pretensions to supernatural communication of both the apostles and the rabbis are correct."[20] Both were in error according to him, but we might believe them if they did not contradict each other. As matters stand we must reject both of them for similar reasons. "Any intelligent reader, on discovering all the superstitions in the Talmud, will at once come to the conclusions that both the authors of the New Testament and the compilers of the Talmud committed one and the same error, viz., they accepted and presented those aberrations of the human mind as matters of fact."[21]

This objection to miraculous prophecy and the irrational was continually stressed. "Christianity starting with inspiration from the supernatural standpoint must consistently maintain that the prophet is the divinely commissioned man to a certain religious end, who predicts future events and works miracles. Therefore, both Jesus and his original apostles, also Paul, according to statements of the Acts of Apostles, and a number of primitive Christians prophesied and wrought miracles."[22] A similar but distinctive statement is found in another book: "The Orthodox Christian . . . believes the New Testament miracles, because they are written in that book. There exists no other evidence supporting them. . . . All those miracles rest upon precisely the same authority of this or that book or tradition; hence one must believe all or none. Believing none of them, one is no orthodox Christian. Believing all of them, one must believe also all the doctrine taught in those books, or he must confess with us that miracles prove nothing."[23] "Whoever believes the miracles of the Gospels must no less believe the miracles of the Talmud."[24]

Nor did Wise find the Biblical proof-texts cited in the New Testament any more reasonable than the stories of miracles. He presented a lengthy discussion and concluded: "So frail are all the references of the New Testament to the Old, where the attempt is made to prop Christology by the oracles of the old prophets in Israel. If you even admit the unreasonable construction of those passages, it would prove nothing in favor of the Messiah which it does not also in favor of Alexander the Great, who was a son of Apollo, or any other Roman or Greek who has a son of some God;

cases of that kind were not rare even in the time when Mary conceived of the Holy Ghost, as you can see in Josephus."[25] Finally failing to discover a hint of Christianity in the books of Moses, the Prophets, or the Psalms, he summarized with the statement: "The New Testament is the fulfillment and continuation of the Old, by the grace of the church and the bookbinder."[26]

Wise did not hesitate to argue from the divisions of Christianity that the basic truth must be in doubt, which was a favorite theme of the deists. "The Jew's argument is invigorated by the protests of millions of Christians in past centuries against the orthodox dogma; and in our century especially, by the dispute and controversies of the hundreds of Christian sects now extant. If you take together the sum of all denials by those sects nothing is left of the whole orthodox Christology. Everyone of them denies something which the others considered essential to true Christianity."[27]

Using these traditional paths and the path which had been prepared by nineteenth-century Biblical criticism, Wise was, then, a rather severe critic of Christianity. In all his books one has the feeling that a portion of this harshness stemmed from the fact that no such expression had been possible to a Jew for a long time. Like someone gone wild after long confinement, Wise used every conceivable argument against a religion that had often oppressed the Jew and was now threatening to postpone the millennium he so sincerely desired.

At the time of his writing he felt that Judaism had not been given sufficient credit for its contributions to the general civilization. This was especially overdue because Christianity had lost many of its old characteristics and was coming closer to Judaism.

Wise insisted that the basic ethics of Sinai were quite sufficient when reason was added thereto. This led him to a strong rejection of vicarious atonement, for he felt it to be contrary to higher ethics. "We also agree that there could be no remission of sins without sincere and genuine repentance. We furthermore agree in most of the means, such as humiliation before God and man, confession, giving alms and the like. But we disagree in other means, and the dogma of vicarious atonement is no more than that. . . . This makes of Christianity a tribal and sectional religion in conflict with man's reason. Therefore, those who believe in the universal and eternal character of the Sinaic revelation and the final triumph of God's truth can hardly doubt that this 'Disagreement' also will be overcome and the religion of the future man will contain no Christology. The future man will need no Messiah and no redeemer, no baptism and no circumcision. . . . ; for neither all these nor other means are contained in the Sinaic revelation or based upon the pure dicta of reason. Whatever is not either in revelation or reason is of the spontaneous generation of fancy and purely accidental."[28]

Yet Wise never underestimated the moral strength of Christianity, and in fact he admired it. "The forte of Christianity is its moral doctrine. All the good it ever did and ever can do is accomplished by the spread of this moral doctrine among such nations or tribes with whom on account of their defective intelligence the standard of morals was low and inadequate to attain that amount of happiness which man is naturally endowed to enjoy."[29] He strongly felt that the ethical insights of that religion ought to be admired and that it must be praised for the good it has done in the world. "Let me add here that Christianity has done so large an amount of good and is doing it now, that it certainly must command respect as the religion of three hundred and more millions of people. Least among all men the religious Jew dare attack Christianity with any weapons except the most rational and most charitable, as he maintains that whatever is true and benevolent in Christianity is taken from Judaism . . ."[30]

In this spirit Wise felt that Christianity was in essence the same as Judaism and that Jesus had added little, if anything, to it. "If Jesus has left the ethics of the Old Testament unchanged and unaltered, without addition or diminution, then Calvary has added nothing to the ethics of Sinai. Therefore what some gentlemen are pleased to call Christian morals or Christian ethics are actually Jewish morals or Jewish ethics, which Christendom accepts and endorses. After all, perhaps, the name does not make much difference, although it is always proper to call things by their right names. It offers the advantage in this particular respect that all of us become aware how numerous, essential and important our 'agreements' are, while our 'disagreements' appear chiefly in names.''[31]

It was, of course, necessary for Wise to discuss the place of the Gospels, the apostles, and especially of Paul. Here again he largely followed the tendencies of his time and added little that was new. The discussion of the Gospels begins with the statement: "The four Gospels, the origin of which is discussed in this volume, cannot be taken as the main sources for the origin of Christianity. They represent it in the second and third stages of its development. The authors were Christians before they wrote their books; hence Christianity preceded them ''[32] In this approach he agreed with many nineteenth-century Christian writers who also sought a rational and nonmiraculous basis for the Gospels. Wise thought that beneath the present Gospel tradition lay a "primitive gospel" in Hebrew or Aramaic, and he several times sought to prove this. On another occasion he proposed a most unusual theory by claiming that the Gospels were composed during the reign of Hadrian, who had forbidden the use of the Jewish Bible. They were intended to serve as a temporary substitute for the Bible, and the numerous Biblical verses they quote were meant to preserve some link with the forbidden Scriptures. On the whole, however, he remained with the earlier notion of a "primitive gospel."

Wise discussed Paul several times, though never in detail. He considered Paul's protests against the Law to be limited to ceremonial law and not to include the ethical statements of Sinai. "Paul's protestations against the law and circumcision were in nowise directed against the Sinaic revelation and covenant, although he goes back to the Abrahamitic covenant; for he preached the same moral doctrine and the same God who should be again 'all in all,' when the Son will return the kingdom to the Father. He held so firmly to the laws of the Decalogue that he commanded the adulterer among his flock to be put to death; and claimed that the covenant had been inherited by the Gentiles. The abolition of the law referred to the political, civil, criminal, ceremonial, or Levitical laws . . . This, I believe, is admitted by the orthodox expounders of the New Testament. Hence it must also be admitted that the Sinaic revelation and the covenant were the fundamental principle of primitive and original Christianity, and the protestations of its founders were directed only against a portion of the laws and institutions of Moses."[33]

He drew the usual distinction between Paul and the other apostles and assigned the radical changes that brought about Christianity to Paul alone. "The apostles themselves maintained that Jesus only protested against the rabbinical laws and the traditions of the Pharisees, and had not come to abrogate an iota or a tittle of the Laws of Moses. . . . Paul, in one bold stroke, abrogated everything in the name of the master, which was in the way of the new system of religion, to be promulgated among the Gentiles, ready then for a change in religion. These two different schools are known in the early history of Christianity as Jewish and Gentile Christianity. Peter was the representative man of the former system, and Paul the founder of the latter."[34]

At one point Wise attempted to prove that Paul was the *Aher* of the Talmud[35] (term applied to Elisha B. Abuyah, a sage of the Mishnaic period who apparently became either a Gnostic, a follower of Philo, or a Christian) and went into considerable detail in the process. In the end he returned to another view of Paul: "So the law is good and just, but Paul and everybody else is a disobedient and rebellious rogue. It must have been quite pleasing and soothing to the incestuous and degraded heathens, to learn that actually all men are rogues and scoundrels, not by their own choice, indeed, but by the will of God who has not given them the capacity to perform that which is good, so that everyone has a devil in his flesh who plays diabolical tricks with a poor man. This was the capital hit of Paul, to win the heathens who felt the burden of their wickedness."[36] This meant then, according to Wise, that Paul abrogated the entire Law but also reinstated the moral law; this, he felt, led Paul into many contradictions—"sometimes entirely astray, to misquotations from the Bible, quibbling on words, and endless contradictions and repetitions."[37]

Yet Wise admired Paul, fully recognizing his greatness as well as the influence he had on the new religion and its growth. "The moral of the thing is, a great man must not resort to fictions, or to any accommodation, however efficient means they may offer for the time being. And Paul was a great man. The idea of demolishing heathenism, and to do it alone, all alone, opposed by Jews and Gentiles, opposed by those whose redemption scheme he adopted and whose master he glorified, shows a great energetic and resolute man. The determination to bring the knowledge of the One God and the pure moral law to debased and corrupted heathens, is holy and admirable. . . . Like all brilliant and successful men in history, he understood his age, stood upon its summit, adopted the most available means to carry out his plans, felt an interest in, and an attachment to, the whole human family. . . . However numerous his imperfections may be, he was a great, energetic and independent man, in comparison to whom Peter and James were monks, visionary Essenes, stubborn and narrow sectarians."[38] And elsewhere: "All Jews of all ages hoped and expected that the kingdom of heaven would encompass all nations and tongues; but Paul undertook to realize this hope, this is his title to greatness."[39]

Wise interpreted Paul as looking toward the end of the world and the imminent Messianic Age; this led to his abrogation of the Law, his support of Roman rule, and his refusal to condemn the evils of slavery. "He did not want to squander the few days before the end in any worldly improvements, in any reform of social or political relations."[40] Wise saw him as an excellent judge of men and his era, very much a man of the world who "made use of all these means, the end of all flesh, the son of God, and other novelties, not because he believed in them; but because he considered them the most effectual means . . . to the true conceptions of God, immortality . . . and moral life."[41] Thus Paul's Jesus was very different from the original figure. "The Jesus of Paul is no more than the superintendent of the catastrophe which was then to come to pass, and after which he should be subject to the Father, and God should be again all in all."[42]

Despite Wise's admiration of Paul and the task he undertook, he felt that Christianity had erred greatly in the manner in which it treated the Law, for in the final analysis law is needed. In the event, a different law was developed. "Christianity, starting out without laws, made its Talmud entirely different from that of the Jews, although it was developed by the same law of evolution as Judaism was. It made, in the course of time, a Talmud of Rome, a Talmud of Constantinople, and at last a Talmud of Protestantism.

With the laws of Moses, also the freedom, quality and stern justice underlying them were relinquished, abandoned to the so-called worldly rulers, which was a great loss to humanity."[43]

Wise's commentary on Acts, which deals with the origins of Christianity, remains an interesting volume, although much of it is highly speculative in nature. It is actually a sermonic critique of Christianity rather than a scholarly work. The proof for many statements is weak and rests on little more than the author's intuition. Wise intended the volume as a popular critical approach to the New Testament, and in a measure he succeeded, but the level of learning he presented in it was inferior to that of contemporary European writers on the same subject.

Wise gave little attention to the development of Protestantism or the great Protestant leaders. He was disturbed by the lack of rationality in both Catholicism and Protestantism. He sought evolution in the Protestant Reformation but failed to find it; instead, there was a system with its own rigidities. Actually, the sectarian development caused by Protestantism was used by him to dispute the dogmas of Christianity since so little agreement on basic principle could be found.

The Reformation was viewed primarily as useful to prepare for later philosophical and scientific advances. "In spite of all the blunders made in the Reformation, the European nations advanced from the dawn in the sixteenth century to the high noon of the nineteenth. . . . The old Christology of supposed fact was changed into speculative Christology, by men like Frederick Schleiermacher, Kant, Schelling, Hegel. . . . The ideas which they represent are sufficient to constitute a satisfactory Christology; . . . this is the last phase of Christian reformation; the next step beyond leads into the Sinaic revelation and the covenant as the sole foundation of positive religion."[44] So the Christianity of the present day seemed to have cast off many ancient dogmas and practices. "The Christianity of Peter and the other disciples of Jesus exists no more; Paul, especially after the fall of Jerusalem, opposed and defeated it. Modern Christianity has more of Paul than of Peter and Jesus, although in the dogmas Paul is also scarcely recognizable. . . . If the Pope is a Christian, Paul was none; if any of our modern congregations are Christian, then the apostolic congregation in Jerusalem was heretic."[45]

Wise's criticism of Christianity was harsh, but it was meant to bring Judaism and Christianity closer together rather than separating them further. Again and again, Wise stressed both his strong feelings of kinship to his Christian neighbors and the common religious heritage shared by Judaism and Christianity. "We love the Christian as our fellow-man and Christianity as a daughter-religion of our own. The injuries of the past we have forgotten long ago, the liberty, justice and humanism of the present day are 'bone from my bone and flesh from my flesh,' as was Eve from Adam, reuniting and fraternizing the discordant elements of society. . . . For all that, and with the best will to please our neighbors, we cannot discover Christology in the Bible, nor persuade ourselves that it is a religion in harmony with the divine principles acknowledged as such by Jews and Gentile."[46]

However, Wise's qualified respect did not cause him to overlook Christianity's weaknesses. "Christology can never become the religion of all mankind because its teachings are contrary to the common sense of man, are discredited in Christendom today, not only by infidels and philosophers, but by the sectarians them-selves, each maintaining to be orthodox; and by the uninterrupted protest against the fabric of salvation by the Jews during all the years of its existence, from beginning to end. . . . It cannot make us better men and better women, as it did not succeed in sixteen centuries in civilizing and humanizing the nations under its sway. . . . Hence Christology is not the mother of these virtues, it can do us no good, it has done more harm than good to the nations of Europe."[47]

Such words may induce the reader to wonder how Wise would have defended traditional Judaism. He did not do so, because he felt similarly about the traditional forms of Judaism. "Both must fall. Rabbinical Judaism and dogmatic Christianity, being exten-sive codes concerning the means of religion, must finally yield to the progress and triumph of the religious idea itself; then God will be again all in all, to speak with Paul, or then God will be one and his name one, as the prophet has it. Whenever they shall have done each of its full service to the cause of religion, they will disappear. Intelligent men in our days need neither rabbinism nor christology. Thoughtless masses need the antiquated means, the child must be coaxed to school, but it is the duty of every good man to diminish the number of thoughtless individuals, by spreading light, information.''[48]

Wise keenly felt that Judaism purified of its rabbinic elements was the religion of the future, not only for Jews but for all men. He was certain that all mankind was on the verge of accepting Reform Judaism. He was convinced that in America, the progress of culture, science, and art would eventually proselytize all people to Reform Judaism. No particular effort by Jews was necessary, for this was the next natural step in the religious progress of mankind.[49] Christianity, therefore, became a religion of the past; its mission was to prepare men for Judaism. Christianity had become enlightened and more rational in the nineteenth century; much Christology had been cast off; therefore it had brought mankind to the threshold of Judaism. Now Reform Judaism was the universal religion of the future and all others could be discarded.

Isaac Mayer Wise added little new to the study of Jesus and Paul. Many of his statements can be found in Christian writings of the time. The novelty lay in the fact that he pursued this course as a Jew and a rabbi. He rejected Christianity as vigorously as any of his forefathers. He began the study through a desire to rebuke missionary efforts. At first he thought little of Paul and doubted the existence of Jesus. Eventually he felt admiration for Paul's vigor, courage, and brilliant use of the opportunity of his age, although he regarded his theology and ecclesiology as harmful. He also felt that Jesus was a historical figure to be admired for "patriotism and enthusiasm,"[50] although rejecting all Christian doctrine concerning him. He was among the Jews who began the task of rediscovering some Jewish elements in the life of Jesus and the Jewish basis of Christianity, especially modern Christianity. The liberal, energetic Isaac Mayer Wise was not satisfied with reforming Judaism but sought also to reshape Christianity and to demonstrate that the new Christianity led directly to the Judaism of the future.

9

Hermann Cohen

Neo-Kantian Critique

The nineteenth and twentieth centuries brought Jews into the mainstream of Western life. Judaism was forced to face a series of challenges from the world it entered. Through the ages Judaism has grappled with various philosophies and systems of science and technology, but the oldest and most enduring challenge came from Christianity. Hermann Cohen (1842–1918) sought to view Christianity as a modern Jew and to reach a new understanding of it.

Cohen was the most influential German-Jewish thinker of the late nineteenth century; for many he was *the* spokesman of German-Jewish philosophy. He was also a *baal teshuvah,* an intellectual who had rejected Judaism and returned to it later in life. Although he had received a thorough Jewish education from his father, the cantor of Coswig, and later at the Jewish Theological Seminary in Breslau, he lost interest. As a student he turned to philosophy and soon became a leader in the Neo-Kantian movement, which dominated German thought at the end of the nineteenth century. His contributions were outstanding, so he rose rapidly in the academic ranks. His gifts led the anti-Semitic academicians to overlook the fact that he was a Jew and he became a leading professor at the University of Marburg, where he remained until his retirement. When he chose to end his career by lecturing at a Jewish institution, the Lehranstalt in Berlin; his disciples were few but notable, among them Franz Rosenzweig, whose philosophy was, however, to follow a different path. Cohen concerned himself mainly with Jewish topics during those decades, and his final work sought to link Neo-Kantian thought and Judaism.

Hermann Cohen's approach to Christianity was more philosophical and less exegetical than that of most rabbis and Biblical scholars. He was not concerned with the details of the Gospels or their historical background, but with their implications for the modern Jew and Christian. Partially his interest was stimulated by Christianity's attractiveness for many emancipated German Jews. Christianity was an alternative to the old-fashioned faith of their Fathers and, as Heine had sarcastically put it: "Baptism was the admission ticket to European civilization." Cohen began his discussion as a defense of Judaism; later he sought a Jewish understanding of Christianity not motivated by apologetics or hindered by fear.

Christianity seemed unsatisfactory to Cohen in that its treatment of God leads to pantheism. Cohen saw the Trinity as a pantheistic effort to bring man closer to God—necessary for Christians, who did not find a sufficiently close bond between God and man in Judaism, but a disadvantage to him as a Jew.[1] To Cohen the Christian solution also fails to bring man close to God because Christian theology links the Holy Spirit and God rather than God and Jesus.[2] There was also the difficulty of properly interpreting the nature of God and man; Christianity, which follows the path of pantheism, confuses the nature of God and man: "Man does not remain man, and God does not remain God."[3] The doctrine of the Trinity is a barrier rather than a bridge to truth.[4] Cohen in another place, however, showed the advantage of pantheism, the love of Jesus and his elevation to the position of the ideal man and the noble role this later thought had played in history. Christianity had contributed to the advance of mankind through emphasizing this ideal man, but Cohen felt that the dangers inherent in pantheism limited the development of the ethical impulse in man.[5]

Ethical considerations led Cohen to a thorough discussion of Jesus and other Christian figures. He criticized the hero worship of Jesus and the saints as detrimental to man's highest ethical ideals. The cult of the hero, he said, was not entirely absent from Judaism, but it was limited to the patriarchs and was never expanded to include later figures. The Church constantly increased the number of saints and through its emphasis on them does not leave perfection as an unlimited goal which can never quite be attained.[6]

Cohen's criticism became sharper when he dealt with Jesus himself, for he felt that Jesus, as interpreted by modern Protestantism, was a threat to Judaism. As he became more a supreme teacher and less a divine being, Jesus was no longer a deity but only an ideal man, a teacher of mankind, and a very appealing personality, especially for modern Jewish youth. Cohen felt that our ethical feelings must arouse a protest in us against the " 'teachings of the life of Jesus' of our age. It is the last defense which the culture and civilization of our time allow (to Christianity), but it posits an even greater danger to us for this reason. As we do not recognize a God of suffering, so we may not recognize *an ideal man* either. For us, man must always remain erring and striving, striving for the highest, but erring according to human fate. For us, there can be no imitation of any man. . . . As men, we are all equally children of the One God; no son of man is the son of God, in no sense no matter how idealized or symbolic.''[7]

Cohen also objected to the current interpretation of Jesus on historical grounds. Jesus is idealized by the Gospels as a man of love and peace, yet one could read an entirely different account of his actions into the New Testament. From a purely pedagogical point of view, Jesus must be rejected by Jews, for his life "fulfilled itself in enmity to the basis of our teachings." Even if he did not claim to be the son of God, he certainly claimed a special relationship with God. Furthermore, the Sermon on the Mount contains statements that must be declared to be falsifications of the Jewish point of view; Judaism has never demanded hatred of our enemies, etc. Even if the Pharisees showed some weaknesses, they surely were not the "hypocrites and vipers" the New Testament makes them out to be. The life of Jesus was of a piece with all these statements, and thus he can hardly be an ideal personality for us. This becomes even clearer in the account of his final days and his crucifixion. Cohen contrasted the dying statement of Jesus on the cross with that of various Jewish martyrs. Jesus asked why God had forsaken him; they died without a murmur. Why must we accept him as *the* ideal personality whom all men must admire?[8]

Cohen had deep respect for Christianity and its religious teachings, but he considered it wrong to attempt to awaken love for Jesus among Jews. We may encourage understanding, but not admiration, he wrote. "We can and should recognize and honor without prejudice, but with esteem and reverence, the utterances which bear that name [i.e., Jesus]; however, we may not mitigate our opposition to the privileged position of this God-Man. Here the fate of our religion is at stake."[9]

Elsewhere Cohen looked more closely at the historical picture of Jesus given by nineteenth-century scholarship. Cohen considered its conclusions irrelevant. Religious beliefs do not depend upon the reality of historical events; they are based upon individual decision, not persuasion by history. Cohen considered the emphasis on the historical Jesus a mistake of Protestantism. "When Christ is honored as an idea rather than a historical person or fact, then the best thoughts of ancient Christianity and the deepest characteristics of the Christian Middle Ages live on. Protestant dogma becomes much stronger, deeper, and purer when thus transmitted than through boasts about the reality of a historical person."[10]

The individual Christian must deal with the problem of belief in Jesus, not belief in God. He must accept Jesus as interpreted by Christian theology. The discussion cannot center around a historical man, but around Jesus as the *unique* man. To Cohen there could be no "unique," unexplained phenomena in history. If such uniqueness were granted Jesus, the problem of his relationship with God would remain unsolved. Jesus, as the source of ethics, would also become problematic. The distinction would no longer be between God and man, but between this unique individual and the ordinary man. The problem would be eliminated if Jesus represented the *idea* of humanity, but as a historical personality—it destroyed human freedom. If one historical man made a decision for all men, ethics loses all meaning.[11]

Cohen protested against the special and ironic relationship between the life of Jesus and the history of Israel. The story of Jesus is tied to Deutero-Isaiah, who portrayed the future history of Israel. Christianity sought to assign the role of a nation to an individual. Thus, the history of Israel and the life of Jesus parallel each other. Nothing akin to this situation can be found in world history.[12]

Cohen also objected to Jesus as the symbol of human suffering.

The Bible has its pessimistic pages, but they do not jeopardize the unity of God. A Jew may recognize the motivation toward social justice inspired by the portrayal of Christ as the Suffering Servant of God, but he must object to this.[13]

There is a similarity between the position of Jesus in the New Testament and Philo's Logos. Cohen felt that both positions would have been unthinkable to the Biblical prophets. The idea of the Logos was attractive and had influenced later Jewish philosophy, but it did not fit Cohen's ethical religion. For the prophets and Cohen, religion was man's ethical yearning; ethics could not flow from God through a series of emanations. God, according to Cohen, could only be the ideal of the highest morality. "Thus, the Jewish idea of God exhausts itself in the ethical meaning of the idea God."[14] This ethical relationship of men with each other and God forms one of the chief distinctions between Judaism and Christianity. Christianity stresses the relationship between man and God, but neglects that between man and man.

To Cohen's mind it was tragic that the God of Christianity can no longer be a pure ideal, but must perforce be partially human. Christianity derives its vigor from this dualism. It seeks to overcome the flesh through the spirit, but since the spirit cannot be detached from matter, all spirituality becomes ambiguous.[15]

He did not minimize the ethical power of Christianity, which can evoke a high degree of morality, but he made it clear that this ethics suffers through concentration on individual salvation and lack of concern with other people. Individual perfection and the individual relationship to God are central and the rest tangential. "Christ is the redeemer of the individual, and only as such can and does he become the savior of mankind. In contrast the Messiah is the redeemer of mankind and only as such does he become the savior of the individual."[16]

Cohen recognized Christianity's contribution to the unification of mankind. The idea of One God awakened the dream of one united mankind. Christianity has stressed this goal through emphasis on its worldwide mission. Although the individual and his salvation are central to Christianity, the thought of a united mankind plays a secondary role on the periphery.[17]

Suffering plays a major role in Christian theology, and Cohen contrasted this to Judaism's view, in which suffering is never an end in itself. Because Christianity had transferred certain pagan elements into itself, it could "portray God Himself as afflicted by human suffering." Cohen admitted the fascination of the idea that suffering reveals a divine purpose, but he rejected it violently: "In monotheism suffering is only a link in the chain of salvation; it may not become the final link. . . . It is just a first step on the path of salvation, to the perfection of mankind in accordance with the attained perfection of the idea of the unique God."[18] Cohen considered Christianity's discovery of a surrogate, upon whom man's suffering, guilt, and finally even his punishment could be placed, as a weakness. Jesus does more than jeopardize the position of man—he also changes and to some extent delimits the nature of God.

Christianity's great emphasis on belief as the path to salvation was also criticized by Cohen. This emphasis substitutes belief for the ancient offerings. He, in contrast to Richard Rubenstein later, criticized sacrifice generally as a form of worship too concerned with the relationship between man and God, at the expense of developing the relationship between man and man. The prophets regarded sacrifices as fundamentally related to idolatry, so they fought against them. This step of the prophets becomes especially noteworthy "when one considers the attachment of the entire ancient world to sacrifice and especially that the thought of sacrifice remains basic for Christianity. Finally, one must also consider that this thought has remained a true and formal expression in the most diversified areas of modern emancipated consciousness, so men reckon their fate and their supposedly voluntary ethical deeds as an offering either to destiny or, if not that, then to duty."[19] The sacrificial cult was abandoned in the course of religious progress, but Christianity, unfortunately, has retained it, so God's essence becomes complete through the sacrifice of Jesus and the rituals of the Church, which symbolically repeat the sacrifice. Cohen held that these rites border on the idolatrous. The Mass and Communion seek to reach the essence of God and the acts of God, without affecting the acts of man. All the Christian sacraments imitate the essence of God; the commandments of Judaism emphasize the ethical imitation of God without seeking His essence.[20]

Paul reawakened the mythology of the ancient world, which had provided a means to discover peace and freedom in a prehistoric age. Paul saw this mythological age as a perfect time before sin and the "Law."[21] Cohen felt that the Law had been misunderstood by Paul and through him by later Christianity. In this area the two religions have taken absolutely divergent paths. To all Jews, no matter how far removed from Judaism, the Law "is a protective wall against the leveling down of pure monotheism, its teachings of the reconciliation of man with God, and the salvation of man by God." Christianity lost this when it eliminated Law from its religion. A visible symbol of this change is Christianity's reinterpretation of the Sabbath. In Judaism it is a reminder of social ethics; in Christianity it is the Lord's day.[22]

Without underestimating the value of the Jewish elements in Christianity, Cohen felt that a loss in the Biblical component had been caused by the Church's transmission of the Bible in Greek and Latin. Some basic concepts were altered and given a different emphasis in Christianity.[23] Cohen found little originality in the New Testament,[24] but he did not enter into prolonged discussions of Biblical themes in any of his writings.

Cohen was, perhaps, the first to emphasize Christianity's influence on Judaism. This may be seen clearly in Jewish Bible translations, which constantly reveal unconscious Christian influence. We fail to recognize even some authentically Jewish ideas. "It is an instructive example that the concept of a savior is not recognized as originally Jewish in many Jewish circles and has become known as a Christian concept in the general conscience."[25]

Moreover, Cohen pointed out, "Much of what we, as modern men, recognize as alive in our Judaism is Christian illumination which arose out of those old, eternal foundations. Would our current notion of the Messianic idea have been possible without the liberation of the German spirit set in motion by Martin Luther? Or would the development of medieval Jewish philosophy, which was responsible for the intensification of religious life and for its philosophical freedom, be responsible for Mendelssohn? Could Mendelssohn's *Phaedon* or his *Jerusalem* be derived historically or intellectually from Maimonides?"[26]

In numerous essays Cohen also commented on other aspects of

Christianity without treating them thoroughly. He raised the question of images used in Christian worship and suggested that the very designation "Son of God" brings an image to mind. "In the case of Christ this only has consequences for our pattern of thought, but each plastic image of God contradicts monotheism; the prophets attacked it at its root."[27]

Paganism and the overemphasis on the individual remained primary objects in Cohen's critique of Christianity. Christianity has narrowed the boundaries of religion and decreased feeling for the rest of humanity; in matters of salvation human equality has ceased. Cohen contrasted this thought with the Talmudic dictum that "the pious of all people will have a place in the world to come." In the Talmudic statement no positive beliefs of any kind are demanded of the pious, but only that they abstain from idolatry and blasphemy. Thus, salvation becomes possible for all men, not for one group alone.[28]

When Cohen approached Christianity from a historical perspective, he was critical of its orientation to the past as not permitting progress. "The focus on Christ meant arresting the religious process through him. It is then claimed that his piety and his teachings cannot be surpassed. However, this point of view contradicts all historical scholarship."[29]

Despite all critiques Cohen also sensed a deep relationship between Judaism and Christianity. Jews feel a kinship to the Protestant emphasis on the believing individual and a tie to the historical emphasis of Catholicism. Though such relationships exist, Judaism stands separated from both Christian groups, and we can view both objectively. "We are part of this religious world and its history, and in it we may see the further growth of the original ideas of our religion within Christianity as well as in Judaism."[30] In Cohen's view, Judaism's ties with Protestantism are especially close due to the fact that Protestantism has thrown off much of Christian tradition. This would surely lead to closer bonds, he believed, which would be important for the development of Germany.[31] We might also borrow methods from present-day Protestantism, such as its successful techniques of teaching the Bible to its followers; through the music and readings of the service, which assist the educational endeavor.[32]

Looking to the future, Cohen saw Protestantism approaching

Judaism; this path had been prepared by Biblical criticism, which had demolished much of the Protestant reliance on dogma. Modern Protestantism ignored the literal story of the Gospels and depended heavily on a theoretical "original document." "Modern piety, particularly in Germany, no longer depends on the text of the dogma, but sees the kernel of belief and seeks its truth in the distinctive elements of religious ethics for men as individuals and for all the nations of the world. The ethical elements of revelation are emphasized and honored rather than philosophizing on the existence of God."[33] The new affinity between Judaism and Protestantism awakens unforeseen problems regarding their distinction. If it no longer rests on different ethics, then it has to lie in their respective concepts of God. Here Cohen saw each religion following a distinct path. He felt that Jews should see the Christian belief in God in its most idealized form as had been the practice during the Middle Ages; in that era the rabbis did not judge Christianity by the beliefs and common practices of ordinary men, but by its highest manifestations. Jews should assist this process of idealization, to bring Christianity nearer Judaism.[34] "Yet we neither await nor promote the abolition or dissolution of Christianity, rather we wish and shall encourage all those profound endeavors which exert themselves to its idealization. We are convinced that all of them will redound to the honor of the Unique God." Cohen considered this Jewish influence on Christianity to be a part of the mission of Israel; he thought it might succeed in the enlightened Germany of the last century.[35]

Cohen pleaded for a better relationship between Judaism and Christianity. "Neither distrust nor patient waiting should govern our relations with Christians, but tender trust in humanity and human nature, even to our current adversary."[36] In return he expected Christianity to treat Judaism not as a stranger in Western culture, for Judaism had contributed and was part of this civilization.[37]

The task of Judaism remains the strengthening and maintenance of monotheism. This takes precedence over all other efforts. "The Jews possess only one 'eternal task,' the *preservation of monotheism.*" They can be aided in this duty by the purer forms of Christianity.

Hermann Cohen sought to define the place of Judaism in German and European culture; in retrospect we must state that he was too optimistic. The position he sought for Judaism was not to be granted, and his people were to be wiped out by the very Germans in whom he vested so much confidence. Even if he did not succeed in bringing the two religions nearer to each other, he certainly provided his generation with a clearer understanding of the remaining distinctions between Judaism and Christianity. Tolerance coupled with the mild anti-Semitism of the last half of the nineteenth century blurred the lines, but Hermann Cohen drew them vividly for the educated, philosophically minded Jew of his time.

10

Claude G. Montefiore

The Grand Friendship*

Despite the modern-day dialogue between Jews and Christians, the basic note sounded remains one of apologetics. Our contacts remain superficial although the foundations for a broader-based understanding have been laid. The initial steps in that direction in the English speaking world were taken at the beginning of this century by Claude Montefiore (1858–1938). He sought to set a pattern for future studies; perhaps he went too far in his sweeping statements, but the friendly tone of his work and the open manner in which he viewed Christianity provide us with a basis on which to build as we seek a better understanding of Christianity.

Claude Montefiore was the first Jew to view Christianity entirely sympathetically. He felt no need to defend Judaism, to emphasize the defects of Christianity, or to write apologetically. The scion of an old British-Jewish family, which had supported Judaism and Jewish causes through many generations, he felt that he could combine the best of Judaism with the noblest elements of Western culture. After graduating from Oxford, where he was strongly influenced by Jowett, he sought to prepare himself for the rabbinate at a Liberal seminary in Germany. However, finding himself out of sympathy with its teachings, he devoted his life to Jewish scholarship rather than the rabbinate. Outstanding Jewish scholars such as Abrahams, Schechter, and Loewe were his

*In its original publication, this essay was dedicated to M. L. Aaron on his seventieth birthday.

93

friends. For many years he edited the leading English-Jewish magazine, the *Jewish Quarterly Review*. He wrote and lectured continually to further the cause of Liberal Judaism in England.

Early in life Montefiore developed a deep interest in Christianity, which led to studies of that religion and its literature. In numerous books he evaluated the New Testament from a Jewish point of view, discussed the founders of Christianity, and sought to introduce Christianity to the modern Jew. The introduction to one of these books stated specifically that it was primarily intended for the Jewish reader;[1] this was equally true of his other works on Christianity. Rabbinic parallels to the New Testament were elucidated by him, but he went farther than the discovery of such similarities to discuss them in detail. His works show a thorough knowledge of Christianity as well as a fine understanding of rabbinic Judaism, despite the modest tenor of his writings.

Montefiore must be understood as a Liberal Jewish scholar whose thought was deeply influenced by late-nineteenth-century Biblical criticism, by Hegelian dialectic, and by the theory of evolution. He believed firmly in progressive revelation and God's gradual enlightenment of man, holding that all religious development is to be seen in this light, and all religious literature and heroes are to be judged by their place in the evolutionary pattern. Progress may come naturally or man may struggle to ascend more quickly; those who make the effort for their own advancement and that of mankind are to be praised.

Montefiore knew that his studies of Christianity, which expressed warm friendship, would arouse hostility among Jews; he considered this a natural reaction due to the centuries of suffering, which could not easily be forgotten. "The teaching of Jesus has not been much discussed and appraised as a whole. And where it has been so discussed, the line has been rather to depreciate or to cheapen. Jewish writers have looked either for parallels or for defects. Considering what Judaism and Jews have had to suffer at Christian hands, this Jewish treatment of the Gospels is not astonishing."[2] In reality the same fault had long existed on both sides. "Both religions, or rather the exponents of both religions, have a tendency to caricature the other. Both have a tendency to judge the other religion from its defects rather than from its qualities."[3] Montefiore felt that it was time for a reappraisal; he wished to begin for the Jewish side. He realized that some would question the need for a modern Liberal Jew to concern himself with this problem since so much else remained to be done: "For us who live in a Christian environment, and amid a civilization which has been partially created by the New Testament, our right relation towards it must surely be of grave and peculiar importance. For this civilization is also ours." This task, which is incumbent upon all Jews, must fall especially heavily upon Liberal Jews because of their attitude toward religion. "Liberal Judaism does not believe that God has enabled the human race to reach forward to religious truth so exclusively through a single channel";[4] therefore other religions need to be studied. Montefiore was to concentrate on Christianity, but he felt that Liberal Jews should also understand other religions. He expressed the desire to be as fair and impartial as possible, but he did not blind himself to inherent limitations. "If you are within, you cannot be impartial; if you are without, you cannot know."[5] Since Judaism and Christianity have much in common, he felt able to understand many aspects of Christianity although acknowledging that he would never see it as intimately as a Christian. He felt that as a Jew he could do better than a Buddhist scholar might. For similar reasons, he thought, a parallel impartiality might be expected from liberal Christians, and they would understand Judaism more readily, especially as the "number of 'essential doctrines' has gradually diminished" for the modern Christian.[6]

According to Montefiore, it is incumbent on Liberal Jews to understand and appreciate elements of the New Testament, especially the Synoptic Gospels, as a part of their religious heritage. He regarded the New Testament as belonging to ancient Jewish literature and thought it should be treated in this manner. "It is a book which, in very large part, was written by persons who were born Jews. Its central hero was a Jew. Its teaching is based throughout—sometimes indeed by way of opposition—upon the teaching of the Old Testament." Most Jews have traditionally thought that the New Testament can add little to the Jewish Bible. Montefiore was unwilling to accept this judgment without thoroughly testing it; he felt others should do likewise.[7] As one

reads the various books Montefiore devoted to the subject of
Christianity, one sees not only sympathetic understanding, but
apologetics in reverse. He became an apologist for Christianity,
seeking to present the best of that religion to his fellow Jews.
Montefiore was often criticized for this, and without doubt this is
partially justified; however, the Christianity he presented to his
readers was much purified, and many essential Christian features
were completely removed by his liberal approach to all religion.

Montefiore's general approach to religion was deeply influenced
by his master at Oxford, Benjamin Jowett, who considered the
only difference between St. Augustine and Plato to be that one was
a "religious genius, the other a philosophical and poetical genius."
Montefiore felt at home with the progressive thought of his time
and used the same method with both Christianity and Judaism. As
a Liberal Jew he approached the New Testament with a special
advantage, for he could look at it selectively, just as he was
selective with the Jewish Bible. "The Liberal Jew at any rate will
not be deterred from gaining all the good he can from the Gospels
(or from the rest of the New Testament) because there are many
things in it which he holds to be erroneous. The Pentateuch also
contains things which he holds to be erroneous. It also contains a
lower and a higher. So too the Prophets, but he does not therefore
reject them."[8] Perhaps Montefiore's feelings were best summarized in his statement that "we have not got to take it or leave it in
the lump. We can accept one bit, and reject another. We can
qualify; we can amend."[9] This point of view would hardly be
acceptable to all Christians, but it allowed him, as a Liberal Jew, to
study the New Testament and to show admiration especially for
the Synoptic Gospels. With Liberal Judaism's belief in continuous
revelation, the teachings of another religion could certainly not be
spurned without detailed study. Baeck was to proceed along the
same road, but in a far more critical manner. He felt that
Christianity must be studied by Jews, but sought primarily to point
out its limitations. Baeck's "Romantic Religion" is a powerful
polemic piece, which contrasted the weak elements of "romantic"
Christianity with the strength of "classic" Judaism. Baeck shared
some of Montefiore's general concepts of religion, but when he
dealt with Christianity he abandoned the apologetic note.

Of course Montefiore rejected the miraculous aspects of the New Testament. In its teachings he saw some new elements, but since most of them can be found in the Jewish Bible, their originality lies in the manner of presentation. "There is much in the New Testament which is great and noble, much which is sublime and tender, much which is good and true. Of this 'much,' the greater part consists in a fresh presentment of some of the best and highest teaching in the Old Testament, in vivid reformulation of it, in an admirable picking and choosing, an excellent bringing together. Not a part consists in a further development, or in a clearer and more emphatic expression, of certain truths which previously were only implicit or not fully drawn out."[10] With this statement Montefiore went farther than previous Jewish scholars, for it admitted an independent original development of early Christianity along Jewish lines. Of course he was familiar with the numerous rabbinic parallels to the New Testament, and he added to the literature in this area in *The Rabbinic Literature and the Gospel Teachings* as well as *The Synoptic Gospels*. Despite these detailed analyses Montefiore felt that such parallels must not be overemphasized. It must be remembered that the Gospels are very small in comparison to the vast Talmud; furthermore, each is the statement of one man. "It is not a combination of a thousand different occasional and disconnected sayings of a hundred different rabbis. Again, as a famous German scholar rather bitingly said, the greatness of the Synoptics, as compared with the greatness of the Talmud, must be measured by what is not there as well as by what is."[11] Equally important was the striking manner of presentation of the New Testament. "We have, however, already seen that the greatness and inspiration of a New Testament passage does not depend upon its being wholly unparalleled. They depend upon its position of importance, upon its stress, upon its form and passion, upon its relation to, and its place in, the teaching as a whole, upon its ultimate effect upon the world."[12] He did not consider the question of originality primary and felt the careful scholar should give weight to the other factors. What mattered was that "we have them brought together in words of striking simplicity and power in the pages of the Gospels. Shall we admire, and cherish, and learn from, these exquisite stories, or shall we sniff and sneer at them and pass them by?"[13] Montefiore also admired the mysticism and the strong sense of personal religion in the New Testament. Here was a new element. "Regarded from this point of view, the mysticism and intimacy of the New Testament do seem to carry us some steps beyond those of the Old."[14] In this he differed markedly from all older Jewish scholarship. Benamozegh, Salvador, and Geiger had all depicted the Gospel's lack of originality. As apologists for Judaism, they could not see the positive elements in this religious work.

However, Montefiore did not overlook the shortcomings of the New Testament. Aside from "certain features of religious advance," he also found "certain features of retrogression . . . from the highest points of religious development attained in the Old Testament," such as the demonology, dualism, pessimism, and so forth.[15] The anti-Jewish sentiments were certainly not noble, but he felt that we Jews "can realize better than the average Christian that even the Synoptics were compiled by writers unfriendly to Judaism and to the opponents of their hero. We can perceive more readily than the average Christian that they make the darkness greater in order to increase the light."[16] Several of his essays in this vein were originally delivered as lectures. Their tone, therefore, tends to be somewhat hortatory, and they may sound stronger than even Montefiore wished. Montefiore could not see the Fourth Gospel in this spirit, and he rejected it entirely as debased monotheism.[17] Here he exercised his right as a Liberal, rejecting this Gospel because it did not fit into the scheme of evolution and progress.

A sympathetic understanding of the New Testament was needed, but not the exaggerated enthusiasm to which Montefiore was inclined. Maintaining that the good features of the New Testament far outweigh its weaknesses, he thought that it should be studied by Jews. "One view which will be incidentally maintained and supported in this commentary is that Judaism has something to gain and absorb from the New Testament, and above all in the Gospels, which supplement and carry forward some essential teachings in the Old Testament."[18] All this was to be said in favor of Jews studying the New Testament alongside the rabbinic literature as a development of Jewish ideas. "But when we compare the achievement of the Old Testament with that of the New, we realize how much greater is our obligation to the Old. When you have won through to your monotheism, and to the doctrine of the One Good God, when you have got your Prophets with their weaving together of religion and morality, when you have got your commands and ideals to love God with all your heart and the neighbor and the resident alien as yourself, when you have reached ideals of justice and compassion, of the clean hands and the pure heart—why, then, it was, in a sense, comparatively easy to supplement, to bring together, to purify, to universalize . . . The achievements of Jesus and Paul (in spite of some sad retrogression) are great achievements. But what we owe to them seems but little in comparison with what we owe to their Old Testament predecessor."[19] The book ought to be read, but should never be used in public Jewish ceremony; too many of its concepts remain alien to Judaism.[20] There was no danger that Liberal Jews might overemphasize the New Testament, for a vast difference remained between the Liberal Jew and the Unitarian. "The Liberal Jew could never feel towards the New Testament in the same way, or receive from it the same religious emotions, as the Liberal Unitarian. A different past has molded them, a different allegiance claims them . . ." An understanding and unprejudiced view of the New Testament ought to be possessed by every Jew; but these were the limits of Montefiore's goal. He made this quite clear in an address on Unitarianism and Judaism, for he remained strongly convinced that there are major differences between even this most liberal form of Christianity and Judaism. Liberal Judaism was the progressive arm of this ancient religion while Unitarianism, in his view, had broken with Christianity.[21]

In the New Testament Montefiore singled out the Gospels for special praise. Montefiore saw their numerous citations of the words of Jesus as the noblest element of the entire work, for he had a high regard for Jesus. He concerned himself with both the personality and the teachings of Jesus, rejecting his Messianic claims and understanding him as a continuation of the long line of prophets. "If Jesus resembled the Prophets in the cause and occasion of his preaching, still more did he resemble them in his temper of mind, and therefore in one great feature and characteristic of his teaching . . . The inwardness of Jesus, the intense spirituality of his teaching, need not be insisted on here. I only emphasize it now to show his connection and kinship with the Prophets."[22] Later, Montefiore suggested that Jesus might have gone beyond the prophets since he interrelated his life and his message so completely; this stands in contrast to the grand, but impersonal, presentation by the prophets, whose lives generally remain unknown to us.[23] As Montefiore emphasized the prophetic element in Liberal Judaism, it was natural that he should be attracted toward it in the life of Jesus. His predecessors may have acknowledged Jesus as a minor Jewish leader, but none acclaimed him so sympathetically as Montefiore. This would not occur again until Martin Buber. Buber, however, approached the study of Jesus very differently. He set him into the framework of the "I–Thou" relationship, but even while Buber spoke enthusiastically about his deep understanding of Jesus, he emphasized that he saw him through Jewish eyes. From the beginning Buber acknowledged the underlying distinctions, which cannot be overcome, at least not "pre-messianically," and so did not place himself into the difficult position of Montefiore. For his Jewish readers, Montefiore's Jesus was not sufficiently human; to his Christian readers, he was not the Christ they knew.

For Montefiore the statements of Jesus must be seen in the context of the prophetic spirit. His critique of contemporary Jewry was exaggerated in order to make its point. "The temperament of Jesus, his 'prophetic' temperament, if I may call it so, led him then to attack, just as Amos and Isaiah attacked oppression and hypocrisy."[24] In like fashion he opposed some aspects of the ritual law, for it was felt to stand in the way of "higher law of compassion and lovingkindness."[25] Yet Montefiore was quite certain that "Jesus still recognized the divinity of the Law; he did not make theoretic distinctions between ceremonial and ritual enactments, but he did so in practice and in conflict."[26] He had no desire to abolish the Law; "it is even doubtful whether, except perhaps in cases or moments of stress and conflict, he sought or desired or intended to put his own teaching in direct contrast with, or substitution for, the teaching of these around him, or the teaching of the Law."[27] The spirit of the moment or the troubles of a crisis may have moved Jesus to an occasional extreme statement which has been misunderstood and misinterpreted by later generations. Montefiore felt an affinity with Jesus in the attitude toward the Law; both intended to emphasize prophecy without absolutely rejecting the Law. "Jesus, as I have said, had to hark back from the Law to the Prophets. His teaching is a revival of prophetic Judaism, and in some respects points forward to the Liberal Judaism of today."[28] In this Montefiore was consistent, for he claimed to have a simple gauge for judging inspiration: "That which is good, noble and uplifting is inspired of God. No longer is something revealed simply because it is found in a particular book. It is, indeed, the contents 'themselves.'" Statements like this were misunderstood by both Jews and Christians. Jews considered them perilously close to Christianity, and some Christians wondered why their author remained a Jew. Montefiore wished to show the somewhat parallel outlook between Liberal Judaism and Christianity, but not at the expense of the major distinctions that remained. However, to do so, Montefiore had to overlook endless centuries of Christian interpretation of Jesus which did not favor his own Liberal outlook.

Montefiore was attracted by many of the controversial statements of the Gospels, such as the paradoxes or the ideal "Love your enemy"; there was a need for such exaggerations. He saw this statement and others akin to it as an "expression of passionate idealism . . . likely to stir and stimulate the imagination."[29] "Paradoxes and passion are needed to get out of human nature all of which it is capable. . . . By arousing his enthusiasm for a supreme ideal you drive him forward upon the road towards it."[30] These statements, he felt, were not properly appreciated by Jews, who had looked upon them as impractical and had shown the failure of both Jesus and later Christians to observe them. To him this was insignificant, for their only purpose was the stimulation of the highest possible idealism.

Despite the element of extremism in some of Jesus' prophetic utterances, Montefiore showed clearly that most of his statements fitted well into the general Jewish thought of the period. When Jesus spoke of the Kingdom of God, he did not consciously broaden it beyond the scope of rabbinic thought. "Jesus did not preach a consciously universalist Kingdom, just as he did not conceive himself sent, or send his disciples to the Gentiles and the heathen. Not Jesus but Paul gave to the problem a conscious and universalist solution. Yet there is good reason to believe that, like the prophets before him, Jesus thought that the place of many excluded Jewish sinners in the new Kingdom would be filled by many Gentile believers." The new element here was not universalism but the personal note of individual salvation, which Jesus began to stress.[31] Yet Montefiore considered the claim of Jesus to be the chief member of this new kingdom as a Messianic claim; that is, Jesus considered himself to be the Messiah.[32] A good deal of Montefiore's discussion of Jesus took this as its basis; Montefiore felt that the opposite hypothesis raised more problems than this one. Naturally Montefiore rejected this claim, but nevertheless he tried to understand its meaning for Christianity.

In matters of theory and philosophy Montefiore felt Jesus had added little new; all the materials could be found in the rabbinic teachings of the time and most of them in the Jewish Bible. Originality and freshness lay in the presentation or in the spirit of social service, which he admired, but he also saw the older foundations on which it was built.[33] The emphasis on social service was typical of Montefiore's approach to religion. As with so many other reformers of the last century, this aspect of the prophetic teachings was given primary emphasis. He saw a kindred spirit in these characteristics of Jesus; to do so, he glossed over the less pleasant statements and acts of Jesus. In addition to these elements there was the highly personal note on which Jesus phrased his admonitions. "Here was a new motive, which has been of tremendous power and effect in the religious history of the world. Even if, in the sentences where they occur, the words 'for my sake' are not always genuine, yet the thought and the motive assumedly go back to the historic Jesus."[34] This was a part of his Messianic spirit; it was given added strength by his tragic death. According to Montefiore, Jesus did not expect to die, but thought he would live to see the new kingdom. He was, however, aware of the risks involved in his task and was not afraid of dying.[35] Since his death was caused by the Sadducean priesthood, which has long since vanished, Montefiore saw no need to examine in detail the tragic last days of Jesus. Almost every other Jewish writer on Jesus has dealt at length with this matter; many have made it their primary concern. Montefiore's avoidance of the crucifixion story is typical of his entire approach to Christianity and accounts for his lack of acceptance by Jews. In the crucifixion lies the basis of most of the Judeo-Christian misunderstandings of the last two thousand years as well as the foundation of much anti-Semitism. Thousands had died because of the charge that Jews had crucified Jesus. The long and terrible history of the charge of deicide could not be ignored or brushed aside. Montefiore, however, did so, probably because he realized that here he could convince neither Jew nor Christian. His view may have been correct, but it was also incredible.

Montefiore assigned many elements in the Gospel version of the life of Jesus to later editors. It was they who broadened the scope of his teaching in various directions; indeed, the personal tone of the Gospel became even more pronounced through their additions. Although Jesus probably believed in damnation, they underlined its importance. The Gospel's opposition to the rabbis may have begun in Jesus' desire to deemphasize the intellectualism of the scholars, but it was broadened by the editors.[36] The composition of the Gospel was subjected to a detailed analysis in several other thick volumes, and individual verses were often given new interpretations. Montefiore stressed the elements that are closest to Judaism. He generally judged the teachings of Jesus himself to be acceptable to the rabbis and very near their own—with a few exceptions, such as the attitude of Jesus toward the family.[37]

What Montefiore admired most in Jesus was the "heroic element." "That heroic element seems to show itself in a certain grand largeness of views and in a certain grand simplicity. Taken as a whole, this heroic element is full of genius and inspiration. We must not always take it literally, and squeeze out of it too literal an application. The letter of even the prophet's teachings may kill; here too we must sometimes look only to the spirit."[38] This gives the character of Jesus a certain grandeur and makes it so attractive. Obviously Montefiore felt a personal attraction to the historical character of Jesus; an affinity of minds existed here and we discover that Jesus becomes an idealized Montefiore in miniature.

Montefiore several times appraised the character of Jesus, but he proceeded with caution, for "that character is a sort of sanctuary to every Christian, whether Trinitarian or Unitarian."[39] His general comments were fair and warmhearted: "We seem to see, through the mist of eulogy and legend, the sure outlines of a noble personality. Here we have a deeply religious nature, filled, as perhaps few before or after have been filled, with the love of God and the consciousness of His presence. A character naturally serene and sunny, but with the most vivid appreciation of, and pity for, the wretched, the unfortunate, the degraded. A teacher stands before us who is not only a teacher, but hero, strong, sometimes even passionate, fervent, devoted, brave. He has a burning hatred of shams and hypocrisies, and also of formalisms and externalities where the spirit is wanting or has departed. He is filled with a true Jewish idealism, for there is no more idealistic race than that of Israel. He is gifted with a deep insight into essentials, a love of the inward, the spiritual, the real. He has no ambition except one; to do the will of his Father in Heaven, and to serve the people to whom he has been sent."[40] Montefiore's admiration for Jesus did not keep him from seeing the other side of his life, which consisted of inconsistencies in his teachings, but, he declared, this is excusable, since few great teachers remain always at their highest level.[41] As long as the inconsistencies were limited to minor matters they were of no great consequence, but there was a glaring weakness in the attitude of Jesus toward other men. "There were two sides in the character of Jesus, one stern and one tender, one forgiving and one severe. He preached and taught that we were to forgive and do good to our enemies, but in actual life he sometimes forgot to put his own precepts into practice; violent invective and denunciation of the sinner, who was also his opponent, rather than his sin, fell sometimes from his mouth."[42] Montefiore understood that these statements were stressed by later editors of the Gospel, who wished to emphasize the separation of the Church and Synagogue, but he considered them to have originated with Jesus.

Seen in this balanced manner, Jesus was never viewed as divine by Montefiore. "I would not deny that the dogma of the incarnation of God and Jesus has had its effects for good as well as evil. But nonetheless Liberal Jews do hold that it rests on a confusion, the confusion of a man with God."[43] We can never associate Jesus with the highest concepts as goodness, for they belong to God.[44] Nor did Montefiore believe that Jesus wished to found a new religion: "If he thought that the end was near, he can hardly have also intended to found a new religion and a new religious community."[45] Those aspects of Christian tradition that sharply remove Jesus from Judaism were, therefore, rejected by Montefiore.

In his view, the original Jesus belonged to the Liberal wing of Jewish tradition and should again be placed and accepted there. In part Jesus can be regarded as belonging as much to Judaism as to Christianity.[46] Throughout his life Montefiore continued to honor him and to give him a very high place among the teachers of mankind. "I cannot conceive that a time will come when the figure of Jesus will no longer be a star of the first magnitude in the spiritual heavens, when he will no longer be regarded as one of the greatest religious heroes and teachers whom the world has seen."[47]

Jesus could be admired and understood within the framework of Judaism; it was much more difficult to deal with Paul. Montefiore tried to understand his life and his contribution to Christianity, attempting to see him within the framework of rabbinic Judaism. Contrary to many Jews he was not offended by the writings of Paul and sought to have Jews overlook Paul's historical inaccuracies. "In spite of his amazing forgetfulness of the Jewish doctrine of repentance and atonement, in spite, too, of the remoteness for us of his opposition 'Law versus Christ,' we may still admire the profundity of his genius and adopt many true and noble elements of his religious and ethical teaching. If we can exercise a careful eclecticism in Deuteronomy and Isaiah, we can also exercise it in the Epistle to the Romans and the Corinthians."[48] By doing this, however, Montefiore destroyed much of the "real" Paul and substituted a new individual. He searched for elements that he as a Jew could admire and found them partially in the "purely ethical side of the Apostle's teaching."[49] Of course he rejected Paul's elevation of Jesus to a divinity. "Paul puts a divine being between us and God, and nothing do we hold to be more false than this." Some teachings, such as that of Original Sin, Montefiore simply judged to be obsolete and therefore necessitating no discussion in modern times.[50] "But, on the other hand, we can find more than one teaching of nobility and of truth in the Pauline epistles, though sometimes the teaching may be cast in an erroneous or inadequate form. Thus the Pauline doctrine of faith contains elements of great value, though also elements of falsity and of danger. Again, it is Paul (and not Jesus) who brings the Prophetic universalism to its full and final conclusion."[51] Although he was aware of its shortcomings, Montefiore stressed repeatedly that this was Paul's most significant contribution. "Judaism had so far not been able to solve the puzzle of the universal God and the national cult. Paul cut the knot. He cut it, it is true, by setting upon dogmas which darkened the purity of monotheism, and opened the door for many subsequent evils both in religion and morality; but he cut it. We will not deny to him his meed of glory." It meant that the "shackle" of the Law was now replaced by the "shackle" of unbelief; finally, therefore, the Gospel became more pitiless than the Law.[52] Montefiore felt the superiority of Judaism's universalism, but he understood the wide appeal of Paul's solution. "Though our universalism is grander and truer than Paul's, we will not ignore the world's debt to him, or forget, in the history of universalism, to assign to him his high and his rightful place."[53] Once more Montefiore sought a solution through an appeal to the progressive thought of this time. Paul may not have measured up to all the standards, but he had a place on the road of religious evolution.

Of greater significance was Montefiore's attempt to solve the problem of Paul's attitude toward the Law; he saw it as within the framework of Judaism, rather than as inimical to it. Paul's view of Judaism appears to be disparaging; his attacks seem to be directed against rabbinic Judaism, from which Paul was generally considered to have come to Christianity. Therefore all Jews have seen him as a foe. Samuel Hirsch, the German-Jewish philosopher, had previously sought to demonstrate that Paul's views stemmed from a limited grasp of Judaism. Montefiore's solution was original and tempting: he attempted to prove that there was no similarity between rabbinic Judaism and the Judaism attacked by Paul. The religion of which Paul spoke was "poorer, more pessimistic . . . it possessed these inferiorities—just because it was not Rabbinic Judaism, but Diaspora Judaism.''[54] The form of Judaism with which Paul was acquainted in Syria "was less intimate and joyous than Rabbinic Judaism on the one hand, and more theoretic and questioning, upon the other."[55] Montefiore rather systematically tried to prove that the Judaism which Paul knew was not rabbinic Judaism. He discussed the basic concepts as presented by Paul and as known from rabbinic literature. If Paul had been a rabbinic Jew, could he have changed his ideas about the Messiah, the Gentiles, the attitude toward the world, and many other matters as radically as he did? "Whatever Paul's individual genius, whatever the effect of the conversion, whatever revolution the new faith wrought upon the materials of the old, is it conceivable that the one could have been built up even on the ruins of the other?"[56]

Montefiore admitted that his conclusions had to be based on the rabbinic Judaism of the year 300 or 500. He felt, however, that the changes in the tradition since Paul's time had not been sufficient to invalidate his conclusions. Even the shock of the destruction of the Temple had produced no radical changes in the essential doctrines of Judaism, but only in its outer forms.[57] "The religion of Paul antecedent to his conversion must have been different from the typical and average Rabbinic Judaism of three hundred or five hundred, but not in that difference more 'liberal and ethnicizing.' . . . It may have been more systematic, and perhaps a little more philosophic and less child-like, but possibly for these very reasons it was less intimate, warm, joyous and comforting. Its God was more distant and less loving. . . . The early religion of Paul was more somber and gloomy than Rabbinic Judaism; the world was a more miserable and God-forsaken place. . . . It needed the poverty and the pessimism of the Pauline pre-Christian Judaism to have produced the Pauline Christianity. From the Rabbinic Judaism of five hundred as basis, many salient doctrines of the great Epistles could never have been evolved."[58] The antecedent Judaism of Paul, then, was Hellenistic Apocalyptic Judaism, which seems to fit Paul's later views much better.[59] This solution enabled Montefiore to see Paul in an entirely different manner than most other Jews, for he did not need to defend himself against Paul. The form of Judaism attacked by Paul had already perished thousands of years before. The "ashes of old controversies" no longer glowed in Montefiore's heart.

Despite a certain appreciation of Paul, however, Montefiore nevertheless rejected almost all the major Pauline additions to Christianity: "Paul's pessimism, his Christology, much in his conception of sin, his conception of the Law, his conception of God's wrath, his demonology, his view of human past and human future."[60] Yet he felt that something would be learned from some of Paul's criticism of Judaism. "It does not follow that Paul's diatribes are of no value even for us. We need both 'law' and 'grace,' both 'grace' and 'works,' and though we do not oppose them to one another like Paul, it is of value to be occasionally reminded now of one portion and now of another." Paul emphasized one and the rabbis the other.[61] Montefiore, anyhow, felt that Christianity tends to emphasize this combination more in modern times than it did in previous centuries; here the two religions might soon agree. Montefiore also found some slight value in Paul's critique of the Law, but generally rejected it even from a Liberal point of view. "Just because we are 'liberals,' we shall not, like Paul, condemn the Law in essence or as such. For we regard Law as a revelation of the divine Spirit continuously at work, and this very conception allows and justifies our freedom towards the details of the written code."[62]

The chief grandeur of Paul lies in the autobiographical passages of his works. "There is always something inspiring in the picture of a great man, convinced of his cause, and pursuing his straight course in the face of constant opposition and trial. Paul not only rises superior to his sufferings, but he exults and rejoices in them."[63] He was admired, but his shortcomings were also fully recognized. "In the Epistles, at any rate, there is very little to be found of kindness and blessing towards those who differed from and opposed him. He knew what he ought to have done, but his lower self in this one respect constantly got the better of him. This we cannot quite forget."[64] The Jewish reader of Paul may appreciate the ethics but must reject much else. Montefiore remained most severe in his treatment of Paul and the Fourth Gospel, finding them to be removed from Judaism. His treatment of Paul was unusual, but has had little influence.

Later events and figures in the history of Christianity were not discussed by Montefiore. He was primarily concerned with the formative period of Christianity and spent his life studying it. He sought to approach Christianity with a true understanding of that religion, and he hoped to reclaim elements of early Christianity for Judaism. He considered large portions of the New Testament acceptable to Judaism. By ignoring this book for so many centuries, he felt, Judaism had lost valuable insights. Liberal Judaism should take the steps necessary to regain this lost heritage. In a broader sense, Montefiore felt that Judaism and Christianity can complement each other.

Since Montefiore took up the New Testament and a discussion of Christianity, we must be astonished by his neglect of previous Jewish writers in this area. He almost never quoted other Jews who had dealt with this subject, either to agree or disagree. Nor is his work particularly satisfying when viewed alongside the vast Christian scholarship of the late nineteenth century. Most of contemporary Christian scholarship was ignored. For example, he never dealt with Schweitzer's works on Jesus or Paul although they had appeared early in the twentieth century. Montefiore was aware of German scholarship and reviewed German books in the *Jewish Quarterly Review*. His work was insular, as if the British Isles lay outside the world of scholarship. His books on Christianity did not win a wide audience. Christian scholars found them curiously outside the mainstream of study; Jews continued to view his efforts with suspicion, seeing him as too much an apologete for Christianity, especially Ahad HaAm, who attacked him bitterly.[65]

Montefiore came closer to a dialogue with Christianity than any other thinker up to his time; many believe he went too far and thus began to surrender important elements of Judaism. He wrote about early Christian documents and heroes with warmth and affection, but he could do so only by ignoring the two millennia of later development. He felt justified in this selective approach because modern liberal Christianity appeared to be reemphasizing the key elements of early Christianity. By retaining the utopian spirit of the Victorian era well into the twentieth century, Montefiore seemed to be an anachronism. He looked forward to a universal religion, which would contain all that was noble and would transcend national boundaries. He longed for an end to whatever was old and narrow in both religions. His idealism blinded him to the horrors of our century. We must acknowledge the nobility of the effort, even while we recognize that his extremely liberal approach, which stripped so much away from both Judaism and Christianity, satisfied neither side.

11

Max Brod

Interreligious Struggle

Among the outstanding modern Jews of Central Europe, few are as forgotten as Max Brod (1884–1968). Although he died only recently, his thoughts belong more to the period between the two world wars than to that of modern Israel, where he spent the last decades of his life. He is recalled today primarily as the literary executor and intimate friend of Kafka.

Born in Prague, Brod early absorbed the assimilationist atmosphere of the Austro-Hungarian Empire, a land split by the struggle of many nationalities. Its Jewish community, which produced such literary figures as Hofmannsthal, Schnitzler, Beer-Hofmann, Werfel, and Kraus, was part of a German isle in a multinational sea. Although the bourgeois Jews of Prague considered themselves Germans, they were not accepted by the Germans; this anomalous position did not become a source of inner conflict until shortly before the First World War. Brod and many of his friends recognized themselves as Jews only when they began to understand their tenuous position in the multinational society of the Austro-Hungarian Empire. By the first decade of this century they had come to realize that the comfortable world in which they lived was a masque, although none knew that it would be stripped away suddenly after World War I.

Max Brod once wrote that three lectures given by Buber in 1909 enabled him to understand the meaning of Judaism. His own struggle for identity began then and was not completed until the war years, when he dealt with the change in his own life in essays as well as his novel *Tycho Brahe's Weg zu Gott* (1915). Brod was impressed by the spirit of the Eastern European Jews, whom he met in large numbers as refugees from the war areas. Though he had never met Herzl, Brod became a Zionist and devoted one postwar novel to an experimental community in Palestine that had been established by some of his intellectual friends. At the same time, as he developed strong feelings for Jewish nationalism, he also fought for universal brotherhood. His Jewishness could not be expressed in national terms alone; rather he sought to answer mankind's problems through Judaism. This attitude is best expressed in *Heidentum, Christentum, Judentum,* a comparative study of three world religious movements and their attitude toward this world and the world beyond.

Brod's approach was philosophical, and he did not concern himself with the history of the New Testament literature or early Christian heroes. His analysis of the pagan, Christian, and Jewish outlooks on life was based upon a very special understanding of evil. Brod believed that misfortune, as he called evil, can be divided into two aspects: noble misfortune and ignoble misfortune. Noble misfortune consists of a man's basic imperfections, which are part of his finite nature. Such conditions cannot be changed, and one cannot successfully struggle against them. Ignoble misfortune represents imperfections and difficulties that can be overcome; some, like social and economic problems, may be due to man's own activities, while others, like disease, are a part of the battle for survival in the world; they may be overcome if the effort is sufficient.[1] Closely related to the question is the problem of the gulf between God and man. Every man is driven to seek a relationship with God which will help him in the struggle against ignoble misfortune.[2] Separate answers are offered by the pagan, Christian, and Jewish approaches to all the vital issues. Brod considered the present-day choice of a path by mankind enormously important, for one of these philosophies is destined to dominate the future of the world. "All depends upon whether paganism, Christianity, or Judaism will rise to become the future ideal of the world. It must immediately be conceded that paganism has the best prospects. More accurately stated, an amalgamation of paganism and Christianity is today rising and threatens to reach the zenith of the world . . . Judaism, misunderstood, lurks somewhere on the periphery."[3] In Brod's understanding, paganism affirms this world. This world is good. It is idle to dwell on what, if anything, lies beyond. Mankind has progressed and will continue to progress in a natural manner. Yesterday's paganism has been transmuted into today's Marxism and other leftist doctrines. Christianity views the world as evil. Original Sin dominates, and man is helpless unless there is divine intervention. Lacking such divine help, man as an individual is lost and the world has no future. Judaism willingly acknowledges the imperfections of the world, but feels that it can be brought to perfection through Messianic activity. This world and all men can be redeemed. Salvation is not in the world to come, but here and now. Man is not seen as a passive creature; he does not sit and wait, but seeks to eliminate "ignoble misfortune."[4] Brod symbolizes Judaism's way through the legend of Simon b. Yochai, who, according to rabbinic tradition, experienced a mystical union with God and thus stood outside the realm of noble misfortune in this world, yet chose to return from his life of contemplation and devote himself to improving the social and political conditions of his day.[5]

Brod felt that elements of the divine exist in all three paths but distinguished the manner in which each conceives the divine within the world. "According to the pagan concept it is used to strengthen the orderly progress within this world . . .; according to the Christian view [the divine] manages to break the limits of this world due to the pressure of its metaphysical power . . .; according to Jewish feeling both this world and the tasks of this world . . . suddenly appear new to the man filled with the spirit of God . . .; henceforth they will be able to continue beside and through God. It will be possible in the here and now to combat the ignoble misfortune without endangering eternal salvation."[6]

In distinguishing these three paths Brod devoted most of his energy to Judaism and Christianity, vigorously denying a positive role to the latter. In *Heidentum, Christentum, Judentum,* and also in a novel, *Der Meister,* he portrayed Jesus as an individual who, unlike all other men, was whole and pure. Jesus sought salvation for mankind but was opposed by Judas Iscariot, who is portrayed as a nihilist.[7] Brod was concerned with the way in which Jesus is used by Christianity in its denial of the "ignoble misfortune."

Christianity chooses a narrow answer and sees God's revelation in a single moment of history, rather than, like Judaism and Paganism, in continuous activity. "The pantheist finds God everywhere, therefore nowhere, for he cannot recognize any distinctive revelation. It is precisely this [revelation] which interests Jews and Christians. For the Jew it is, in principle, possible everywhere and in all circumstances of life, although it is realized only very rarely, here and there. The Christian possesses his prescribed route; he awaits the appearance of God from one particular direction and in a particular form—in Christian belief."[8] For Christians all experience is determined by this single experience; all other moments lose their significance. The Christian must conclude that pre-Christian experiences are inadequate and that earlier men wrestled in vain with "ignoble misfortunes." "Man need experience only Christ" for his salvation; all other experiences are insignificant.[9] It was this aspect of Christianity which Brod criticized most severely. It views only a single moment and refuses to gaze upon the broad horizon for the divine redemption of the world.

Brod felt that Christianity weakens man's drive toward useful activity in the world, but a pagan might similarly criticize Judaism with its Messianic emphasis; Brod realized this and did not further emphasize it.[10] In the realm of ethics, Brod saw a basic distinction between Protestantism and Catholicism. For the Protestant only belief is significant, and man remains a sinner. Despite man's belief in Jesus, which leads to salvation, he remains sinful. Catholicism always has tried to leave room for good deeds and has made them a requirement of the path to salvation.

Brod readily admitted that these are the theoretical paths of the two religions, but that human realities fortunately change matters somewhat. "Protestantism presents itself as the logical structured system of Christianity; indeed, therefore, it collides even more violently with the ethical realities of the world and of the heart of man. It is simply unwilling to allow itself to be debased. In contrast, Catholicism is a more elastic machine of divine grace. It would allow reality its place and would fit itself to the truth, however, without abandoning the false premises of the prescribed route of its march to divine grace."[11]

Man's freedom of will is eliminated by both forms of Christianity and his range of action strictly prescribed. A century earlier Abraham Geiger had expressed this thought, but had not developed it fully. If Jesus died for the sins of the entire world at all times, then nothing is left for individual action. Judaism also awaits the salvation of God, but found it not in one cosmic moment but in the infinite variety of individual experiences, so the individual possesses a realm of useful action.

Religions which have stressed salvation have been accused of moral indifference; according to Brod the charge was correct for Christianity, but not for Judaism. The conclusions which were applied to salvation are equally true of free will. "Freedom of will can, as I claim, exist besides 'grace,' but only when enunciated in the Jewish manner, as grace derived directly from God. It is not possible alongside grace comprehended in the Christian man-. ner."[12]

Brod's view is attractive because of its simplicity. His division of the world's problems into two categories still appeals to us, although we might criticize it now, some fifty years later, with the thought that "ignoble" misfortune has become predominant. The troubles which man has brought upon himself certainly encompass the major categories of modern human misery.

We might also criticize Brod's oversimplification of each of the philosophies which he described. His delineation of the "pagan," or as we might call it, "secular" world, was good; it has become predominant in the course of this century. In his attitude towards Christianity, he seems to have continued the polemic of the previous century. In German-Jewish thought two basic patterns of discussing Christianity evolved in the first half of this century. One was followed by Brod and Baeck; the other by Buber and Rosenzweig. Each in his own way sought a new approach to Christianity. Buber's approach may be summarized as one of deep friendship and respect. "It behooves both you (Christians) and us to hold inviolably fast to our own true faith . . . This is not what is called 'tolerance,' our task is not to tolerate each other's waywardness, but to acknowledge the real relationship in which both stand to the truth."[13] One might categorize Buber's approach, a reevaluation of Christianity, which enabled Jews to understand its place in the world in a new fashion. Rosenzweig went even further and found in Christianity one of the possible paths to truth, although it was not to be the path chosen by him. These new approaches, with their ramifications, brought the possibility of Christian-Jewish dialogue to a new level.

Brod chose a different road, akin to that of Leo Baeck. Baeck used the new and more relaxed atmosphere of the twentieth century to attack some of the differences between Judaism and Christianity. On the surface, some of Baeck's writings appear unusually friendly, for he concerned himself with a reconstruction of the Gospels and devoted long studies to a detailed analysis of Christian thought. Yet the Gospels, as purified of later elements by Baeck, no longer were Christian documents at all; they had become Jewish books. Furthermore, Baeck's essay "Romantic Religion" was a strong critique of the essence of Christianity.

Brod's discussion was similar to Baeck's. He criticized the inability of Christianity to deal with current problems outside the framework of the "single event," which occurred so long ago. The "otherworldliness" of Christianity is an unsatisfactory approach to the modern world. All modifications attempted nowadays fail because Christianity is tied to the saving act of a single individual long ago. Brod attacked Christianity's predominant emphasis on faith as not sufficiently considering real works in this world. He was equally critical of Christianity's limitation of freedom for man, which he found intolerable to a modern person.

Unlike Baeck, Brod was not a philosopher or historian, so he did not concern himself with precise documentation. One might almost say that the documentation for Brod can be found in Baeck. Brod's polemic was harsher and not as clearly defined; it avoided discussions of distinctive elements in Christianity. Brod, like Baeck, saw and understood only the Christianity of Central Europe, and not the variant patterns fashioned in England and North America. Baeck modified his thought after becoming acquainted with the denominations of England and the United States; Brod, as an emigré to Israel, learned little new about Christianity after he left Europe.

When Brod contrasted Christianity and Judaism, we must say that he emphasized the liberal strands in Judaism. His view of the

Messianic Age—which he saw as at least partially initiated by man, rather than as a miraculous act of God—would be denied by some Jewish thinkers. It was, however, a part of liberal Jewish thought and found wide acceptance.

Brod continued his long and discursive discussion of modern man's three basic attitudes to the world in an effort to discover their origins. Like many other students of Christianity, he saw its beginning in the work of the Apostle Paul, whose thought became the dominant factor in the final redaction of the Gospels. Christianity's dogmatic belief in Jesus developed directly from Paul; Brod considered it a universalization of the belief that Paul had discovered for himself. "Paul believed in the redeeming Christ, for himself. That, however, was his personal salvation, his individual path to salvation and so religiously appropriate. He generalized this path and that was religously wrong . . . "[14] Brod noted that Christianity was developed by an authentic Jew; the thought of Paul was completely Jewish when applied to himself as an individual, but its universalization went beyond the realm of Judaism. Brod was opposed to "the attempt 'to correct all men' from one point, to let them all reach salvation through only one path . . . "[15] The root of Paul's thought lay in his personal view of Jesus. Jesus was not merely an exemplary man whom he wished to emulate to attain salvation, but "it was precisely through the deed of Jesus, through his sacrificial death" and belief in it that he reached salvation. Paul felt that Jesus had died for him, and so he concluded that the event was valid for all men. That meant that the "free salvation of the infinite deity was narrowed to a specific belief in a definite historic event." Paul's own mystical experience was to become the experience of all men. Brod considered the elevation of Jesus to the status of Son of God to be a natural continuation of Paul's thought. Jesus certainly did not believe himself the Son of God in any sense other than the traditional Jewish view, which considers all men to be children of God.[16]

Despite Paul's responsibility for the division between Judaism and Christianity, Brod felt an admiration for him and for some of the ideals he had stressed. He felt that Paul represented a noble Jewish type, which extended from Moses to Herzl. Judaism seemed to produce such individuals rather than the brutal heroes of other people. In contrast to others, the Jews "produce the type of active martyrs, martyrs of their cause rather than martyrs who are an end in themselves or whose martyrdom is the crown of their life; for them it is incidental . . . " Their work always remained more important than their lives. Paul was of this series, and Jews had removed him from it only because of the doctrine Christianity had taken from his life; "however, although Judaism remains incalculably rich in its humane heroes, it can never be so rich as not to miss a figure like Paul in its midst. It would be parochial and petty to exclude him because of the consequences his actions unwittingly brought forth."[17]

Brod understood Paul as a Pharisee who had internalized the psychic characteristics of this group. "The life of this Pharisaic youth and son of a Pharisee crystalizes around two axes: anger and kindness . . . " He expressed both emotions constantly; only because he possessed this nature was his life so full of accomplishments. As a Pharisee he did not deny the Law, but he did not consider it sufficient for salvation.[18]

According to Brod, Paul did not believe that the Jewish state was to be destroyed and expressed himself clearly about the eternity of Israel and Zion. Paul was not opposed to the state, but was indifferent to it. He separated his mission to the pagan world from Jewish universalism. He did not realize that the restrictions, the "fence around the Law" imposed by Jewish teachers, were meant to maintain Judaism; Paul saw these laws as unwarranted demands and ignored them.

Brod felt that the modern world misunderstands the Jewish expression of nationalism, which he regarded as a reaction against pagan nationalism. Nationalism need not lead to eternal warfare as it had under paganism, he wrote, nor need it be dissolved in abstractions, as in Christianity; there is a Jewish path, which offers a third alternative. Paul himself did not oppose Jewish nationalism; such opposition only developed later in Christianity.[19]

According to Brod's view, the main elements of Paul's own teachings—not those derived from him—could have reinforced traditional Jewish thought, but this did not happen. Jews were unable to look at Paul dispassionately—and for good reason. "Judaism has suffered too much on account of Paul, that is the purely human reason. Obstacles must be overridden in order to mention his name without bitterness—if one considers the indescribable ignominy and the ghastly misery which the Church founded by him has heaped upon us."[20]

Jews cannot acknowledge Paul's path as a universal path. "We understand the belief in Jesus of the Apostle Paul as his individual way to salvation, and naturally no further critique of it can be allowed." However, all conclusions that go beyond this point were rejected by Brod.[21] As Jesus did not consider himself the Messiah, Jews have rejected Paul, not Jesus.[22] Jesus was seen as a Jew by Brod and must be so viewed by the Church; Brod noted that the nationalistic Jewish statements of Jesus and his interest in the Jewish people cause the Church considerable difficulty. The Jewishness of Jesus and his interest in the Jewish people Brod stressed in his novel *Der Meister.* Jesus showed no particular interest in the pagan world or its conversion.[23]

The attention Brod gave to Paul was not unusual. Many Jewish writers had dealt with him at length. In 1914 Montefiore had published a book devoted to Paul; earlier others had dealt with this interesting figure. This fascination on the part of Jewish writers had two roots; a need to explain the origin of a separate Christian religion, and a desire to explain Paul's "defection." Brod admired Paul; he felt that such an inventive individual could not be dismissed by our tradition and that we should reclaim him.

As Brod's argument proceeded, he sharply criticized early-twentieth-century Christianity as an amalgamation of traditional Christianity with paganism. (The Holocaust and the excesses of Nazi Germany prove his argument to have been prophetic.) Up to the sixteenth century, Brod asserted, Christianity fought with some success against paganism; its way may have been erroneous, but it was a forceful opponent to the pagan path. Since then an amalgamation has dominated both the private and the public realm. "This Christian-pagan cultural amalgam, which in time sequence is the last link in the development of Christianity, absolutely rules the present-day world. It has formed and conquered this period as no other pattern of thought before. Perhaps it is the exclusiveness and omnipresence of its role which makes it invisible and neutral; it is hardly noticed and, therefore, rarely demands analysis. For only where there is friction does one notice power."[24] With this statement Brod damned current Christianity. He echoed the feelings of Formstecher and Steinheim, who concentrated on this fault in Christianity. Paganism is to be found in all forms of materialism; it has no real god, but deifies supermen, akin to the ancient Greek deities.[25] The current combination of paganism with Christianity has not been successful, and, as with many a mongrel, the offspring possess the worst qualities of both parents. "For paganism the temporal is everything, for the Christian it means nothing. Out of these two points of view the following conclusion emerges: leave earthly matters to themselves."[26] This kind of attitude was responsible for the First World War, and for the cruelties of the modern political state. Superficially viewed, Christianity favors love, nobility, and other virtues, and contains countless allegories about these qualities, but on a deeper level it remains indifferent to everything of this world.[27] Therefore, it has not been difficult to misuse this religion in war, politics, and other pagan ways.[28]

Christianity is weak in the twentieth century; it has been losing ground ever since, centuries ago, it gave up the battle against paganism that it had waged so successfully when it was true to its Jewish heritage. The Reformation, which generally has been considered a struggle against foreign elements within Christianity, actually led to pagan domination.[29] This does not mean that Christianity is dead; "I have never thought of looking upon Christianity as a lost cause." Counterforces are at work; externally they are represented by Judaism, but possibilities of internal change also exist. Protestantism has brought about the amalgamation with paganism, but it also has liberated the individual Christian from the all-inclusive grace of the Church. The rejection of this world has weakened in Protestantism. Brod found the thought of Kierkegaard, with which he disagreed in many ways, most encouraging. He felt that the Danish thinker had led Christianity closer to Judaism.[30]

Max Brod provides us with a sharp and original analysis. He intended to be critical. "I would rather write a one-sided book than one which will 'contain something for everyone.' "[31] In his view, Christianity has unquestionably contributed to mankind but its failures outweigh the benefits. He wished to present the three competing forces in vivid contrast because, he believed, the future depends on the outcome of their struggle.

Brod has remained largely ignored, and his major work has only recently been translated into English. His analysis of the religious situation and his critique of Christianity contain much stimulating material. His statements about Christianity continued the classical Jewish pattern, but he developed them further. He did not strike out on new roads, as did Buber or Baeck, but restated the Jewish position in terms of the twentieth century. He did so with greater clarity and impact than Baeck and so provided the Jewish world with a modern approach to Christianity.

12

Franz Rosenzweig

A New Relationship

As a young man, Franz Rosenzweig (1886–1929) considered converting to Christianity. This was more than a whim of a moment, and it reflected the German-Jewish mood of assimilation at the turn of the twentieth century. German Jewry entered this century with considerable confidence, and it did not permit temporary defeats to divert it from attaining the goal of complete equality in Germany. For example, in the first quarter of the century, my grandfather, Jakob Loewenberg, began two anthologies of his own poetry with a poem entitled "My Fatherland"; it spoke of the difficulties faced by the German Jew, but concluded that despite these he could not be robbed of the feeling "Deutschland über alles . . ."

Jakob Loewenberg expressed an opinion that was widely held. In this atmosphere a young man would not convert merely to open social and economic doors, for that was not felt to be necessary. Instead, the decision would often represent deep intellectual and philosophical introspection. This was certainly so of Rosenzweig. His friends, Rosenstock-Huessy and Ehrenberg, wished him to follow a path already taken by them; however, Rosenzweig rejected Christianity and became instead a leading exponent of modern Jewish thought. After his decision for Judaism, he spent several years studying, for he wished to deepen his understanding of it. The remainder of his life was devoted to Judaism; he developed a new Jewish philosophy, translated the poetry of the Spanish-Jewish poet Judah Halevi, began a modern German translation of the Bible with Martin Buber, and helped to transform adult Jewish education in Germany. All of this was done despite a serious illness, which gradually paralyzed him and eventually made work all but impossible.

Rosenzweig's approach to Christianity differed from that of his predecessors. The intense interest of his youth undoubtedly led to a greater recognition of Christianity than most Jewish thinkers were willing to grant. On the other hand, his rejection of Christianity was vigorous and his critique, firm. Like Hermann Cohen before him, he was interested in the current philosophical overtones of Christianity. He felt this was more important than a historical approach to events that had occurred some thousands of years before. The problems of the nineteenth century and the historicity of Jesus did not concern him. Furthermore, he felt no hesitation about dealing with the entire subject area in a free and open manner. The fears of the previous century were gone. He did not feel it inappropriate to discuss the religion of the surrounding world and simply began to seek an understanding of it in relation to Judaism. He was interested in building a new relationship with Christianity and made the first attempt to do so without polemic.

Perhaps it was easy for Rosenzweig to move in this direction because he had considered conversion to Christianity. Furthermore, many of his thoughts were expressed in letters to a wide circle of friends—primarily to Ehrenberg, who had converted to Christianity. The unusual correspondence the two men developed was an almost ideal Jewish-Christian dialogue. Both were enthusiastic about their respective religions; to the discussion they brought the excitement of discovery or rediscovery, the vigor of deep faith, but also a spirit of enduring friendship. This combination has not been found again in any Jewish-Christian relationship.

In one of these letters Rosenzweig discussed his basic attitude toward Christianity, which could be tolerant despite its intolerance. "You, of course, correctly see that my extensive interest in Christianity is unique. My interest, but not my 'tolerance'; not only 'ethical' but also 'theological' tolerance. How else can religions be tolerant or intolerant except in theological terms. Christianity as a missionary religion is intolerant due to its nature. Judaism has abandoned the missionary effort, due to its national mystique—or whatever you may wish to call the dogmatic kernel of Judaism. It is, therefore, naturally tolerant and promises 'eternal bliss to the pious of all people.' So it is not the tolerance, but the interest, which is individual with me. Christians generally do not realize how limited it is, and they are usually very perplexed if one responds truthfully to their question: 'What does Judaism think about Jesus?' with the answer: 'Nothing.' "

Rosenzweig felt that as a Jew he could view Christianity impartially since no missionary thoughts were involved. On the other hand, Christianity always had to stop its understanding of Judaism at the point where its essential missionary impulse became dominant. "Precisely here the missionary obligation throttled the obligation to understand."[1] He felt safe to generalize on the specific relationship that existed between himself and his friend. One had attempted to convert the other but met firm resistance. This was the classical Jewish position in Western history; the pattern was so old that it had become almost impossible for a Christian to look at Judaism without thoughts of missionizing. Rosenzweig developed his thoughts on tolerance further in another letter in which he analyzed the past as governed by a rhythm which marked certain periods as tolerant and others for struggle. "Both tolerance and strife have an allotted time; if the period for spiritual struggle has not yet arrived, then spiritual tolerance is in order." Yet some of the greatest antitheses would survive these periods of rhythmic alternation and would find no solution till the end of history; he considered the distinction between Judaism and Christianity in this category. One lives with these differences even if they often remain unexpressed and will continue without solution through all history.[2] For Rosenzweig, his era was a period in which understanding was possible; he might well have considered the events of the Nazi period to be part of the natural rhythm of history. As Judaism and Christianity view each other they must ask only understanding, not change. This was to put an end to missionary efforts so discussion could begin. Rosenzweig sought to understand Christianity and to make Judaism clear to his Christian friends.

He wished to explain Judaism to his friend, but saw how difficult it was. "Now, as I attempt to continue writing, I realize that everything I must write is beyond my power to express to you. For

I should now need to show you Judaism from within, hymnically, just as you would have to show Christianity to me, an outsider. Just as you cannot do this, neither can I. The soul of Christianity lies in its expressions; while Judaism shows only its hard, protective shell to the outer world; only within can one speak of its soul."[3] In this expression of inability to understand another religion from the outside, Rosenzweig joined a number of other thinkers who expressed similar reservations. Martin Buber and Claude G. Montefiore stated the same position clearly, but both, like Rosenzweig, felt this should not stop them from trying to understand Christianity.

As Rosenzweig understood Christianity in its relationship to Judaism, it had a special status granted to no other religion.[4] This did not mean that no truths had come from the pagan world, but paganism did not possess a system of truths. Paganism had no real approach to God, as had been granted to Judaism and through Judaism to Christianity. At best it could be classified as the prehistoric beginnings that led to the development of a higher form of religion.[5] In this way Rosenzweig ended any further discussion of pagan religions or pagan influence in the modern world. The whole problem was treated very differently by Max Brod, who felt that however one might classify the pagan elements in the modern world, they threatened to become predominant. In this matter, and in many other areas, Rosenzweig remained on a lofty philosophical plane without much consideration for realities. He still felt that Christianity was the way of the pagan to the God of Judaism. True as this might have been in the past, it did not reflect the conditions of the modern world. Rosenzweig never seriously considered the growing weakness of Christianity but continued to see it as a major force in twentieth-century life.

According to Rosenzweig, Christianity can claim to be on the same level as Judaism, and this claim derives from its acknowledgment of the Bible. If the Bible was given by God, then both religions have a true source of revelation. Jews and Christians share revelation, God, prayer, and the final redemption.[6] Though both religions possess these eternal verities, Christianity is a combination of pagan elements and true religion. This enabled it to approach and conquer the pagan world.

Rosenzweig attempted to present the common basis of both

religions symbolically with Israel as the "star" and Christianity the "rays"; this was central to his understanding of Christianity. "The truth, the entire truth, belongs neither to them nor to us. We bear it within ourselves, precisely, therefore, we must first gaze within ourselves, if we wish to see it. So we will see the star, but not its rays. To encompass the whole truth one must not only see the light but also what it illumines. They, on the other hand, have been eternally destined to see the illuminated object, but not the light."[7] Truth, then, appears to man only in this divided form—the Jewish way and the Christian way—but before God it remains united. The unity exists, but only in the eyes of God; therefore, in our life and in the world there remain two truths.

The attempt to show the unity of the two religions was noble, and no one else has taken this path. Rosenzweig was the first Jew to grant Christianity such recognition. Yet this does not mean that he considered the two religions equal and interchangeable. The distinctions between them remained; Rosenzweig tried to reduce these to one basic point: their relationship to time.

Rosenzweig considered Christianity a religion on the way to a goal—the beginning of eternity, a world which is with God at the beginning of the Messianic Age. Judaism has already arrived at this destination; this is the essential meaning of Israel's election as God's people. Christianity's eternal beginning has been continually emphasized by the Christian stress on the birth of Jesus; that event was the beginning, but the Messiah has not yet come. "The Christian lives at the beginning and the Jew at the end of the interregnum . . . and the Christian's relation to the interregnum is affirmative while that of the Jew is negative."[8] For a Jew the Kingdom of God has already begun. Rosenzweig found this Christian attitude expressed in Christianity's religious forms—for example, in the change of the Sabbath from the last day of the week to the first day. "The Christian is the eternal beginner; completion is not his task. If the beginning is good then all is good. In that lies the eternal youth of Christianity; every Christian, even today, really lives his Christianity as if he were the first."[9]

For Rosenzweig this eternal way was noble and represented the only alternate path toward God. For the pagan it was the only path. Thus, Christianity has accomplished a missionary task that

Judaism could not have successfully undertaken. This approach to Christianity was unique, although the twelfth-century thinkers Maimonides and Halevi approached it, assigning Christianity an important place in the world. Judah Halevi presented the three world religions—Judaism, Islam, and Christianity—on an almost equal footing in the story that begins the *Kuzari*, his chief work. The framework of this philosophical essay is the tale of a king of the Khazars who is faced with the choice of a new religion for his subjects. A debate among the three religions is then presented, and the king chooses Judaism because it was the source of both other religions. In essence Halevi concluded his discussion of Christianity at this point and rejected it, but the very placing of it in such a setting of near equality was unusual for the Middle Ages.

Maimonides wrote somewhat differently about Christianity. He, like many other medieval figures, felt that basic Christian belief is very similar to basic Jewish belief. We share the Bible and only differ in the interpretation of Scripture. Again and again he stressed the Talmudic tradition that all Gentiles who follow the Noahide laws have a place in the world to come. Viewing Jesus and his followers as men who help prepare the world for the Messianic kingdom, Maimonides saw Christianity in a more positive light than many of his contemporaries.

Rosenzweig undertook some discussion of the life of Jesus, which for Christians represents the eternal way. The Christian must believe that the goal will be attained when Jesus comes again. "In this covenantal brotherhood of Christianity, Christ is both the beginning and the end of the way; therefore, he is both the content and the goal, the founder and the master of the covenant."[10] Therefore, the cross is the symbol of the beginning and the end to Christians; both remain of equal significance to them. In contrast, the Jew looks only to the end of the path, to the appearance of David's offspring.[11]

Judaism's arrival at the goal and the Christian way are best described through Rosenzweig's contrast of the sacrifices of Isaac and Jesus. He came to this discussion through a letter from Rosenstock, who had compared the sacrifice of Agamemnon with that of Abraham. Rosenzweig objected: "Abraham did not just sacrifice something, not a child, but his 'only' son, more significant—the son of the promise. He sacrifices this son to the God who made the promise, and through this sacrifice the content of the promise becomes impossible in the eyes of man. . . . The son is returned: now he is only a son of promise. Nothing else occurs; Ilium does not fall, the promise simply remains valid. The father's readiness to sacrifice was not prompted by some Ilium, but was 'without cause.' Agamemnon sacrifices something 'that he has,' but Abraham, everything that he could be; Christ everything that he is. . . . Thus the sacrifice of Abraham is the prototype for Israel, which establishes concretely and corporeally the special status of the Jews before God and man. . . . This differs from the access open to the pagan through Christ's sacrifice of the New Covenant." Later in the correspondence Rosenzweig continued: "The sacrifice of Isaac has eternal significance for us precisely because of its once-and-for-all character. No Jew can give up his son, the son of promise. So Abraham's renunciation was done for all generations to come, so that henceforth no one would need to imitate it. Just as the death on the cross occurred for all future Christians, so that they might live."[12] This was an original and striking parallel, which he then interpreted as having created an eternal brotherhood for the Jew, and an eternal man for the Christian, through belief in whom the goal can be attained. One path depends on the inheritance of an ancient promise and the other on belief. The Jew is a member of his religion through birth and he must follow the commandments; the Christian is not really a Christian by birth, but only upon acceptance of the right belief. Prior to that he was a pagan. The Christian's personal "experience," which is properly stressed, is not necessary for us. "We possess what the Christian will one day experience; we have it from the time of our birth and through our birth it is in our blood. The antecedent of the experience goes back beyond our birth to the antiquity of our people."[13] This emphasis on genetic heritage was an element of early-twentieth-century German thought. While Rosenzweig sought to use it in a positive vein for Jews, the Nazis emphasized it for the Nordic race and its qualities. Of course, they also felt that the characteristics of Jewishness were passed on through the blood of the Jew. As these were considered to be negative, even a small amount of Jewish ancestry was sufficient for exclusion and persecution.

Since a Jew is born into this special relationship, Rosenzweig held, it is impossible for any Jew to consider conversion to Christianity, although that religion may be considered to represent the outer ramparts of Judaism. "Shall I leave the castle in order to strengthen the imperiled outer works? Shall I 'convert,' I who have been among the 'chosen' from birth? Does this alternative exist for me at all?"[14] Here Rosenzweig continued the struggle against all efforts to convert him. Although he had already come to a final decision, he still felt the need to defend himself. Thus he maintained that in the basic approach to life the two religions differ, and it is only possible for one to supplement the other. Each has a definite purpose; they do not compete, nor can members realistically convert from one to the other.[15]

This means that the individual has to be markedly different in each religion. It leads to a unique position for all Jews in their relationship to Christianity or any other religion. This is the second major distinction between Judaism and Christianity. "This then is the deepest distinction between the Jew and the Christian: The Christian is by nature, or at least by birth, a heathen, while the Jew is a Jew. So the path of the Christian must consist of a discarding of his self; he must constantly leave his self and oppose his self in order to become a Christian. By contrast, the life of the Jew does not lead him from his self; he must strive to live more fully within himself. The more he finds himself, the more he abandons paganism, which lies outside of him, not within himself as with the Christian." Although the Jew is a Jew by birth, this must be developed through continual effort, while the Christian must begin entirely from the outside.[16] Perhaps the distinction is even clearer in the attitudes of Jew and Christian toward belief. "Those who know that their own life is on the way from Christ, who came and who will come again, belong to Christianity. . . . This knowledge is belief in something; this is precisely the opposite to the belief of the Jew."[17] Rosenzweig's statement later became the central thesis of Martin Buber's *Two Types of Faith,* in which the distinction between the Jewish and Christian forms of belief is traced historically and explained in detail.

Rosenzweig's interest in Christianity led him deeper into Christian theology than any Jew before him, and he tried to deal with the relationship of Jesus to God, which certainly belongs to the inner core of Christianity that cannot be understood by the outsider. "What is your reality, the basis upon which you act? Jesus or God? As you consider Jesus the Messiah and believe yourself to be part of the interregnum, so God only represents truth to you and Jesus alone reality. But then you are merely a Christian without the Christian phraseology. For this a minimum of Christology is necessary, far less than you possess. For me God alone is reality, and I am part of the interregnum only because of the coercion of nature, not because of free choice. Jesus is part of the interregnum. Whether he was the Messiah will be shown when the Messiah comes. Now he is as problematic to me as the entire interregnum. Only God and His kingdom are a certainty to me, not the interregnum. For that reason I am a Jew and you a Christian."[18] Of course, to a Jew the entire system dealing with the nature of "father" and "son" is unacceptable; yet because this is the basis of Christianity, it has to be understood in any discussion of Christianity. "The Christian way into the land of God is divided into two paths—a dualism which is plainly incomprehensible to the Jew, but nevertheless forms the foundation of Christian life." The Jew also understands the contradictions within God and the various qualities attributed to him. It is difficult to conceive of those characteristics within a single being, but this never leads to a division in the concept of God. "For the Christian, in contrast, the division between 'father' and 'son' indicates far more than a mere distinction between divine sternness and divine love. . . . However, Christian piety follows separate paths when it deals with the father and with the son. The Christian approaches only the son with the confidence that is so natural among us toward God. It is hardly conceivable for us that there are men who do not possess this confidence. Only while holding the hand of the son does the Christian dare to approach the father; he believes that he may only come to the father through the son. If the son had not been a man, then he would be useless to the Christian. He cannot conceive that God Himself, the holy God, could descend far enough for his needs." Subtly, as on other occasions, Rosenzweig has moved here from a friendly exposition to an attack on the most essential feature of Christianity; however, elsewhere he balanced this view with the apologia that this "pagan" influence on Christianity, which weakens it, has proven advantageous in gaining converts. The son is invaluable for the missionary aspect of Christianity. Otherwise, the son represents the Christians' way to God; they are to be satisfied with him and do not need to know anything of God beyond the fact of His presence. No direct contact is necessary or desirable, for all can be accomplished through the son.[19]

When Rosenzweig evaluated this conception of God in the light of the "interregnum" of Christianity's path to God, he felt that the idea was valid for the present period, but that it would cease to have meaning at the end of history. When the final day arrives, these thoughts will no longer exist and all men will return to the Jewish conception of God. "Christianity acknowledged the God of Judaism, not as God, but as the 'father of Jesus Christ.' It holds itself to the 'master,' because it realizes that he alone is the way to the father. He will remain the master in his Church through all time to the end of the world. Then, however, he will cease to be the master and he will also become subservient to the Father. He will then be all in all. We are agreed on the meaning of Christ and the Church in the world; no one can approach the Father except through him.

"No one can approach the Father—but it is different if one need no longer come to the Father, if one is already with him. This is the situation of the people of Israel (though not of the individual Jew). . . . At that juncture where Christ ceases to be the master, Israel ceases to be elected."[20] These distinctions will not be altered by the rhythm of history; they will only be dissolved on the last day of history. Despite the statement that "the entire truth belongs neither to them nor to us," here Rosenzweig returned to the classic Jewish position that Judaism will be the final form of man's religion. Rosenzweig differed from the medieval Jewish thinkers only in the matter of timing; they would have stated that the world is ripe for Judaism at any time, while Rosenzweig postponed this event to the "final day."

Just as Judaism and Christianity have a definite relationship to each other, so do their institutions. The Church and Synagogue need each other and can be helpful to one another. By asserting this, Rosenzweig sought to provide some practical aspects to Jewish-Christian relations.

More important, Rosenzweig used his analysis of Church and Synagogue to renew the confrontation between Judaism and Hellenism. Greek philosophy and Jewish thought had encountered each other more than two thousand years earlier; the Maccabean Wars marked the beginning of the struggle. In Jewish philosophy it soon took the path of accommodation followed from Philo through all the medieval thinkers who sought an adjustment between Greek thought and Judaism. The Jewish philosophers of the nineteenth century had ignored the Greeks; Rosenzweig now attacked again.

As we follow his discussion of the Church and the Synagogue, we also see an original interpretation given to the Christian idea of Israel as a witness. Rosenzweig accepted the idea, but turned it around so that the witness became the admonisher. In Rosenzweig's view, the desire to expand had brought problems to the Church, putting it always in danger of being overwhelmed by the world. The function of the Synagogue, he maintained, is quietly to remind the Church of its duties. "The Church, with its unbreakable staff, with its eyes open to the world, a victorious warrior, constantly faces the danger that the conquered will impose their law on it. Sympathetic toward all it shall nevertheless not lose itself in generalities. Its words shall always remain foolishness and a stumbling block. The Greeks will see to it that it will remain a foolishness then as now and in the future. They will always inquire why precisely this statement should represent the power of God and why another or a third statement should not be equally good—why Jesus and not (or, not also) Goethe. Their questioning will continue to the last day; however it will become fainter with every external and internal victory of the Church. For the wisdom which believes itself wise falls into silence in the face of examination. When the last Greek has been silenced through the operation of the Church, then the statement from the cross—at the end of time, but still within time—will appear as foolishness to no one. But it will remain an eternal stumbling block even at that moment. It was no stumbling block for a Greek to recognize a power of God in the world; the Greeks saw the world full of gods. Only one matter remained inexplicable to him: that he should worship the one Savior on the cross; so it is now and so it will be in the future. But the Synagogue had her eyes blindfolded; she saw no world; then how could she have seen gods in it? She saw only with the inner eye of the prophet; thus she saw only what was last and most distant. Therefore the demand that she see the closest and that which was present in the same manner as she saw the most distant became a stumbling block to her. So it is now and so will it be in the future. Therefore whenever the Church forgets that it is a stumbling block and would adjust itself to 'the human condition' . . . , whenever this occurs the Church finds the Synagogue as the dumb admonisher who has not been enticed by the human condition and only sees the stumbling block. . . . For this reason the Church knows that Israel will be preserved until the day when the last Greek has perished, the work of love has been completed, and the final day, the day of the harvest of hope, dawns. But that which the Church willingly admits for all Israel it refuses to grant to the individual Jew. Upon him it shall and should test its strength to see whether it may win him.''[21] Unless the Church heeds these admonitions and carries the teachings of the Bible into the world, Israel cannot recognize it. "Our recognition of Christianity rests precisely upon the fact that Christianity recognizes us. It is the Torah which is spread by Bible societies to the most distant 'islands.' ''[22] Rosenzweig indicated that both religions must understand each other and the place each occupies in the world. Christianity needed an additional revelation to find a place, but it must also recognize the older revelation to Israel. Israel in turn must understand the function of the Church in the world. Turning his attention to the old Christian idea of the "stubborn Jew" who continues to believe in his election by God, Rosenzweig reversed its meaning in an original manner. He made it serve as a Jewish characterization of Christianity. The widely accepted concept of Christianity as a daughter religion to Judaism served to express the thought clearly. "The dogma of the Church about its relationship to Judaism calls for a corresponding dogma of Judaism and its relations with the Church. It exists in the theory known to you only from modern liberal Judaism, of the 'daughter religion' which shall gradually prepare the world for Judaism.''[23] He demonstrated the ancient roots of this statement and showed that elements of it could be found in the Talmudic literature, although it was clearly stated only in medieval times. Christian power may fill the world, but finally it will serve to bring all men to Judaism; this is Jewish dogma—just as much as it is Christian dogma that Judaism survives only as hardhearted stubbornness and that its adherents will finally be converted. Here the two religions will always clash sharply; this must not be hidden and should rather be clearly noted. To the Jew the wrath of God did not begin in the year 70 C.E. with the destruction of the Temple, as implied in the Christian dogma, but it has always been a part of Israel's election; Israel has suffered God's special love and His anger.

Rosenzweig did not provide a detailed analysis of the Jewish and Christian doctrines of man, but he gave an illuminating insight. "Man who as a Jewish man with all the irredeemable clashes of his love of God, his Jewishness and his humanity, patriarch and Messiah—with all these contradictions he remains one, a single unified living being. This man appears in Christianity as two beings. Not as two figures who must necessarily exclude or battle one another, but as beings who will follow separate ways, divided even when, as may always occur, they find themselves together in the same person."[24] Aside from this, Rosenzweig also saw the danger of hero worship directed toward one form of man. This peril exists in the relationship to the priesthood, which may be idolized and raised beyond ordinary humanity. The soul of man plays a very important role in Christian thought. "It is significant for Christianity, as the religion of the interregnum, that it has expended so much strength upon the concept of the redemption of the soul; here it is also the legitimate heir of paganism, whose inheritance it accepted in order to freely transform it. . . . In Judaism this concept remained firmly imbedded in the folklore, but did not penetrate into the theology."[25]

A major difference also exists in the attitude of the two religions toward nationalism. The sense of nationhood has remained a natural part of Judaism; a Jew's religious development is not impeded by his being a member of the Jewish people, for both individual and people are elements of Judaism. Christianity, on the other hand, had to destroy the myth of the pagan nations, for it found them opposed to its teachings. It could not have succeeded in any other way, but in so doing an important element of national life had to be sacrificed. Judaism, by combining individual ethical-religious demands with the cohesive force of nationalism, brought about a natural unity, which need not be broken in order to attain the noblest goals of religion.[26] Rosenzweig made it clear that the long Christian struggle between Church and State has no meaning for Judaism. The bitterness engendered by these controversies can only be viewed by the Jew as an outsider.

Only on a few occasions was Rosenzweig led to deal with some other great personalities of Christianity. One of these was a discussion of faith and law. He wished to show that Marcion's Gnosticism forced the Church to adopt Paul's personal theology of the simultaneous rejection and election of the Jews and of the connection between the Old Testament law and the Gospel faith. The historical significance of Paul's doctrine has to be understood before it can be discussed in contemporary terms.[27] Here again the points of departure of the two religions differ markedly. Jews have to begin with duty—the Law—and this must not be misunderstood; Christians must begin with faith, and that too must not be misinterpreted. "From this our duty may be derived; we shall not wait until the experience awakens within us, but we must step backward into the experience that has already occurred and is part of our heritage. No sentimentality then! No anxiety about the purity of the experience—all that is Christian. The Christian must begin with *kavvanah* [devotion], but we must without sentimentality begin with *mitzvah* [commandment], with Talmud Torah [study] in some form; the *kavvanah* will then come."[28] The beginnings of Baeck's distinction between "romantic" and "classical" religion lay in these remarks. Baeck went much farther and developed a long polemic out of this difference. Rosenzweig was also not enamored of Christian "sentimentality," but he felt it was a path Christianity had been destined to take, and should be viewed in that light.

A leading motif through the entire discussion was the powerful conviction that Christianity would lead to a universal Judaism. At times Rosenzweig felt this era was near; the revolutions of the preceding centuries had weakened the Church, and had brought it closer to Judaism. There had been a kind of return to Johannine Christianity, which was very near Judaism. Furthermore, Judaism had also moved forward in this century through the Messianism of the Zionist movement.[29] As Rosenzweig approached the end of his life he remained optimistic about the future of the two religions. Even when he did not discuss the matter in such imminent terms, he felt that Christianity would eventually change, that Jesus would cease to be significant for it, and that in every way it would become Jewish. "The completed Judaizing of Christianity would mean the exclusion of Christ. Expressed in a different manner: the year zero has a relationship to time. Therefore, Christianity will only reach its absolute state as Jewish-Christianity, in the Johannine state.

"Its absolute state: It is the 'essential dogma of Christianity' that I, the one who has been sent, am the way, the truth, and the life. This makes the absolute state of Christianity an absolute within time, but relative in the face of eternity. It is no distortion of Christianity, as you feel, to place God at the final goal. . . . As long as the statement 'I am the way' stands as its main dogma—that means forever—till then there is no room for the living God." The two religions have separate tasks: Christianity must deal lovingly with the realities of the world, and Judaism must concern itself with the final truths. Neither religion must attempt to follow the path of the other, for then they "will both postpone the coming of the Kingdom of God."[30]

Franz Rosenzweig cast a new light upon the relationship of Judaism and Christianity. He did not abandon the old distinctions and the historic differences, which had been discussed so often, but he tried to view them in a creative way. Some of his insights parallel those of Buber and Baeck, whom he several times influenced directly. Rosenzweig built on the medieval Jewish thinkers; he did not reject their evaluation of Christianity but placed it in a different perspective. The ultimate distinctions and the final aim of Judaism remained the same; but because these elements had been transferred to the future, it was possible to achieve a much greater degree of understanding in the present.

13

Leo Baeck

Modern Polemic

Leo Baeck (1873–1956) is generally considered to have been the last great exponent of Liberal Judaism in Germany. Until his deportation to the concentration camp at Theresienstadt in 1943, he was the representative of the Jewish community to the Nazi government. Aside from being a scholar and a notable thinker, he was for many years the president of the World Union for Progressive Judaism, and in that capacity he was a leading international spokesman and exemplar of Liberal Judaism.

A single event may often have a dominant effect on a man's life. This was certainly the case with Baeck, who was propelled into an examination of the historical relationship between Judaism and Christianity by the publication in 1900 of Adolf Harnack's *The Essence of Christianity*. This work embodied the mature thought of one of the leading German-Protestant theologians of the late nineteenth century; it consisted of a series of lectures, which later appeared in a widely read and often reprinted book form. The volume provided an ethical-humanistic view of early Christianity and a very liberal account of Jesus—depicting him as "the Jesus of the anti-Jewish liberal Germany of the early twentieth century."[1]

Baeck criticized Harnack's work as purely apologetic and lacking a historical or scientific basis—in fact, of totally neglecting the rabbinic literature in its evaluation of the period of the origin and rise of Christianity. He first attacked the volume in a lengthy review,[2] and a few years later he published *The Essence of Judaism*, the very title of which indicated that it was in part an answer to Harnack's earlier book.[3] In this work Baeck sought to

137

present a modern approach to Judaism that would show the religion as it really was to both Jew and Gentile and would subtly answer Harnack. In the very best sense of the word this is a major work of apologetic literature, and from the outset it was intended to serve an apologetic purpose. The book was successful and brought renown to its author. Leo Baeck, therefore, is somewhat indebted to Harnack for stimulating his enduring interest in Christianity. Indeed, it remained a compelling interest for the rest of his life, and at regular intervals Baeck concerned himself with Christianity, placing special emphasis on its earliest formative stage. He wrote about the Church, about Jesus, about Paul and Luther, and also touched on the later development of Christianity. Each of his collections of essays contains segments of his developing thought in the study of Christianity.

Baeck especially wished to establish a genuine dialogue, for which there had been no previous opportunity, and he was rather regretful about the path the Church had taken, which did not permit a real understanding or a dialogue to develop. In fact, as he pointed out, the relationship that had existed between the surrounding cultural world and Judaism in the early centuries was not permitted to continue in the medieval world, which was dominated by the Church. "The only way this would have been possible would have required self-renunciation. Even the Book, the old Hebrew Bible, which might have led to unity, was forced to be a source of divisiveness." Thus, during the medieval period Judaism had to defend itself and its right to the Bible against the Church.[4] "In retrospect it seems tragic that the Church, with all the riches of its inner world, with all the depth and fullness of its piety, confronted this people often, if not always, as Imperium. Thus it did not see the world of this people, nor was its own world seen by them."[5] Of course, this spirit continued during the period of the Crusades.

Most of the essays in which Baeck concerned himself with Christianity were historical and expository. At first he sought a Jewish understanding of Christianity; later he wished to discover a road of reconciliation between the two religions, which both believed themselves to have the final answer and had stood face to face through nineteen centuries of history without thoroughly examining each other. "And the usual, and inevitable, result of any talk was an increase in the feeling, on the Christian side, of being uncompromisingly rejected by the Jew, and, on the Jewish side, of being forcibly summoned and violently accused by the Christian—let alone the fact of the restrictions and burdens imposed on the Jew, or on behalf of, the Church."[6] There had been times to keep silent, he felt, but this was an age for attempting to speak, and it would be very wrong not to fully utilize the present-day situation, which encouraged such discussion among all religions. It would have to be completely honest, however, for Baeck was well aware of the difficult position forced on the Jew in earlier times, when discussions took place without freedom of expression. "These were discussions in which the result to be attained was already set at the outset. These were not occasions of free speech. At times, though rather rarely, Jews wrote books about Christianity, such as Lipmann of Mühlhausen and others. These books, however, concerned themselves solely with the interpretation given to certain Biblical verses by the Church; they did not deal with Christianity as a religion or with the dogma of the Church."[7] Now, in modern times, all this has changed; Judaism has to view itself in a different light and must take greater cognizance of other religions.

The new dialogue in our age must be free, honest, and willing to pose all questions as well as to receive all answers. Although these sentiments were expressed late in Baeck's life, they contain the essence of his method of discussing Christianity.

In *The Essence of Judaism* Christianity is hardly mentioned by name, nor are the significant personalities of its beginnings singled out for marked attention. Yet a comparison between the two religions is almost continually implied. This is what Mayer, in his critique of Baeck, called the "polemic of silence."[8] However, at times Baeck rather clearly pointed to the major distinctions between the two religions, in such instances leaving nothing to suggestion and, without hesitation, criticizing Christianity for its weaknesses. However, since the study of Christianity was not a primary purpose of the book, his thoughts in this area were rarely fully developed; they served mainly to show the careful reader what might be expected in later essays devoted entirely to the subject of Christianity.

In essence, Leo Baeck's approach to Christianity can be divided into two periods. Until middle life he saw it as an antagonist and thought the best method of approach to be a vigorous attack. He did not state this in so many words, but it is perfectly clear in numerous writings, especially in the essay "Romantic Religion." Later in life he muted his criticism somewhat, emphasizing the Jewish elements of Jesus and Paul. He was also led in this direction by the form of Christianity he encountered in England and America, which possessed its own special characteristics. Still, he remained sharp and unrestrained in his attitude. In one of his last essays he posed some of the questions that Judaism is obliged to ask the Church. "They will not be designed to challenge dogma or articles of faith: the other's creed is his sanctuary that cannot be queried or disputed here. The subject of our questions is not the 'what' but the 'how'; that is to say, not the belief in itself, in its contents, but so to speak the conduct of the belief; not what the belief wants to say, but how it is saying it. Every religion claims its place and asserts its task in the world. It also wishes to strengthen this place and to confirm this task. It cannot dispense with it."[9] Baeck was concerned with "the style of the Church." He began by viewing the historical treatment of the Jew and asked whether the Church addresses itself to the Jew as a religious faith or as a great power. Is it "the voice of the messenger of the religion or that of an envoy of a regime?"[10] He discussed the dangers of corruption through power, which had often occurred within the Church. Shall the meeting of the two religions be similar to that of a great power meeting a small country? For a true reconciliation can only be expected if they meet on the religious and spiritual level, not on that of power. "Without this wide outlook onto that common ground, any meeting, however important, would be an isolated event leading nowhere."[11]

Judaism must have other concerns about a meeting with Christianity, for "in the religious sphere, especially from the Jewish point of view, any question, while starting from the past and the present, has its full truth only when aiming at the days to come."[12] The Church, on the other hand, faces the world with the satisfied view of one who possesses all understanding and with a greater emphasis on its early historical past than on the present or the future. So Baeck had to ask a painful question: "Has not the

Church, as a whole, extensively or intensively, played an unimportant part in the historic, painful endeavors for human liberation and emancipation? Was it not comparatively late in the day that what others achieved by great exertions and sacrifices was finally somehow acknowledged by the whole of the Church? . . . What, on the whole, was the attitude here, the attitude of mind and action, adopted by the Church when peoples started to right the wrong that for so long had been done to Judaism and to the Jew?"[13] He reminded the reader, however, that it was not proper to overemphasize the past—one should stress the future that may grow from the present common ground.

Leo Baeck's basic attitude toward Christianity is best expressed in his long polemic essay "Romantic Religion." In this piece he contrasted "classic" Judaism with "romantic" Christianity. The discussion was executed on a lofty philosophical level, but the tone remained militant in the characterization of Christian thought: "Feeling is supposed to mean everything: this is the quintessence of romanticism. . . . Its danger, however, which it cannot escape is this: the all-important feeling culminates eventually in vacuity or in substitutes, or it freezes and become rigid. And before this happens, it follows a course which takes it either into sentimentality or into the phantastic; it dodges all reality, particularly that of the commandment, and takes refuge in passivity when confronted with the ethical task of the day. Empathy makes up for much and gives a freedom which is really a freedom from decision and independence from inner obligation."[14] Radical as this statement sounds, it appeared in a much briefer form earlier in Baeck's career when he discussed the lack of dogma in Judaism. "In it there was no need for a constant, inviolable formula; this is necessary only in those religions at the heart of which lies a mystical, consecrating act of faith—an act which alone can open the door to salvation and which therefore requires a definite conceptual image to be handed down from age to age. Such acts of salvation and gifts of grace are alien to Judaism; it does not pretend to be able to bring heaven to earth. It has always maintained a certain sobriety and severity, demanding even more than it gives. That is why it adopted so many commandments, and refused sacraments and mysteries."[15] Naturally he felt that mystery and faith were not entirely absent from Judaism, but they were properly balanced. Judaism did not make the mistake of resting upon only one of the two pillars of religion; it did not choose commandment or faith, but both.[16]

In "Romantic Religion" Baeck traced the romantic development in Christianity, which originated with Paul, who brought the Oriental mystery cults with their essential romanticism into Christendom; these elements then remained dominant through its long history. Baeck began with a description of the Roman Empire in the days of Caesar and his successors, during which a need for a new religious orientation was felt because the old classical Greek cults were losing their hold on the people. New faiths, such as the Egyptian mysteries and the cults of Mithras, Adonis, Attis, and Seraphis "shared the sentimental attitude which seeks escape from life into living experience and turns the attention towards a phantastic and marvelous beyond."[17] This showed a great yearning, and "the way was prepared for a new faith without limits or boundaries." The great romantic tide thus swept over the Roman Empire, and the ancient world drowned in it. Even as the old, naive poetry of the gods perished in the sentimental myth of the redeeming savior, so what was classical vanished, along with its sure sense of law and determination, and gave way to the mere feeling of a faith sufficient unto itself.

"What is called the victory of Christianity was in reality this victory of romanticism. Before Christianity took its course, that through which it eventually became Christianity—or, to put it differently, whatever in it is non-Jewish—had already become powerful enough to be reckoned as a world faith, as a new piety which united the nations. The man with whose name this victory is connected, Paul, was, like all romantics, not so much a creator of ideas as a connector of ideas."[18] Paul had grown up in the Jewish and the Roman cultural environments; he had known the Jewish longing for a Messiah as well as the myth of the mystery cults where deities were constantly reborn. He finally combined both religions, which meant a union of the Jewish and the pagan world and according to his thought would lead to salvation for both through the figure of Jesus and the mystery connected with him. "In a heavenly-earthly drama, in the miraculous mystery that took shape between the here and the above, the meaning of world history and of the individual human life stands revealed. . . . This myth was the bridge on which Paul went over to romanticism."[19] This step was final for Paul, although he continued the struggle between the new romantic feelings and the mood of Judaism within his own soul.

As the new religion gained form, and as its theory was developed by Paul, it became a religion of passivity. Man "is pure object; fate alone is subject. In this way, religion becomes redemption from the will, liberation from the deed."[20] Baeck conceded that this attitude became somewhat softened in medieval Catholicism, which gave man a certain sphere of action. "But Luther then returned to the purer romanticism of Paul with its motto, *sola fide*, through faith alone."[21]

Having outlined in a brief manner the growth and development of this idea, Baeck continued by demonstrating its significance in Western culture. It led to the concept of the "finished man" in which an individual may feel that he possesses the entire truth and can rest in peace on that assumption. This was perhaps his chief criticism of Christianity. "Since the end of the ancient world, the intellectual life of the Occident has in many ways been determined by this notion. It has established that orientation in which the answer precedes every question . . . "[22] This, of course, was the pattern of scholastic philosophy, which was dominant until the Enlightenment.

The Middle Ages may well be called the Christian "finished" world, the world of "regularity without any exception, a world of absolute symmetry in which everything fell into its precise place." Furthermore, the Reformation under Luther hardly changed this fact. "The Protestant state is its ultimate result, a state without inner problems."[23] Only the French Revolution broke out of this pattern, while enlightenment and its modern successors have been faced by a continual struggle against the credo *quia absurdum*, the ultimate result of all forms of romanticism, which destroys the inquiring mind and even the privilege of inquiry. For Baeck the necessary tension and questioning that permit a true future were missing in both Greek thought and in Christianity, which was largely conquered by Greek thought;[24] so "philosophy and experience, gnosticism and sacrament amalgamated in the conviction of the finished, absolute man who is the redeemer and the redeemed."[25] The man who lives with tension possesses the future, although he may remain most uncertain in the present. The completed man possesses the present and may continue as a powerful force for many centuries; but when death comes it is absolute, while that which is unfinished and incomplete possesses the future. "The religion of tension, the culture which lives in it will not perish. It may be pressed to the ground, it may become weary, it may slumber, but it cannot die; it will always be reborn."[26] This tension was also stressed by the individualism present in Judaism but lacking in Christianity and the Church. "For this reason the congregation is something different than the Church, which has grown from different soil, from the fellowship of the sacrament. The Church exists as a separate entity with its own claims and pretensions. Therefore the tension and the discussion between the individual and the group, which exists in the community, is not present in the Church." The contrary gives the free state its moral and spiritual foundation.[27] Baeck furthermore clearly showed that the romantic mind is completely dependent on the moment of inspiration and takes its presentation as a completed process which needs neither analysis nor further development. Finally Baeck was led to make the statement: "Even the love of man which is glorified in romantic religion is merely the gift of grace which is the share of those who have faith. The only activity of the genuine romantic is self-congratulation on his state of grace."[28] Thus, in the first portion of his essay Baeck demolished much of the foundation of Christianity by demonstrating its weakness as a "romantic" religion.

Baeck then continued by portraying the history of groups within Christianity that had struggled against the romantic impulse and sought to reestablish the classical elements of the religion; he especially discussed the Calvinists and the Baptists, as well as other groups in which a social conscience had been awakened. They all mark a decided contrast to romanticism, which depreciated all human effort, as had much of medieval Catholicism. Whatever drives these forms of modern Protestantism toward reform and social conscience has its origin in the Old

Testament, according to Baeck. In the realm of culture, romantic religion became all-embracing and attempted to take it entirely under its wings with the consequential loss of freedom to culture and science. Only with the advent of modern times "could the classical, ethical idea of history be regained—this idea of becoming, of the never-quite-finished, of the direct ascent."[29] As a consequence, "movement and becoming appear as an alienation from religion, an alienation from the faith which is everything."[30] In the realm of history this means a constant definition of the past and the present in the light of one event, the life and death of Jesus; all other history ceases to be significant and there can be no meaningful study of history.

As romanticism depends upon experience, each follower of its tenets must have the experience; in Christianity this is accomplished through the sacraments, which become the instrument of grace. They bring the mystery into daily life. Here again the weakness of romanticism is clearly pointed out, for "the human being in whom the miracle takes place need not participate either through action or through knowledge."[31] Baeck was also aware of the dangers in the materialization of this psychic and spiritual event; when it becomes a substance and its attainment is further simplified, the spiritual dangers are increased. Naturally Christianity has constantly fought this tendency through the monastic movement as well as by other methods which seek to make the religious experience wholly a part of man's life. Baeck drew a distinction between Judaism, which emphasized miracles in its early days but slowly overcame them, and Christianity, which has continued this pattern, pointing out that "its cult with its ceremonial is the drama of the miracle."[32]

The problems raised by the need for religious experience soon led to dogma as a necessity for the Church, according to Baeck. "What such formulations grant to faith is that it need no longer be ecstatic or seek transfiguration."[33] Of course this means that the personally experienced must give way to the general formulation, which leads to the development of an orthodoxy. "Truth and lie now receive their preeminent meaning from the finished ecclesiastical doctrine and not from any infinite ethical duty; they are no longer a matter of conscience, but rather a matter of dogmatic

definition; . . . love of truth now becomes love of the ecclesiastical truth, and a lie now becomes a deviation from the dogma."[34]
"It is no mere accident that the command of truthfulness so rarely
finds expression in the Pauline and the subsequent Christian
literature. The precepts of faith and humility, of suffering and
hope, of pity and charity occupy a spacious sphere, but our simple
virtue generally disappears behind them. And it is lacking not only
in the literature; the turning away from it is one of the chief traits
of the entire romantic Middle Ages."[35] All criticism and all criteria
of truth disappear in this system of thought, which has been
characteristic of much Church history.

Within the Church there has always been a contrast between the
complete adjustment to the miracle and the partial adjustment, the
former made by the priests and the members of the hierarchy, and
the latter made by the laity. This, of course, has led to great
passivity on the part of the layman. Passivity consequently brought
the need for authority in all realms of life; there must be a firm
guardian of the faith in any romantic religion, but a classical
religion may use faith to build and rebuild without reference to the
past, as was expressed by the prophets.[36] The step from this to the
tyrannical state is simple. "The alliance between ruler and believer
has been readily formed wherever romantic religion has held sway;
every reaction has been consecrated and every forward drive been
damned."[37]

Within this romantic system "works" are always in danger of
disappearing, however much the Church may follow the emphasis
of James on "faith and works" and thus give a certain sphere to
human activity. Luther also defined the path of salvation as
attainable entirely through faith. Sinfulness and guilt are seen as
part of the essence of man; only an act of grace could change this,
and man's individual deeds can accomplish nothing.[38] Ethics,
therefore, becomes superfluous in the dichotomy of "Either faith or
ethics!"[39] Man can become good only through the miracle of faith.
Baeck proceeded to show the dilemma in which the Christian
romantic is placed by this dichotomy; various thinkers have
emphasized one or the other position, but the predominant emphasis
has been on faith, as indeed it must be. Ethics, therefore, has been a
source of some embarrassment to the Church, for it has no organic

relation to faith. Romanticism has always found ethical demands difficult: "Ethics evaporates into exaltation. The place of the determinate ethical commandment is taken by the aureolo-surrounded image which is to be adored."[40] Which leads to the adoration of saints rather than individual striving for saintliness.

"Everything that is characteristic of romantic religion makes a united front against the idea of a moral law. All its multifarious tendencies coalesce in this opposition. Justice is to be reduced to a mere feeling and experience; the good deed is effected, not by human will and action, but by divine grace. . . . "[41] This means that virtue is lacking where the right faith does not exist, and that it cannot exist outside a Christian. Thus, this religion has been able to witness a great deal with equanimity and has often become highly intolerant. Baeck went so far as to assert that "it is difficult to say what has been more pernicious in the course of time: the intolerance which committed the wrongs or the indifference which beheld them unperturbed."[42] This leads to such indifference to the fate of others that even missions are largely a remnant of the Hebrew Bible rather than an essential part of Christianity and are to be found only as a late addition in Lutheranism.[43]

Perhaps one of the most telling arguments in this long and discursive essay is directed against the exclusiveness of the Church. This too grew from the concept of romantic religion, in which there was only one truth and one world-dominating event. All mankind became divided into two segments through the interpretation of a statement in the Fourth Gospel—"No man cometh unto the Father, but by me"—"the harshest and most denominational sentence ever spoken. It furnished the basis for much mercilessness . . . This sole way of loving God has often left little room for loving man. . . . Corresponding to the finished man of romanticism there was the finished mankind, the Church."[44]

In contrast, "classical religion finds in the irrational the revelation of the existent which summons the self; . . . In classical religion, the irrational appears as the holy, the covenant between the Eternal and man." This aspect was always shared by both aspects of religion, but in classicism it moved forward rather than being a mood which turned only on itself. "In classical religion, longing strives ever again for the goal which is to unify men and impels them to follow the commandment of God."[45]

This highly polemical essay subsequently met criticism in Richard Mayer's long monograph, which attacked many of its points.[46] Surprisingly, no one else has really challenged it. Mayer felt the designation "romantic" was not used correctly and that Baeck actually wrote more about romanticism than Christianity, for, he claimed, the connection between Baeck's statements and the Church often seemed weak. Mayer also felt that some elements of Christianity were overemphasized at the expense of others. He also stressed Baeck's polemic of silence in *The Essence of Judaism*, for he felt that Baeck often criticized Christianity quietly by omission. This certainly is an unusual and correct insight. However, for all Baeck's polemic excesses, the essential religious dichotomy seems to be correct. It may not be acceptable to a Christian, but it will need a stronger reply than Mayer gave it. Despite his critique, Mayer appreciated Baeck's efforts to understand various special elements of Christianity, though he felt that Baeck saw them in a Jewish manner.

Leo Baeck also investigated specific aspects of Christianity and concerned himself with an analysis of early Christian sources in a number of cases. He sought to distinguish the elements that stemmed from Judaism and those that were borrowed from the Oriental mystery religions. His major effort in this direction was *The Gospel as a Document of the History of the Jewish Faith*, published in 1938. This book fitted well into the general Christian discussion of the life of Jesus, which had continued for more than a century. The book grew out of Baeck's desire to demonstrate the Jewish background of the Gospels, and it offered the conclusion that the essential Gospels are a piece of "not inconsiderable Jewish history—a testimony of Jewish faith."[47] In arriving at this view Baeck stripped the Gospels of all the late accretions and attempted to reconstruct the original documents. He justified his method of analysis by showing that the Gospels were derived from oral tradition and had been written down only after a number of generations had passed. Baeck tried to analyze the changes that might have taken place in the transmission of this or any other oral tradition due to piety for a teacher, through the love of the disciples, through omission of ideas which did not appeal to the next generation, and so forth. He demonstrated that these factors were important in the transmission of all oral traditions.[48] Finally, he attempted to demonstrate that the outlook of the men who wrote the Gospels was similar to Jewish tradition; Baeck summarized: "These men, too, experienced everything in terms of the Bible, and the words of Scripture directed, commanded, and exerted an inner compulsion. For these men, too, a fixed content, a fixed religious doctrine, was there to begin with and was most vividly real and the whole truth. For them, too, and for those who received the tradition from them, their master's lot and fate had long been revealed and always preordained. . . . The tradition of the Gospel is, first of all, in every one of these respects, simply a part of the Jewish tradition of that time."[49]

Later, as he pointed out, the thought pattern of the Greco-Roman world slowly influenced basic Christian ideas and led to changes in the interpretation of the original Gospel message about Jesus; this caused the eventual rift between Judaism and Christianity. Despite all difficulties, Baeck felt, it was possible to discover the original layer of the Gospels. "On the whole it is nevertheless possible to get back to the original tradition. If one notes the special characteristics of each of the three authors and, so to say, eliminates them, the procedure and method to be followed after that can be shown quite clearly. . . . The following, on the other hand, must be part of the old original tradition: whatever is completely different from the tendencies and purposes of the generations which came after the first generation of disciples; whatever contradicts the tenets which later became part of the faith; whatever is different from, or even opposed to, the intellectual, psychic, and political climate in which these later generations gradually found themselves; whatever, in other words, exemplifies the way of life and the social structure, the climate of thought and feeling, the way of speaking and the style of Jesus' own environment and time. In all this we are confronted with the words and deeds of Jesus."[50]

After this had been accomplished in the more technical portions of the essay, which examined the life of Jesus in some detail, Baeck proposed the conclusion: "In the old Gospel which is thus opened up before us, we encounter a man with noble features who lived in the land of the Jews in tense and excited times and helped and labored and suffered and died: a man out of the Jewish people who walked on Jewish paths with Jewish faith and hopes. His spirit was at home in the Holy Scriptures, and his imagination and thought were anchored there; and he proclaimed and taught the word of God because God had given it to him to hear and to preach. We are confronted by a man who won his disciples among his people: . . . men who then found him and clung to him and believed in him until he finally began to believe in himself and thus entered into the mission and destiny of his age and indeed into the history of mankind. . . . In this old tradition we behold a man who is Jewish in every feature and trait of his character, manifesting in every particular what is pure and good in Judaism. This man could have developed as he came to be only on the soil of Judaism; . . . Here alone, in this Jewish sphere, in this Jewish atmosphere of trust and longing, could this man live his life and meet his death—a Jew among Jews. . . . When this old tradition confronts us in this manner, then the Gospel, which was originally something Jewish, becomes a book—and certainly not a minor work—within Jewish literature.''[51] To Baeck this original Gospel was a Jewish book lying entirely within the realm of Jewish tradition, like so many thousands of other Jewish books. Therefore, ''Judaism may not pass it by, nor mistake it, nor wish to give up all claims here. Here, too, Judaism should comprehend and take note of what is its own.''[52] In this manner the Gospels were reclaimed by Baeck for Judaism—however, only in the severely abridged forms that Baeck considered authentic. In the final portion of the essay his proposed text of the original oral tradition was presented.

Many Jewish scholars before Baeck had pointed to the Jewish elements of the New Testament, but none had tried to actually reclaim the Gospels as a Jewish book. Of course, this effort was also criticized. It was not.acceptable to Mayer, who felt, with some justification, that Baeck had abstracted the most beautiful traditions of the Gospels, claiming them for Judaism and discarding the rest.[53]

In this most interesting essay Baeck not only reclaimed a major segment of Christian literature for Judaism but he attempted also to reclaim Jesus. The statements he made about the "Jewish" Jesus certainly were as admirable as any made by a Jew, but one must remember that Jesus emerges as a Jew from this essay. Baeck had no quarrel with the founder of Christianity and clearly admired the "Jewish" Jesus who appeared once the Greco-Roman accretions were removed. Jesus spoke primarily to Israel, as Baeck stated in his *Essence of Judaism.* "It bears witness to the power of the words of Jesus rather than indicating any narrowness of outlook, that he limited his message to Israel. But it is fortunate that his exhortation is neither in the Old Testament nor in the Talmud, for it would have found small grace in the eyes of those austere Protestants who would have dubbed it as yet another manifestation of the narrow-minded national religion of the Jews. . . . The prophets speak of the world and its salvation, but they speak to Israel. Only the later colorless imitators were to summon all mankind as their audience."[54] This was stated with greater clarity later. "In the old Gospel which is thus opened up before us, we encounter a man with noble features who lived in the land of the Jews in tense and excited times and helped and labored and suffered and died: a man out of the Jewish people who walked on Jewish paths with Jewish faith and hopes. His spirit was at home in the Holy Scriptures, and his imagination and thought were anchored there; and he proclaimed and taught the word of God because God had given it to him to hear and to preach. We are confronted by a man who won his disciples among his people; men who had been looking for the messiah, the son of David, who had been promised; men who then found him and clung to him and believed in him until he finally began to believe in himself and thus entered into the mission and destiny of his age and indeed into the history of mankind. These disciples he found here, among his people, and they believed in him even after his death, until there was nothing of which they felt more certain than that he had been, according to the words of the prophet, 'on the third day raised from the dead.' In this old tradition we behold a man who is Jewish in every feature and trait of his character, manifesting in every particular what is pure and good in Judaism. This man could have developed as he came to be only on the soil of Judaism; and only on this soil, too, could he find his disciples and followers as they were. Here alone, in this Jewish sphere, in this Jewish atmosphere of trust and longing, could this man live his life and meet his death—a Jew among Jews. Jewish history and Jewish reflection may not pass him by nor ignore him. Since he was, no time has been without him; nor has there been a time which was not challenged by the epoch that would consider him its starting point."[55] Although Baeck first encountered Jesus when he undertook his reply to Harnack, he found a Jewish figure; actually in both periods of his Christian studies he was able to meet the Jesus of the Gospels with "love and reverence."

Mayer criticized Baeck here for having created a special person of Jesus from whom the Christian characteristics had been removed. This presented an erroneous and oversimplified view of early Christian history, Mayer felt; nonetheless, he admitted, the picture of Jesus that emerged was truer and more sympathetic than the one given by many Christian scholars.[56]

A discussion of the beginnings of Christianity would be far from complete unless it presented a detailed account of the changes that soon led to the separation of Judaism and Christianity. If such matters were not treated, the reader would be left with an admirable account of Jesus as a Jew and a polemic essay against the Christian religion as it finally emerged—with nothing about the transition in between. Of course Baeck touched upon this question also, although not in a single separate work. Like many others he saw Paul as the figure responsible for the basic change in Christianity, recognizing in him much that was contrary to the basic Jewish spirit of the earlier Christian tradition. In a sympathetic and cogent manner Baeck described the background of Paul, who was versed in Judaism and the mystery religions of his Asia Minor home. Somehow Paul began to combine elements from both paths and thus provided an answer to the problems of the time, also promising triumph over death. Baeck saw both elements as conceptions that "were really pointing toward each other."[57] Baeck felt that the four letters that can be attributed to Paul show that "one day, this man, Paul from Tarsus, joined the congregation of Jesus' adherents; and one day he began to preach and spread his own new faith and a new theology which was designed to furnish a biblical foundation for his faith; . . . What found its place here was not the doctrine of Jesus, but a doctrine about him, not his own faith which he had communicated to his disciples but faith in him. What is central here and determines everything is not the commandment or the comfort which Jesus had offered the distressed, the suffering, and those who had gone astray, but the sacrament that the believer is to receive in his name; not his life and work and passion but his incarnation, his death and resurrection; not his divine service to men, his preaching of the kingdom of God, but a salvation which is the share of those that believe in him; not a task and a confidence but a grace that is fulfilled; not a demanding faith but a doctrine of salvation."[58] All of this radically changed the Christian religion and left its dogmatic imprint on the Gospel account of earlier Christianity.

Paul, as the real founder of Christianity, merited a long and thorough discussion by Baeck in a number of his essays. He emerged as the central figure in Baeck's polemic on "romantic" and "classic" religion, for the distinctive "romantic" characteristics were original with him; he derived them from the pagan mystery cults. "Alongside the one God before whom the gods of the pagans were to vanish, it now placed the one redeemer, the one savior before whom the savior of the nations could sink out of sight: it placed the oneness of the savior alongside the oneness of God. Thus he experienced it: paganism, with its deepest aspirations and thoughts, was led to Judaism; and Judaism, with its revelation and truth, was bestowed on the pagans, too."[59] To Paul the divided world was now unified, and he had brought about this union through his new theology. He preserved what was most essential in the pagan mysteries and united it with Judaism.

Baeck admired Paul for the clear view of his inner struggles that he presented in the letters giving us his vision.[60] Essential for an understanding of this vision is the fact that it was Christ-centered. "A turning point in the history of religion, of monotheism, is seen here. The old theocentric faith of Judaism is superseded by the new Christ-centered faith. The belief in God, the One, has receded before the belief in the Christ. Here is a parting of the ways in religion." In this way then God is "removed into the background. He became the *Deus absconditus* surrounded by the dark and tremendous mystery. The bright light, the broad glory shines now round the Christ. His is the eternal drama, where God has only eternal existence."[61] Baeck discussed some of the general trends in the study of Paul, who at the turn of the century was almost depicted as the founder of a new mystery cult. A later reaction against this scholarly opinion denied any such influence, but to Baeck there remained "conformities pointing to influence."[62] He showed that the resurrection and the essential sacraments—baptism, unction—were taken from the mysteries. Although there were Jewish rites similar to baptism, they meant something completely different within the Jewish context. Paul, furthermore, reinterpreted various Jewish ideas, such as the "Kingdom of God," which in Jewish tradition referred to the "days to come," but for Paul meant the present time. "The faithful was in the midst of the days of promise, in the midst of the days of the messiah. Here was the core and the strength of Paul's faith."[63]

Paul faced another problem, which Baeck refreshingly analyzed: According to Jewish tradition, the Torah was not to govern the world forever, but only until the days of the Messiah.[64] Therefore, if the Messiah had already come, the Torah had to be discarded. This meant that Paul's struggle was not against the Law, but against its present validity. If that were not denied, the Messianism of Jesus would be denied. It was a misunderstanding, according to Baeck's interpretation, to state that Paul rejected the Law. "There is an interconnection between them [Law and redemption], the same as there is between the route and its goal, or that between what is 'written' and what is 'fulfilled.' The two together prove the truth, and display the nature of the divine ordinance and dispensation."[65] This doctrine as such did not separate Paul from Jewish tradition, for the same transition would have to come at some moment in history; the question was, had it already come? Baeck showed that Paul did not reject the Jewish people—indeed, they were a necessary element in his theology, the people who had received the revelation of God. It was only when the Jews rejected the "now" of Paul's doctrine that he turned to the Gentile world.

Yet, as Baeck showed, Paul retained a Jewish view of Scripture. "As a Jew, his life was contained in the Bible, and as a Jewish scholar he had to justify before the Bible whatever he would say and do. . . . It is a principle in Judaism that truth has to be discovered in, and through, the Bible."[66] On the other hand, the Bible caused him much difficulty. "For Paul, Judaism had to cease to be religion, the religion of the present and of the future, and the Bible had to cease to be the Bible, i.e., the Book of the present and of the future."[67] Yet, he was faced by the contradiction that he had to retain the Bible as proof for all that he said about Jesus. "It was for him the divine revelation, the announcement of Christ, and it is therefore 'holy' and 'just and good' in his eyes."[68] Furthermore, the statement that always remained crucial to his Scripture-centered theology was: "It was written." So Paul remained inconsistent, but those who came after him often were consistent, according to Baeck, and thus opposed Judaism and all that was Jewish within the Church. Baeck showed this in his discussion of the directions taken by Barnabas and Marcion, though, of course, both of these tendencies were fought and overcome by the Church. These were logical conclusions for the pure Pauline: "It was a choice either of faith or of ethics, either of the savior or of the Law. This is the fundamental alternative which Paul places before the individual. With reference to Paul himself, his Jewishness was still too strong in this respect likewise. His ethics the same as his attitude towards the Old Testament in general is the result of this inconsistency."[69] Yet the Church rejected pure Paulinism by placing the Epistle of James, which is a polemic against Paul, at the head of the Epistles, thereby stressing works alongside faith as does that Epistle.

Church history, for Baeck, thus becomes a struggle between the Jewish element and the Pauline element within the Church. "One may say that the history of the dogmas of the Church is actually a history of Judaism within the Church, that it has its various phases, according as the active ethical-psychological element of Judaism with its emphasis on the personal, or the passive magically sacramental element of faith of Paulinism, with its dissolution of that which is individual into the metaphysical, is brought more strongly into prominence.[70] In all of this the Papacy kept the compromise alive with great skill. Baeck traced some of the occasions of compromise in the history of the Church. He showed that the same problem had to be faced by Martin Luther, who in the final analysis made another compromise by keeping the element of faith within the Church while leaving practical ethics to the State.

Yet Baeck recognized in Paul a man who could not quite abandon his Jewish heritage. "Even after his conversion to mystery and sacrament, he only too often found himself again on the old Jewish ways of thought, as though unconsciously and involuntarily; and the manifold contradictions between his sentences derive from this above all. The Jew that he remained in spite of everything, at the bottom of his soul, again and again fought with the romantic in him, whose moods and ideas were ever present to him. But in spite of this, if we are to label him as he stands before us, the apostle of a new outlook, then we can only call him romantic";[71] for faith was everything to Paul—man was passive, and this was to be explained by the doctrines of Original Sin and Election. Still, Baeck was friendly enough to Paul to once remark that "Paul the great Jewish apostle who came from this people was correct: Where men believe and love, there they hope."[72] Baeck claimed that Paul had influenced Judaism although his name was not mentioned in the Talmudic literature. "His 'antinomism,' and more so that of his successors, provoked a strengthening of 'nomism' within the Jewish sphere."[73] Baeck described the Jewish influences on Paul and almost reclaimed him for Judaism, but on the other hand, he remained hostile to him for having left Judaism. "This is why Paul left Judaism when he preached *sola fide* (by faith alone) and thereby wound up with sacrament and dogma. . . . The boundary of Judaism was crossed only by Paul at the point where mystery wanted to prevail without commandment, and faith without the law."[74]

Mayer was especially critical of Baeck's view of Paul, for he saw that Baeck found little relationship to Judaism in him. He felt that Baeck overstressed the Oriental mystery background of Paul, especially in "Romantic Religion," but he was more appreciative of Baeck's "The Faith of Paul," which stressed somewhat the Jewish element in him. Mayer felt that Baeck, in this and other essays, was really only able to see the relationship to Judaism and that as a result Paul became less Hellenistic and more Jewish in Baeck's writings. Mayer recognized that it was unusual to have a

Jew show such a sympathetic understanding of Paul and to see him in a Jewish framework, and he believed that this was an enduring contribution to scholarship and understanding which could lead Jews to a better understanding of Christianity and Christians to an appreciation of Judaism.[75]

Baeck also discussed Martin Luther at some length, portraying him as caught up in the same dilemma of romantic religion. Luther, like most Protestants, was depicted as a "romantic"; for Luther, too, man's salvation was primarily an act of grace and, therefore, a sacramental act. "While he decreased the number of the sacraments, he placed beside them the 'word,' which is for him the great instrument of grace in which the power of salvation dwells—that which, by its sheer presentation effects the miracle of faith. It does not merely *mean* something, but it *is* something and is therefore effective solely by being preached, *ex opere operate;* its influence is not anything psychological, but supernatural, magical. Man stands before it absolutely dependent, purely passive and receiving. The affirmation of the word through faith comes over man without his action and without his aid, as a miracle; faith cannot be won, but only be given by grace."[76] Baptism and Communion were similarly interpreted. According to Baeck, Luther, in his earliest period, stressed the passivity of man more than Catholicism did and emphasized the experience of faith, but later he saw the value of the sacraments. For him they were a reality—not a symbol, as they were for Zwingli and the Baptists; therefore, Luther fought vigorously with these men over this matter, following Pauline principle. "This complete passivity demanded a sacrament that, being no mere symbol to which man must find meaning, is a supernatural reality that gives man everything as a gift. The romantic faith cannot in this world do without the designated instrument of grace."[77] In this system the universal priesthood again gave way to the priest, who was an instrument of the state church. The reestablishment of the basic duality of priest and layman was the natural result of Luther's emphasis on the sacrament.

Baeck was troubled by the practical implications of this willingness to leave all power to the State. Luther began with a priesthood of all believers, but ended with religion entirely under

the wing of the State, a difficulty which Catholicism sought to
overcome by becoming dominant over the State. "Furthermore,
Catholicism, due to its ancient established ecclesiastical organiza-
tion, could dispense with the State; Calvinism could do likewise
due to its development of the free community, but Lutheranism
could not dispense with the State. Visible Church and State here
are intertwined."[78] In this philosophy of the State there was a
strict division between the ruled and the rulers. The former remain
as passive objects of the will of the ruler, just as in the religious
realm they must live by faith alone. "This bond between rigid
concepts of ruler and ruled with a Christian philosophy of life left
all that was ethical and religious to the private sphere of life. This
became a matter so marked and characteristic that one historian of
Protestantism ventured to speak of it as the 'Prussian Religion.'

"The Lutheran conception of the State has succumbed to the
events of world history. If one seeks its basic defect, it may be
found in the absence of the Old Testamental element, the Jewish
element. Absent is a strong sense of the religious confidence that
believes in the future. There is no social or Messianic conviction,
no urge to improve or rebuild the world as in our Bible."[79] In place
of all this there is only a deep pessimism. Here also is the great
contrast with Calvinism, for in Calvinism there is strong optimism,
Messianism, hope for the future of the world. Calvinism provides
religion with a very firm ethical basis: "In Calvinism, unlike the
religion of Luther, faith does not have its purpose in itself, but its
goal is the determination of moral effectiveness and activity."[80]
Baeck even termed the First World War a struggle of the
Anglo-Saxon forces of Calvinism and the other Protestant groups
against the Lutheranism of Germany. He admired the Anglo-Saxon
churches of the West and felt them to be much closer to Judaism.[81]

Baeck demonstrated that Luther followed Paul's view of the
Law completely, carrying it to its logical extreme in which ethics is
of secondary significance beside proper belief. "Even his oft
quoted word 'fortiter pecca—sin bravely,' which he wrote to
Melanchthon in 1521, does not by any means stand alone as if it
were an expression of casual irony. It is purely Pauline in its
essence; and it is typically romantic. . . . The more sin there is,
Luther thought moreover, the better can divine grace prove its

power. In the demand for good deeds as something decisive, he
perceived the tempting voice of the devil who would pit human
activity against grace . . .''[82] Baeck, in contrast to other
opponents of Luther, clearly stated that despite such statements
Luther remained highly ethical in his personal life. "His
conscience and his life condemned sin in spite of everything and
exalted man's duty to be virtuous and ethical. Only his faith was
ruthless and amoral."[83] Lutheranism, Baeck pointed out, never
until fairly late felt the need of missions, for its energy was spent in
searching for individual salvation. "The romantic idea of salvation
could only produce the demand for unlimited ecclesiastic power
and the missions that relied on coercion."[84] Mayer mildly criticized
these views of Baeck's.

Leo Baeck did not discuss other periods or personalities of
Christian history in detail; his primary interest was the early period
of the Church. As he approached the modern world he realized that
there was another level of contact, which was not bothered by such
considerations of principle. In the everyday contacts common in
modern times, the Christians "will accept him as such, [a Jew] in
spite of what the Church has preached and taught. . . . Daily life
often involves convenient evasions; it moves about the peripheries
rather than towards the center."[85] But Baeck was interested in
more than this and above all in future generations, so he felt
obliged to ask whether the Church would fully recognize the path
of Judaism and its right to a future. The Church must be willing to
recognize the crucial distinction between the two religions; the
Christian "had an assured place and he [the Jew] had this certainty
of the way."[86] Judaism in this spiritual sense has, of course, had
more than its share of days of trial, but they have kept it on the
religious path. In its history there were, of course, periods of quiet
and great awakening, for the real test of any religion is its capacity
to reawaken. "Christianity can point to many a wonderful rebirth
and is entitled to take pride in each of them. They are the essence
of Christian history. But may they not also be regarded as an
inheritance—and not the only one—from the Jewish religion, like
that power to withstand trials which is also such a heritage?"[87]

Baeck realized that every religion has to have a mission as its
essential center, and that this task must not be denied to any

religion. "There can be no monopolies here, nor reserved regions."[88] But he was concerned with the methods used in this endeavor: are they to include political and earthly power or only spiritual persuasion? He was willing to honor the sincere convert, but despised him who changed merely because of outside pressure or the desire for power. Both religions must stress dignity in their missionary endeavors. "This dignity must essentially be the hallmark of any relations between Christianity and Judaism; between the two there will be noble relations or no real relations at all."[89] However, Christianity has largely denied Judaism the right to a mission in the world. Moreover, according to Christianity, Judaism is "the dark shadow cast by the past upon the present. It has no real, no living history. It is but a bearer of a religion which has now no present task, no proper aim, and no right to a future of its own."[90] Baeck, in other words, protested against this image of a fossil people, which has been a common Christian portrayal of Judaism.

Baeck pointed to the Christian debt to Judaism for the Bible, and this led him to further questions. Christianity was given the Old Testament and had to fight on its behalf; this Bible had made the Christian religion into the City of God, the Communion of the Saints, "and at the same time, [enabled it to] strive to penetrate the sphere of the state and to lay stress upon 'natural law.' One could ponder on whether without the Old Testament the Church had ever lived to see true history."[91] There could hardly be a New Testament without the framework of the Old; one could not exist without the other. Yet the Church has not always been willing to acknowledge this fact and discuss its significance.

Baeck once more pointed to the history of the Jewish elements within the Church, which were also part of the Biblical heritage. "In a great measure the history of the doctrines that have been striven for within the Church is, one might say, a history of Judaism within the Church. All this is a part of the Jewish drama in the world. Insufficient attention is paid to this phenomenon. But the more the Church becomes aware of it, the more it will become cognizant both of essential elements of its own life and of the unique significance of the survival of the Jewish religion. On the other side, Judaism itself while considering the matter, will grow more conscious of its proper peculiarity."[92]

He concluded this essay on an optimistic note, which may suitably conclude our study as well: "On the whole, both sides will truly benefit by considering all these questions. While questioning Christianity, Judaism must pass on to questions that, in all honesty, it has to put to itself."[93] Thus both religions will grow and develop. This self-examination will lead to a fine conclusion: "Inner voices will be heard. To each other Judaism and Christianity will be admonitions and warnings: Christianity becoming Judaism's conscience, and Judaism Christianity's. That common ground, that common outlook, that common problem which they come to be aware of will call them to make a joint approach."[94]

Leo Baeck's contribution to a Jewish understanding of Christianity was very great. He and Montefiore were pioneer workers in this field, which had been touched by only a few other serious Jewish scholarly efforts before the turn of the century. Baeck's analysis of the Jewish elements of early Christianity was to be followed by other students; it has led to a greater understanding of Christianity by Jews. His polemical critique of Christianity clearly demonstrates the position of Judaism in basic theological matters.

14

Joseph Klausner

A Nationalist View

Joseph Klausner (1874–1958) was one of the first to write about Christianity in modern Hebrew. His studies began in Russia and continued in Israel after 1926. A professor at the Hebrew University in Jerusalem, he wrote at length on Jewish literature, history, and philosophy. His doctoral dissertation on the Messianic ideas of the Tannaitic period led to an enduring interest in Christianity. His books on Jesus and Paul expressed a distinctly nationalistic point of view—he saw everything in the light of Zionism.

As Klausner explained in the introduction to his *Jesus of Nazareth*, he wished to be objective in his attempt to show "how Judaism *differs* and *remains distinct* from Christianity . . . every effort has been made to keep it [his book] within the limits of pure scholarship . . . avoiding those subjective religious and nationalist aims which do not come within the purview of scholarship."[1] He may have begun in this spirit, but many sections of his study on Jesus, and of his subsequent one on Paul, are partisan. Klausner criticized both Jesus and Paul for their lack of nationalist interests,[2] concluding each of several chapters with the challenge, "What could Judaism have to do with such views as these?"[3] Few could accept Klausner's subjective approach, and this led to many angry reviews of his works.

Klausner's volumes on Jesus and Paul were neglected by the general world of scholarship until their translation from Hebrew into English. He was fortunate in having Herbert Danby, a well-respected figure, as the translator of his *Jesus of Nazareth*.

162

This translation, published in 1925, led to reviews that were more favorable than one might have expected of such a polemic work. On the other hand, Jewish reviewers attacked Klausner's books without mercy, especially Armand Kaminka in a lengthy discussion in a Hebrew periodical.[4] Both the scholarship of the works and the conclusions were vigorously criticized. Many Jewish scholars—Samuel Sandmel the latest among them[5]—felt that Klausner was often wrong, that his understanding of rabbinic statements was poor, and that his conclusions were not warranted. Despite these major shortcomings, Klausner's books have been influential in Jewish circles. As they were written in Hebrew, Jews who might not have read similar works in German or English —such as those of Montefiore—read these volumes. Sandmel states that they influenced him in the direction of Christian studies; undoubtedly that was true of other modern Jewish scholars as well.

The first portion of Klausner's books on Jesus and Paul, was devoted to preliminary matters, which began with a history of the period. He continued with an analysis of the sources. Finally, there was a section devoted to previous Jewish and Christian scholarship. Klausner's judgments on his predecessors were often harsh and unfounded; his own works were destined for similar severe critiques.

Klausner's more strictly biographical treatment began with John the Baptist. At the outset he made it clear that our lack of facts about John's life is not unusual when compared to what we know about contemporary Jewish figures, such as Hillel. "As with Jesus, so with John the Baptist: history showed no interest in his origin or his life before he came to the front and became an historic figure."[6] From the evidence Klausner concluded that John the Baptist was not an Essene, but a Nazarite. The Essenes may have been a society of Nazarites, he explained, but they eliminated all contact with the world, did not welcome disciples, and did not interfere in political affairs. John's personal life may have been akin to that of the Essenes, but his public manner did not fit the Essene pattern. According to Klausner, John considered himself the forerunner of the Messiah, although he did not openly proclaim this.[7] "John continued a true Jew, imitating the Prophets and showing himself akin to them in spirit." He did not begin a new path like Jesus, but his following seems to have been large enough to arouse Herod to kill him.[8]

In considering the life of Jesus, Klausner made some interesting minor comments. He thought that despite the early death of Jesus' father, love of his father remained a stronger emotion in Jesus throughout his life than love of his mother: "His father's memory was more precious to him than his living mother, who did not understand him. . . ."[9] Turning to the Gospels, Klausner stressed their authors' lack of interest in history or biography, noting that as a result many facets of the life of Jesus will never be known.[10] Klausner refrained from speculating about the vague early years of Jesus.

From the outset, according to Klausner, Jesus was "obsessed by his idea that he was the Messiah." His activities and teachings must be understood from this point of view. Jesus did not announce himself as the Messiah at the beginning of his career because none of the three Messianic ways of contemporary Judaism seemed likely to succeed. It was not his nature to be a revolutionary. He did not like the Law, so he could make no new contribution and claim leadership as a scholar. He rejected the path of material prosperity as too gross. The elimination of these roads forced Jesus to conceal his Messianic aspirations.[11] He became "a wandering Galilaean 'Rab' and preacher" similar to other homilists, but he stressed the Messianic Age, emphasized the moral law over ritual, preferred parable to Scriptural interpretation, and used miracles to attract disciples. Except for these differences Jesus followed the path of rabbinic preachers.[12] Klausner analyzed Jesus' use of parables, which he praised highly; Jesus showed himself to be poetic, a skillful story-teller; and the use of the parable gave his teachings an esoteric flavor.[13] Klausner was troubled by the miracles attributed to Jesus and attempted to distinguish five categories of miracles, but this analysis was not successful.[14]

According to Klausner, most of the followers of Jesus were *ame ha-aretz*;[15] as members of this poor, ignorant group, they were not immediately aware of Jesus' antagonism to the Law. Jesus did not actually reject the Law, but he opposed it subtly and so came into conflict with the Pharisees. As the Pharisees became cooler toward Jesus, his following diminished, for the *ame ha-aretz* venerated the Pharisees. "The Pharisees instilled into the people a dislike of Jesus: they said that he was a transgressor and a friend of transgressors . . . "[16] The antagonism became mutual, and Jesus' manner of expression toward the Pharisees was hardly tender or loving.[17] However, his views remained very much akin to the views of the Pharisees. Jesus' attitude toward the Temple incurred the enmity of both Pharisees and Sadducees.[18] The Sadducees eventually tried and condemned him, for they were aroused by "the 'cleansing of the Temple' and by his reply concerning the Law of Moses and the resurrection of the dead," as well as by fear of the Roman authorities. Nothing in the teachings or activities of Jesus would have made him criminally guilty to the Pharisees. Klausner attributed the differences between the trial described by the Gospels and the procedure set by the Mishnah to the fact that the Mishnah portrays a Pharisaic court while the Gospels describe a Sadducean court, which no longer existed when the Mishnah was written.[19] This solution of the trial is similar to Zeitlin's. "A few only of the priestly caste had condemned Jesus to death and given him up to Pilate, primarily because of their dread of this same Pilate, and only incidentally because of their annoyance at the 'cleansing of the Temple,' . . . No Jews took any further part in the actual trial and crucifixion." Klausner regarded Pilate's opposition to the crucifixion as unhistorical, maintaining that the Gospel story about it was prompted by fear of Rome and later by the successful conversion of Romans to the new religion. "The Jews, *as a nation,* were far less guilty of the death of Jesus than the Greeks, as a nation, were guilty of the death of Socrates; but who now would think of avenging the blood of Socrates the Greek upon his countrymen, the present Greek race?"[20] Klausner disagreed with those who doubted the resurrection. "Here again it is impossible to suppose that there was any conscious deception: the nineteen hundred years' faith of millions is not founded on deception. There can be no question but that some of the ardent Galilaeans saw their lord and Messiah in a vision," which assured the continuation of his memory and formed the basis of Christianity.[21]

Klausner devoted a long section to Jesus as a teacher, judging him to have been akin to the Biblical prophets and the rabbis of the Talmud rather than to philosophers.[22] This was severely criticized by Kaminka and was found unacceptable by many other Jewish readers.[23] According to Klausner, Jesus' teachings were thoroughly Jewish in most respects; his attitude toward the Law remained positive even if unenthusiastic. "Jesus was a Jew and a Jew he remained till his last breath. His one idea was to implant within his nation the idea of the coming of the Messiah and, by repentance and good works, hasten the 'end.' "[24] Details and a different emphasis separated him from the other Pharisees. Jesus opposed ceremonial excesses; but at the same time he underestimated the nationalistic importance of these rites.[25] Jesus' ethical pronouncements lacked originality and paralleled Tannaitic teachings. Klausner acknowledged that the Gospels have preserved "one of the most wonderful collections of ethical teachings in the world";[26] yet because they are nonetheless insufficient, Christianity has been forced to preserve the Old Testament to supplement the New Testament. Jesus may have been more ethical than his contemporary Hillel, but his ethics were too exalted, and as a result they were "relegated to a book or, at most, became a possession of monastics and recluses who lived apart from the paths of ordinary life."[27] Klausner considered exaggeration to be the chief danger of Christian ethics, which can really only be applied to the Messianic Age and not to our world.[28] Klausner often criticized Jesus' failure to stress the national elements of Judaism and his emphasis of the individual over the nation.[29] Jesus offered nothing extraordinary to the Jew; on the contrary, he restricted the scope of Judaism, but "for the pagan world, there was a great gain in the belief in the one God and in the prophetic ethical teaching which was perpetuated in Christianity owing to the teaching of Jesus the Jew."[30]

The secret of Jesus' influence lay in the unique combination of strength and weakness in his personality. "The contradictory traits in his character, its positive and negative aspects, his harshness and his gentleness, his clear vision combined with his cloudy visionariness—all these united to make him a force and an influence, for which history has never yet afforded a parallel."

Later Jesus' terrible death "added a crown of divine glory both to the personality and to the teaching."[31] The meaning of Jesus must remain limited for the Jew; but "no Jew can . . . overlook the value of Jesus and his teaching from the point of view of universal history." To the Jewish people he remained "a great teacher of morality and an artist in parable." His ethical code remained distinctive and original in expression if not in content—so much so, in fact, according to Klausner, that "stripped of its wrappings of miracles and mysticism, the Book of the Ethics of Jesus will be one of the choicest treasures in the literature of Israel for all time."[32] Like many other Jewish scholars before and after him, Klausner admired Jesus and his teachings as they were revealed after the Christological elements were removed.

Klausner also felt admiration for Paul and tried to appraise his personality fairly. He approached Paul the same way he had Jesus, but could not quite succeed in reclaiming him for Judaism. He began by describing the historical background and reviewed his conclusions about Jesus. Klausner emphasized the Hellenistic Jewish background of Paul and evaluated the Greco-Jewish sources as well as the New Testament, judging Acts the best source for the life and teachings of Paul. Klausner found Paul (or Saul-Paul, as he sometimes called him) a singular personality inclined to extremes, who combined "lofty ideals and base passions . . . Saul-Paul was lacking in humility, exceedingly confident of himself and boastfully condescending. But he knew his own shortcomings, fought against them, and sometimes conquered them. He had great energy and courage, he never retreated, he was even willing to suffer martyrdom for his opinions."[33] Despite a sickly nature, he willingly risked the hardships of missionary travel. Sometimes the lack of success led to melancholy, but generally Paul was hopeful and ready to engage anyone opposed to him. In some ways he was a mystic; on the other hand, Paul had outstanding talents as a "preacher, controversialist, and debater." He was also adept at compromise. "Paul was, therefore, a 'clever politician,' and he was far from being a saint, particularly in the Christian sense of that word."[34]

In Klausner's view, early Christianity, as found by Paul, "was nothing more than an adjunct to Pharisaic-Essenic Judaism."

However, "it was quickly felt that if the new faith did not wish to remain only a small Jewish sect, it would have to make its righteousness *less* than the righteousness of the scribes and Pharisees, and not *more*. "[35] The group had to turn to pagans and divorce itself from the declining Jewish state if it sought success. "These things had to be done by a non-Palestinian Jew, a Hellenistic Jew, who, although he had received some instruction in Palestine, had also imbibed doctrines and learning from the Gentiles . . . He had to be sufficiently denationalized so as not to care about the damage to the nation caused by the putting aside of the belief in political redemption." Paul was the right man for the task.[36] Klausner's discussion of Paul's life followed liberal Protestant scholarship. He believed that Paul had received his early education from Rabban Gamliel the Elder (the Gamaliel of the New Testament) and that a mystical experience had led to his conversion. Paul always felt inferior to the other disciples because he had not seen Jesus alive according to Klausner. Subsequently he undertook missionary journeys and had a controversy with Peter. Finally Paul was executed by the Romans. Often with surprising naivete, Klausner accepted most of the New Testament traditions as authentic.

He became critical, however, when he turned to Paul's teachings and religious innovations. In his view, Paul's elevation of Jesus to a position "but a little lower than God" had its seeds in the early apostles, whose fear of the Romans led them to interpret Jesus as a purely ethical Messiah without political overtones. Later, when they wished to stave off disappointment, they emphasized the resurrection. As Paul had experienced the resurrection through the mystical experience that led to his conversion, and had seen Jesus only in this spiritual form, he could "conceive Jesus as entirely spiritual."[37] Klausner considered this view to have resulted from the combination of Paul's own inferiority feelings and his mystical nature. The cultural factors of Hellenistic Judaism, which was more universal than Pharisaic Judaism, were added to the personal elements. Philo and Paul emphasized universalism, but Paul was also keenly aware of the pagan longing for salvation.[38]

As a Hellenistic Jew, Paul felt that he had recast Judaism to fit the needs of his coreligionists and the pagan world. "Paul never felt himself a non-Jew . . . For him Christianity was a new and improved kind of Judaism, like Essenism, for example; except that in this new Judaism it was possible and necessary to include Gentiles, and therefore it was proper for this Judaism to be distinguished from the old and unbelieving Judaism by a special type of congregation made up of both believing Jews and believing Gentiles."[39] Paul's Christianity was unconsciously influenced by non-Jewish thought; Paul followed this path because he was a Jew of the Diaspora, "detached from the *authentic, living Judaism* which was rooted in its own cultural soil." All his teachings, including the most mystical, can be traced to Jewish sources, but he often unconsciously gave them a non-Jewish flavor.[40] This conclusion made him an erring, but almost acceptable, Jew.

Paul's spiritualization of Jesus changed the crucifixion from an obstacle to the central doctrine. As a result of this new spiritual view, Jesus was soon considered as standing next to God. Paul never consciously accepted the doctrines of the mystery religions, nor is there any evidence that he studied them.[41] However, the "mixture of pagan-philosophic beliefs and opinions, which *hovered in the air* in the Hellenized cities in which Paul lived and preached,"[42] influenced all his formulations of Christian doctrine. His conception of the dualism between spirit and flesh stemmed from this source, as did the idea of life *in* Christ.[43]

According to Klausner, Paul never understood the Law and found its total observance impossible. Generalizing from his own difficulties with the Law, Paul considered everyone a sinner. He maintained that the death of Jesus annulled the Law. Again he was generalizing; obviously death annuls the Law for any man, but in this case it was claimed that the Law had ended for all who believed in Jesus, whose death had voided the Law. Klausner criticized Paul's inability to grasp the importance of the Law for the Jewish nation and the national culture.[44] Despite these feelings, however, Paul often quoted from the Law, using it to buttress arguments. Faith in Jesus and ceremonials to make this faith concrete were Paul's substitute for the Law. Through this emphasis he came to the thought of vicarious suffering and the atoning death of Jesus.[45]

The ethical and social teachings of Paul contain the same difficulties as the statements of Jesus, for they presume the speedy arrival of the Kingdom of God. Paul's ethics was intended to replace the morality of the Law, which he had abrogated.[46] Klausner found these teachings akin to Judaism with all national elements removed. He vigorously criticized Paul's treatment of women as conservative and his views on marriage as strange,[47] as would Sandmel and others later on. "All these views about the government, woman, marriage and divorce, slavery, and the importance of work are by no means unethical. . . . But in any case, from the standpoint of ethics, Pharisaic Judaism had nothing to learn from Paul."[48]

Klausner was more sympathetic to Jesus than Paul. Jesus remained an authentic Jew, while Paul lacked the national background of Palestine and the "genuine authority" and natural understanding that characterized Jesus. Jesus may unwittingly have changed Judaism, "but the ideological and organic structure of the Christian faith as a *religion* and as a *church* was built by Paul. . . ."[49] The separation of Judaism and the new religion came through Paul, whose foundation may have been Jewish, but "his *own* teaching is both the *contradiction of the Jewish religion* and the *rejection of the Jewish nation* ";[50] without nationalism he could not be fully accepted by Klausner. Since Paul's time the two groups have lived apart, "there being between them no relation except that of kinsmen who have grown apart; hence animosity and conflict between them increased."[51]

Klausner as a Jew could not accept the teachings of Paul, but he considered certain sayings beautiful and felt they could be made acceptable by removal of the theological overtones.[52] Paul's merit, from a Jewish point of view, was that he "based all his new teaching upon the 'Old' Testament"; he forced Christianity to include the Old Testament in its canon. Through this emphasis the influence of Judaism was enormously extended.[53] Jews may thus regard Paul as one who prepared the way for Judaism, which will eventually spread through the world—thus Klausner returned to the hope so often expressed by nineteenth-century Jewish thinkers.

Klausner did not concern himself with the development of

Christianity, except for occasional references. Looking ahead, he felt that "Judaism will never become reconciled with Christianity . . . nor will it be assimilated by Christianity; for Judaism and Christianity are not only two different religions, but they are also *two different world-views*. . . . Judaism is a more practical faith than Christianity, it is more capable of realization in actual life."[54] Eventually Judaism will become the universal religion, but it will acknowledge a debt to Christianity.

Klausner has been severely criticized by New Testament scholars, who have properly stated that he was eclectic, unoriginal, polemical, biased, and often wrong in the use of Jewish sources, and therefore that his books must be used with reservations. Unquestionably, though, he did a service to Judaism by writing in Hebrew. Countless Israelis have received an introduction to Christianity from him. His conclusions often echo those of Montefiore, who, however, was a better scholar. Montefiore went farther in his positive assessment of Jesus and Paul, which alienated many Jews. On the other hand, he did not approach early Christianity from a nationalist point of view and so appealed to a different Jewish group. Both of these scholars, Klausner and Montefiore, despite their respective weaknesses, made the serious study of Christianity more easily possible for the next generation of Jews.

15

Martin Buber

Philosopher to Christians and Jews

Martin Buber (1878–1965) was the most influential Jewish thinker of this century. While he was still quite young, two men, Theodor Herzl and Georg Simmel, profoundly affected the direction of his life and thought. Herzl brought him to Zionism, while Simmel made a deep impression on his philosophical development. Buber, though born in Austria, spent much of his youth in Poland with his scholarly grandfather, Solomon Buber, who exerted a strong lifelong influence upon him; later he settled in Germany and finally in 1933 left for Israel, where he spent the rest of his life teaching at the Hebrew University in Jerusalem. Martin Buber had a major effect on several fields of Jewish study. Through him the literature of Hasidism was reintroduced to Jews and Christians. Together with Franz Rosenzweig he made a revolutionary translation of the Bible into German; he also wrote a number of significant Biblical studies. His most important contribution was made in the realm of philosophy. He exerted a great influence upon both Christians and Jews, though for many years he had a larger following among Christians than Jews.

Martin Buber studied Christianity for more than sixty years and wrote many essays on it. His approach was basically historical, with some of the philosophical overtones found in Brod and Rosenzweig, his contemporaries. Jesus and Paul were the subject of special studies. He also engaged in one of the earliest Jewish-Christian dialogues—with the theologian Karl Ludwig Schmidt in 1933 in Stuttgart. The statements of both men were published; Buber subsequently expanded his presentation into a full book. Ironically, this forthright confrontation between the two religions occurred at the beginning of the Nazi period. In this dialogue Buber clearly presented his approach to Christianity: "We may attempt something very difficult, something very difficult for the man with religious ties; it strains his ties and relationships or rather seems to strain them. It seems to strain his relationship with God: We can acknowledge as a mystery that which someone else confesses as the reality of his faith, though it opposes our own existence and is contrary to the knowledge of our own being. We are not capable of judging its meaning, because we do not know it from within as we know ourselves from within."[1] Herewith Buber set the limits of his understanding of Christianity and any other religion, for it would be based only on external knowledge, which is deficient. Buber thus recognized the reality of Christianity as a path to God, as had Rosenzweig. This implies a demand for similar understanding and self-limitation by Christians who discuss Judaism.

Buber gladly acknowledged the inner sanctuary of Christianity and respected it. However, to preserve the place of Judaism, he had to reject the Christian claim to the sole power to redeem the world or the statement that it had been redeemed. The people of Israel did not reject these ideas merely because of hard-heartedness, but based upon its experience in the world. "We understand the Christology of Christianity throughout as an important event which has taken place between the world above and the world below. We see Christianity as something the mystery of whose coming into the world we are unable to penetrate. But just as we know that there is air which we breathe into our lungs, we also know that there is a space in which we move; more deeply, more genuinely, we know that the history of the world has not yet been shattered to its very core, that the world is not yet redeemed. We feel the lack of redemption of the world." He denied that this was merely a feeling possessed by Jews because they had not been redeemed, for redemption was obviously missing in the world; it had to be absolutely and complete; partial redemption of a group or individual souls had no meaning. "We do not perceive any caesura in the course of history. We acknowledge no mid-point in it, but only a goal. The goal of the way of God, who does not pause upon his way."[2] Buber undoubtedly realized that it is much easier for Judaism to make such a statement than for Christianity, for the latter sees itself as possessing a world-conquering mission. By recognizing other paths, Christianity would partially deny this mission and permit not only Judaism, but also Islam and other faiths, to thrive. Yet Buber felt that such a statement is the basis for true understanding and meaningful dialogue. He knew that any discussion had to be "between the Church, which does not recognize the mission of Israel, and Israel, which is conscious of its mission. There can be a genuine dialogue, in which the participants do not reach an agreement, but understand each other for the sake of the one true being, who is understood as the reality of faith."[3] This was Buber's point of departure. He also clearly stated his relationship to Christianity and his hopes for the future: "I have already stated: What joins Jews and Christians together is their common knowledge about one uniqueness. . . . Every authentic sanctuary can acknowledge the mystery of every other authentic sanctuary. The mystery of the other one is internal to the latter and cannot be perceived from without. No one outside Israel can understand the mystery of Israel. And no one outside Christendom can understand the mystery of Christendom. . . . How is it possible for the mysteries to exist side by side? That is God's mystery. . . . We serve, separately and yet together, not by avoiding the reality of our belief nor by surreptitiously seeking togetherness despite our difference. Rather we should acknowledge our fundamental difference and impart to each other with unreserved confidence our knowledge of the unity of this house, a unity which we hope will one day surround us without divisions. We will serve, until the day when we may be united in common service. . . . "[4] Thus Buber expressed his desire for understanding and respect now and for unity within the mystery of God in the future.

In his writings Buber dealt with many elements of Christian faith, but his most systematic discussion was presented in *Two Types of Faith*. There Buber concentrated on Jesus and Paul, judging their contributions to the development of Christian thought.

Buber appreciated Jesus but rejected Paul. Like Montefiore and

Baeck, he attempted to reclaim Jesus for Judaism, emphasizing the Jewish elements in his sayings. He made a number of statements very friendly to Jesus: "From my youth onwards I have found in Jesus my great brother. That Christianity has regarded and does regard him as God and Saviour has always appeared to me a fact of the highest importance which, for his sake and my own, I must endeavor to understand. . . . My own fraternally open relationship to him has grown ever stronger and clearer, and to-day [in 1950] I see him more strongly and clearly than ever before. I am more than ever certain that a great place belongs to him in Israel's history of faith and that this place cannot be described by any of the usual categories."[5] Buber examined Jesus and his sayings in the setting of rabbinic Judaism, and was greatly concerned with finding a means of understanding the Messianic claims of Jesus in the framework of Jewish history. Jesus' view of himself and of the nature of Messiahship was influenced by Deutero-Isaiah. "If we view the connexion rightly Jesus understood himself, under the influence of the conception of Deutero-Isaiah, to be a bearer of the Messianic hiddenness. From this follows straightaway, the meaning of the 'Messianic secret.' The arrow in the quiver is not its own master; the moment at which it shall be drawn out is not for it to determine. The secret is imposed. It is put by Jesus into the heart of the disciples. . . . Only when in sight of the end does the attitude of Jesus appear to change."[6] Until he revealed himself he spoke and worked in the Jewish tradition, but with his Messianic aim he stepped outside it.

In another essay Buber compared Jesus to the long line of pseudo-Messiahs in Jewish history. "Jesus is the first in the series of men who acknowledged to themselves in their words their messiahship and thus stepped out of the seclusion of the servants of God, which is the real 'messianic secret.' That this First One . . . was incomparably the purest, most rightful of them all, the one most endowed with real messianic power, does not alter the fact that he was the first, yea, it belongs rather to it, belongs to that awful and pathetic character of reality which clings to the whole messianic series."[7] Buber considered this step of Jesus wrong; Jesus had harmed the world by his Messianic claims. All Jews must, therefore, reject Jesus. On the other hand, Buber acknowledged the meaning of Jesus for the Gentile world. He could understand and feel a kinship to the figure of Jesus, but no more.[8]

For Buber, there was nothing alien in the teachings of Jesus, and he considered them to be almost entirely within the realm of Judaism. The faith of Jesus was akin to the faith of Isaiah. "Both the word of Isaiah and the word of Jesus demand in a similar way, not a faith 'in God,' which faith the listeners of both possessed as something innate and as a matter of course, but its realization in the totality of life, and especially when the promise arises from amidst catastrophe, and so particularly points towards the drawing near of God's kingdom. The only difference is that Isaiah looks to it as to a still indefinite future and Jesus as to the present."[9] This was the path taken by Jesus in his first message; its words followed the essential pattern of Isaiah: "realization of the kingship, the effecting of turning to God, a relationship of faith towards Him." They were "an heirloom of the religiosity of Israel."[10] As the thought of Jesus followed the prophets, so did his demands of faith. He required not the Greek *pistis*, which is faith in a proposition, but the Jewish *emunah* [trust in God]; a change only came about later through Paul, who demanded faith in Christ. "In this way he did precisely what Jesus, in so far as we know him from the Synoptic tradition, did not do, and, whatever was the case with his 'messianic consciousness,' obviously did not wish to do." Faith meant something else to him; it was "merely that unconditional trust in the grace which makes a person no longer afraid even of death because death is also of grace. Afterwards Jesus does indeed ask whom he is considered to be, but he does not desire that a man should hold him to be anyone in particular."[11] This distinction was the major thesis of *Two Types of Faith.* Judaism and early Christianity took one path while Pauline Christianity, to its detriment, took the other.

Buber believed that Jews could understand much about Jesus better than Gentiles. He wrote: "We Jews know Jesus internally in his Jewish motivations and moods; this path remains closed to the nations which believe in him."[12] This was an extraordinary claim; it had never been made before, nor did it find an echo among Buber's Jewish contemporaries. This belief of Buber's was reflected in his treatment of the relationship of Jesus and the Pharisees. Buber asserted that Jesus and the Pharisees were close in many respects, although in some vital matters they misunderstood each other. "Jesus misses the mark when he treats the Pharisees as people who close their eyes, and they miss their mark when they treat him as one subject to hallucinations; neither party knew the inner reality of the other. Much in the stories in which 'the Pharisees and scribes,' half chorus and half spiritual police-patrols, 'test' Jesus, are snubbed by him and then begin their testings again, is certainly unhistorical, and originates from the polemical tension of early Christianity . . . yet there remains enough of real difference over against the true outlook of the Pharisees, even if never quite so great as to exceed the bounds of the dialectics within Judaism."[13] In most matters Jesus did not exceed these boundaries; therefore Buber commented on Mark 10:17 that Jesus believed "God alone is 'good,' He alone is the good Master, He alone gives the true answer to the question about eternal life. And He has given it, in the commandments of His 'teaching,' the Torah, . . . man only needs to grasp the original intention of the commandments of God, and what that means thou [the questioner] wilt come to know sufficiently if thou goest with me. God teaches His doctrine for all, but He also reveals His way directly to chosen people . . . So Jesus knows himself to be a qualified means to teach the good Master's will, but he himself does not will to be called good: there is none good, but God alone." This continues "the great line of the Old Testament proclamation of the non-humanity of God and the non-divinity of man in a special way, which is distinguished by the personal starting-point and the point of reference."[14] Buber felt that Jesus never wished to destroy the Law; he may have intended to interpret it in a different fashion than the Pharisees, but generally he considered himself a teacher following the path set by Jewish tradition.

Buber felt this was true even about Jesus' Sermon on the Mount. "The attitude of the Sermon on the Mount to the Torah appears to be the opposite of that of the Pharisees; in reality it is only the sublimation of a Pharisaic doctrine from a definite and fundamental point of view."[15] He analyzed the statements in the Sermon and found that "three of them (murder, adultery, oaths) derive essentially from three of the Ten Commandments and transcend them, but what they demand is to be found also in Pharisaic teachings, yet without these approaching the forcefulness of his address. The other three (divorce, formula of the talion, love to one's neighbour) . . . refer to commandments and precepts outside the decalogue, and either contradict them (the first two) or contradict at least an accepted, apparently popular interpretation (the third); rabbinic writings present either no analogy to them or none sufficient." Nevertheless, Buber held, Jesus meant even these statements to fit into the tradition. This could be done by considering the Torah as subject to change through interpretation rather than as fixed law. Or, as in case of his statement on divorce, one could appeal from the Mosaic Law, which permitted divorce, to the statement of God in Eden that man should "cleave to his wife" (Gen. 2:24). "Therefore in the end it is the same with the second group [of statements in the Sermon on the Mount] as with the first: starting from the inwardness of the divine claim Jesus demands that the inwardness of men shall surrender to it. The divine claim in its outwardness has been made known in the historical situation and has reached the externality of man, the outward conduct of man; the inwardness from above presents itself in the eschatological situation and the inwardness from below can now appear before it. Fulfillment of the Torah accordingly means here disclosure of the Torah. . . . Jesus speaks throughout as the authentic interpreter: as long as he remains standing on Sinai he teaches what the Pharisees teach, but then Sinai cannot satisfy him and he must advance into the cloud-area of the intention of the revelation." He did so in the extremely personally worded statements that began "But I say unto you."[16] Jesus spoke in this manner, but the Pharisees considered it their duty to continue working toward their goal within the framework of the specific, the historical situation. Jesus felt that the "eschatological-present" had arrived. Here the difference between Jesus and the Pharisees became decisive, yet it was evident to Buber "that Jesus, as he speaks in the Sermon on the Mount, considers the Torah capable of fulfillment, not merely in accordance with its wording, but in the original intention of its revelation. The first he has in common with Pharisaic Judaism, in the second he meets it in certain points again and again."[17] Jesus and the Pharisees criticized the Law, but they generally agreed in their approach to it.[18]

Buber gave special attention to the phrase "Love thy enemy." Seeking to show its roots in Judaism, he pointed out that it had developed from the older Jewish statement "Love thy neighbor as thyself." Buber concluded his discussion: "All in all, the saying of Jesus about love for the enemy derives its light from the world of Judaism in which he stands and which he seems to contest; and he outshines it. It is indeed always so when a person in the sign of the *kairos* [the opportune moment] demands the impossible in such a way that he compels men to will the possible more strongly than before. But one should not fail to appreciate the bearers of the plain light below from amongst whom he arose: those who enjoined much that was possible so as not to cause men to despair of being able to serve God in their poor everyday affairs."[19] Buber admired the power of Jesus' statements and believed they gave additional force to some of the ideas of the Jewish Bible. On the other hand, he rejected their extremism, which could have only limited success in a world destined to continue and not standing at the edge of the Kingdom of God.

Jesus did not reject Israel nor did he intend to sever the bonds of the Covenant. According to Buber, Jesus was part of the continuing Jewish tradition; this was later changed by Paul. "For Jesus, who was concerned with the individual human soul and with every single human soul, Israel was not a universal entity with such and such an appointed function in the plan of the world, nor was it for him the mere totality of Jews living in his day and who stood in a certain relationship to his message: every soul which had lived from Moses to himself belonged in concreto to it. In his view for everyone of them, when they had gone astray, turning was allowed, and everyone of them when they did turn back, was the lost son returned home. His God was the same Who, though He might at times also 'harden' and perhaps even at times give a statute which was 'not good,' yet answered in every generation to the person interposing for Israel."[20] Israel was not shut out or excluded; it was not merely a rejected element in the larger plan of salvation.

Buber felt that he understood the Christian tradition and was capable of evaluating it fairly from the Jewish point of view. He considered Jesus a part of the Jewish tradition and wished to reclaim him for Judaism. He realized, however, that such reclamation was possible for Jesus but not for the later stages of Christianity. "If we consider the Synoptic and Johannine dialogues with the disciples as two stages along one road, we immediately see what was gained and lost in the course of it. The gain was the most sublime of all theologies; it was procured at the expense of the plain, concrete and situation-bound dialogicism of the original man of the Bible, who found eternity, not in the super-temporal spirit, but in the depth of the actual moment. The Jesus of the genuine tradition still belongs to that, but the Jesus of theology does so no longer."[21] Franz Hammerstein criticized Buber for his inability to understand the Jesus of the resurrection—in other words, the theological Jesus.[22] This was correct, but Buber himself willingly admitted it. The theological Jesus must remain outside the scope of any Jew's understanding if one accepts the opening premise of Buber's studies: we cannot know or understand the mysteries of another religion because we cannot experience them. Hammerstein was criticizing Buber for approaching the Old and the New Testaments in a different manner, for looking upon the former as a theological unity and the latter as divided into many fragments.[23] Yet Buber recognized the contradictions and tensions in the Jewish Bible.

Buber was especially concerned with Paul and the point of Christianity's separation from Judaism. Paul was the "gigantic figure . . . whom we must regard as the real originator of the Christian conception of faith."[24] Though Buber admired Paul's greatness, he did not discuss his personality at length, for he was primarily concerned with the transformation in Christian thought brought about by Paul. The most important elements in Paul's theology were the change in the nature of belief from *emunah* to *pistis* and the total emphasis on the latter. Faith in God and Jesus became decisively important, as compared with the simple sense of trust emphasized by the Jewish Bible. In this way arose the doctrine of justification by faith, which separates Judaism and Christianity. "Faith, as the divine activity in man, gives rise to the condition of being righteous, which the 'works,' proceeding from men alone, the mere fulfillment of the 'law,' are not able to bring about. The simple face-to-face relationship between God and man in the Genesis story is replaced by an interpenetration which comes about by faith and faith alone, the dialogical by the mystical situation; but this situation does not remain, as nearly always in mysticism, an end in itself; it is grasped and discussed as the situation which alone can place the individual in that state in which he can stand the judgement of God.''[25] This doctrine not only established a new relationship between man and God, but it also radically departed from the Jewish emphasis on law as the path to a better life. Buber felt that the change was especially wrong when viewed from the philosophy of dialogue. As a mediating figure now stood between man and God, dialogue was no longer possible for the Christian. The intimacy between man and God was further destroyed by Paul's view of a God who "no longer cares about the men and the generations of men . . . but . . . uses them up for higher ends. Contrary to the Old Testament Paul's God does not have regard for the people to whom He speaks out of the cloud, or rather causes His angels to speak.''[26] Only a world process exists, and individuals are of insignificance. Buber rejected this view, as he did Paul's conception of a God filled with wrath, with the attribute of love largely left to Jesus. In Paul's theology there was a straight path from creation through revelation to the final goal of salvation. Nothing could obstruct this grand plan, certainly not the frailty of the human sinner. "Creation and revelation have taken place as they are for the sake of salvation; for God's way to salvation leads through the 'abounding' of human sin and through its propitiation. Paul does not pray, as Ezra does again and again, for the mitigation of the judgement on humanity; God's sense of justice inexorably demands the appropriate, i.e., measureless, punishment for the 'sin which is sinful beyond measure.' Only God Himself can effect the propitiation of an infinite guilt, by making His Son, the Christ, take the atoning suffering upon himself." Buber recognized that this thought had given "power and consolation to Christian people during a thousand years of development and a thousand years of their struggles.''[27] It answered the question of suffering by saying that man deserves whatever is inflicted on him. This was a sublime and fascinating religious idea, but because it destroyed the relationship between man and God, which had been so carefully nurtured by the Jewish Bible, it had to be rejected. Buber saw God's punishment as akin to the correcting chastisement of a loving father rather than similar to an impersonal force.

Buber could not accept the helpless state of man in Paul's theology, which held man to be entirely dependent on outside forces for his salvation. Whatever man did within the world was unholy, especially when he fulfilled the elemental forces of life, among which Buber listed "hunger, sex, and the will to power." Paul's world was divided into the physical, which was unholy, and the spiritual, which was sacred. "A fundamental dualism in existence resulted: Spirit and world became subject to different laws: man can accomplish nothing by himself. All he can do is surrender to the other, to redemption which has come from the beyond and has assumed bodily shape in his earthly sphere. The corollary of this dualism in principle was a factual dualism between human life as it is intended to be and as it *is* lived, the great rift which was expressed only in the confessions of a few great devout men: up above, a miraculous dome—once more painted in golden colors—arching life, comforting and sating the gaze of man; and below, actual life, governed by the elemental which is at core unhallowed, even when it has been consecrated."[28] Buber admitted that Christianity also contained other elements inherited from the Jewish Bible, but they had become subordinate. Christianity had created a dualism in the nature of God, and Buber rejected both of these contributions of Paul.

According to Buber, Christianity was weakened when it ceased to address people and nations, but spoke only to individuals or to the assembly of individuals. Benamozegh had emphasized this weakness a century earlier. Jesus had primarily addressed the household of Israel, while Paul changed the emphasis to the individual. "Christian Pistis was born outside the historical experience of nations, so to say in retirement from history, in the souls of individuals . . . Paul often speaks about Jews and Greeks, but never in connexion with the reality of their nationalities: he is only concerned with the newly-established community, which by its nature is not a nation. The conception of the 'holy nation' in its strict sense has faded altogether, it does not enter into the consciousness of Christendom, and soon that of the Church takes its place. The consequence of all this is that . . . the individuals, as individuals, not the nations, became Christian . . . the nations . . . remain in their own nature and their own law as they were." This did not matter as long as the individual was able to maintain himself against the "power of public affairs." Yet when the individual becomes weak, as in our time, Christianity faces a real crisis and can offer no solution.[29] Christianity's lack of concern with the nation led to the endless struggle between popes and kings in the Middle Ages. Attempts to correct this situation were attempted; but in our period the Church has lost whatever power it once accumulated over nations. "In the very era which made such technical development possible, Christianity itself as well as its secular derivatives have ceased to be effective as a political supernational authority."[30] In the history of the Church attempts have also been made in the opposite direction, so that—in the eyes of the Church—there would be no connection between the individual and the State. Marcion's extreme dualism took this course; it would have sanctioned a "life of the redeemed soul on the one hand, and that of existing society on the other. In the former there is not justice, but there is loving-kindness, while in the latter there is not even true justice."[31] The Church rejected this path as too distant from the Old Testament foundations of Christianity, but the very suggestion was made possible by Paul, and through the centuries Christianity often followed it in practice.

Buber rejected Paul's basic thoughts, especially his pessimism, which was based upon his views of God, man, and the Law. This outspoken rejection was criticized by Hammerstein, who felt Buber was unable to understand certain elements of Christianity and therefore misinterpreted the nature of Jesus in the theology of Paul, which led him to a one-sided view of Paul.[32] That criticism may be justified, for Buber chose to criticize the Hellenistic elements in Paul and largely passed over the Jewish ones; the latter were not predominant, but they were present. Buber was highly selective in his appraisals of Jesus and Paul. Like many other Jewish scholars he was able to find a kinship to Jesus. The elements in early Christian theology that displeased him were attributed to Paul, with whom he could find no relationship.

This attitude toward Jesus and Paul also colored Buber's views of later Christianity. As he considered Paulinism wrong, he rejected the periods of history dominated by it. "The periods of Christian history can be classified according to the degree in which they are dominated by Paulinism . . . in this sense our era is a Pauline one to a particular degree. In the human life of our day, compared with earlier epochs, Christianity is receding, but the Pauline view and attitude is gaining the mastery in many circles outside that of Christianity. There is a Paulinism of the un-redeemed, one, that is, from which the abode of grace is eliminated: like Paul man experiences the world as one given into the hands of inevitable forces, and only the manifest will to redemption from above, only Christ is missing."[33] He admitted that this spirit had affected Judaism occasionally. The only hope for our age of Paulinism lies in a change of emphasis—from Christian *pistis* to Jewish *emunah*. Buber was hopeful that this might occur: "There is a way which leads from rigid Paulinism to another form of Pistis nearer to Emunah. The faith of Judaism and the faith of Christendom are by nature different in kind, each in conformity with its human basis, and they will indeed remain different, until mankind is gathered in from the exiles of the 'religions' into the Kingship of God. But an Israel striving after the renewal of its faith through the rebirth of the person and a Christianity striving for the renewal of its faith through the rebirth of nations would have something as yet unsaid to say to each other and a help to give to one another—hardly to be conceived at the present time."[34]

Buber was not only interested in a historical investigation, but also in the modern relationship between the two religions. He discussed Calvin and Luther briefly and wrote at length on Kierkegaard. In all his discussions he remained concerned with the misinterpretations of Judaism by Christianity. "Judaism has been misinterpreted from two utterly different standpoints. Christianity couples it with heathenism and claims that both are incapable of transcending the world and looking into a beyond that is over and above the world. Heathenism, on the other hand, and today this means 'neo-heathenism,' couples it with Christianity, arguing that it denies the great vital powers and has no sense of the secret of reality.''[35] He returned to his opening premise, which dealt with the element of mystery in all religions. "Religions are mansions into which the spirit of man is fit in order that it might not break forth and burst open its world. Each of them has its origin in a particular revelation and its goal in the overcoming of all particularity. Each represents the universality of its mystery in myth and rite and thus reserves it for those who live in it.''[36]

Because Martin Buber's philosophy has had a great impact upon Christianity, a number of Christian thinkers have discussed his thoughts critically. This is proper, for genuine dialogue cannot come from one participant. Some of Hammerstein's comments were mentioned in the preceding pages. A more detailed study of Martin Buber was undertaken by the Swiss Catholic theologian Hans Urs von Balthasar. He accepted portions of Buber's thought, but he did not feel that the two religions had come to the point of irreconcilability indicated by Buber in sections of his *Two Types of Faith*. Balthasar directed considerable attention to an analysis of Buber's view of the people of Israel and their position in the world,[37] rejecting Zionism as a solution for the unique position of Israel in our age[38] and Israel as "the suffering servant, one of the arrows hidden in God's quiver.''[39] Both Jews and Christians, according to Balthasar, are to be considered part of the chosen people: the schism between them has led to sad consequences for both—it leaves Christianity without a real tie to the older Covenant and it leaves Judaism isolated and alone in the world. "Israel is therefore immobilized and cruelly isolated, and that isolation inevitably infects the Church to a certain extent. That isolation is the first and fundamental Schism which robs the Church of the unity intended by providence, causing the rift between the Old and the New Covenant." Much of the remainder of Balthasar's book dealt with a reworking of the "familiar fundamentals of Christian theology" in an original manner.[40] It really was a continuation of the dialogue Buber began with the Protestant theologian Karl Ludwig Schmidt two and a half decades earlier. The significance of both statements—Schmidt's and Balthasar's—was the willingness to engage in serious dialogue rather than in mere criticism of the other religion.

Buber looked hopefully to a future in which the two religions would come closer to each other, with Jesus eventually recognized by Jews as a great religious figure in the history of mankind, even though he could never be accepted as a Messianic figure. This was Buber's position now, and he hoped other Jews would gradually adopt it. The two religions would continue to develop, although along divided paths. "Pre-messianically our destinies are divided. Now to the Christian the Jew is the incomprehensible obdurate man, who declines to see what has happened; and to the Jew the Christian is the incomprehensibly daring man, who affirms in an unredeemed world that its redemption has been accomplished. This is a gulf which no human power can bridge. But it does not prevent the common watch for a unity to come to us from God, which, soaring above all of your imagination and all of ours, affirms and denies, denies and affirms what you hold and what we hold, and which replaces all the creedal truths of earth by the ontological truth of heaven which is one."

Elsewhere Buber wrote: "It behooves both you [Christians] and us [Jews] to hold inviolably fast to our own true faith, that is to our own deepest relationship to truth. It behooves both of us to show a religious respect for the true faith of the other. This is not what is called 'tolerance,' our task is not to tolerate each other's waywardness but to acknowledge the real relationship in which both stand to the truth. Whenever we both, Christian and Jew, care more for God himself than for our images of God, we are united in the feeling that our Father's house is differently constructed than our human models take it to be."[41] Both religions must continue along the paths set by their traditions, and they must leave the mystery of their simultaneous existence to God. Both will understand elements within each other's structures that are akin to their own, but they must learn not to condemn the rest. Buber hoped to interpret Christianity for Jews and to seek genuine dialogue with Christianity. Like Baeck, he did not allow the events of the twentieth century to destroy his hopes for better Judeo-Christian relations.

16

Hans Joachim Schoeps

Dialogue in Europe Today

Hans Joachim Schoeps (b. 1909) is the leading contemporary European-Jewish student of Christianity. He has written major works and many smaller studies on the early development of Christianity, the Judeo-Christians, and Paul. He has written about Jewish-Christian relations during the Baroque period, Jewish theology, and nineteenth- and twentieth-century intellectual history. He has also participated in contemporary political affairs.

Schoeps's interest in dialogue is rooted in youthful confrontations on the basic questions of Judaism and Christianity with a friend studying Protestant theology. His study of the Jewish-Christian dialogue reviews past encounters to ensure that we do not repeat worn old themes. "The purpose of this book [*Israel und Christenheit*], therefore, is to assist in bringing the witness of the centuries to the Judeo-Christian dialogue of our own day." Brave words for 1937 in Nazi Germany; a few years earlier Schoeps had felt that dialogue might succeed. The initial mood of that exchange with the young nationalist theologian, Hans Blüher, was angry, but later a grudging, understanding discussion developed. It is astonishing to find such books published at all in that decade in Germany.[1]

Hans Joachim Schoeps spent the Second World War as a refugee in Sweden, but he returned to Germany afterwards to teach at Erlangen. When his book on dialogue was reissued in 1949, he extended the dedication to his parents, who had died in concentration camps, and stated: "I ask myself today whether the period of religious dialogue may not perhaps be past; whether with these senseless exterminations, something quite different has begun. However the case may be, the questions discussed in this book, as well as various essays, was devoted to that theme.[3] He world."[2] In his introduction to the third edition Schoeps returned to his earlier optimism; the hopeful tone of the original text was left unchanged.

In his *Jewish-Christian Argument* Schoeps provides an introduction to the history of dialogue, seen from a theological point of view. He clearly stated that he did not seek originality, but rather a brief and general survey. To this task he brought his own research on the first Christian centuries, as well as special studies of Baroque figures who were forerunners of modern dialogue. A later book, as well as various essays, was devoted to that theme.[3] He concluded his work with a summary of the most significant figures of the last two centuries, an area in which he has also written.[4]

Schoeps states in the opening chapter that he is seeking more than history, for these questions "cannot be answered unconditionally on the basis of 'historical significance' alone."[5] He himself stands within traditional Jewish thought. The Tanakh is the sole revelation of God to Israel; it needs no supplement. The Bible speaks of God's covenant with Israel, which "goes through history ever since that occasion of grace as a covenant community, completely distinct from other nations."[6] On the other hand, he acknowledges Christian belief in a new covenant made with the world; both Christian and Jew know "that the revelation which has come to each—and come in a different way to each—is truth which comes from God." Both are united in confessing the same God, who is the source of both revelations. There is only "one truth, although the modes of participation in the truth differ"; neither group should surrender its special way or its unique claim until the end of days when both paths will unite to attain the final goal of mankind.

The older orthodoxies would not permit such mutual recognition; nineteenth-century liberalism simply blurred the lines and attempted artificial synthesis. In our century we need mutual acknowledgment of each other's truths, for we are "confronted with a world which for two centuries now has set itself against the word of God, per se, to a degree which increases terrifyingly, the

Church and Israel—each in its proper way and in its place—have a common witness to bear."[7] The Church especially finds itself in a difficult position today and thus might be more open to dialogue and understanding; it has experienced "the bitterness of being 'only' a wanderer on the face of the earth."[8] Its former power is gone; those who are called Christians in the modern world are hardly distinguishable from non-Christians. Both Judaism and Christianity now stand humbly awaiting fulfillment; Christianity of the apocalyptic eschatology and Judaism of Biblical Messianism. "Both are united by one common expectation that the truth, which we do not know, which we can only guess, is yet to come, in that hour when the beginning is swallowed up in the end."[9] Schoeps has a mystic hope which foresees a new relationship, but he cannot point out the precise way.

Schoeps's survey of Jewish-Christian relations is too optimistic and perhaps, as Manfred Vogel has stated, not realistic. Can we really expect a "hands-off" attitude and continue as vital faiths?[10] In his lengthy chapter on the first Christian centuries, Schoeps provides a good summary of the development of Christianity and its struggle with Judaism. He then rather quickly passes over the next thousand years, which causes his book to be unbalanced —because those miserable centuries of encounter and disputation are minimized, past conflict is glossed over. A good deal has been written on Judeo-Christian relations in the Middle Ages, but Schoeps chooses to omit most of it. The remaining half of his book is devoted to the Baroque period and the last two centuries; his presentation is strongest when he turns to Mendelssohn, Steinheim, and Rosenzweig, although other figures are also well discussed. His work is a good introduction to dialogue, and, since optimism is necessary in this field, perhaps it will serve a good purpose.

According to Schoeps, if progress is to occur, it will be necessary for both sides to acknowledge each other's truths, something they have never yet done. Although we Jews will continue to reject the essence of Christian belief—that God, "out of his infinite love for mankind, came down into flesh"—we must change our attitude toward this event. "What is basically new—and at the same time also the utmost limit of what is possible—is this: We believe it when they say it. Therein lies the Jewish acknowledgement we have alluded to, namely to grant belief to the Christian witness that God has dealt with the world and a new revelation has taken place outside the covenant with Israel and the revelation to it.'' This will neither change nor abrogate Israel's special relationship to God. "The recognition of other covenants outside of Israel (sc. the covenant of Christ, and, in principle, that of Mohammed) even fills a gap in Jewish knowledge, since according to Jewish belief, not only Israel, but all mankind belongs to God, and is called on the path to God.''[11] Judaism cannot go farther than this, and it can only take this step if Christianity is willing to acknowledge the truth of Judaism in a similar manner. Following Buber and others, Schoeps adds that neither we nor they can understand each other's inner mystery.

Schoeps is both a historian and a theologian. He began his studies with first-century Christianity, producing major works on the Jewish-Christians, the earliest Jewish followers of Jesus, that have stimulated considerable scholarly discussion. This Jewish-Christian group, variously called Ebionites and Nazarenes by the Church Fathers, is described in surviving fragments of Christian literature and by hints in the Gospels. Schoeps's studies of Ebionite theology eventually led him to envision new possibilities for a Judeo-Christian dialogue, for the Ebionites did not recognize the divinity of Jesus and granted more importance to Moses than was allotted him by normative Christians. The ideas and history of the Ebionites must be carefully reconstructed, a task Schoeps set himself in his *Theologie und Geschichte des Judenchristentums*. In this work Schoeps outlines the relationship between the Ebionites and earlier sectarian movements centered on Galilee—the Rechabites, Kenites, and Essenes.[12] Because the North had a long tradition of sectarianism, the Ebionites, once the mainstream of Christianity, were able to survive there, and also on the other side of the Jordan, long after Paul led Christianity toward success among the Gentiles. The relationship of the Ebionites with various early Christian figures, including Paul, is discussed, their literature is carefully analyzed, and their history outlined.

Pella, the Ebionite center across the Jordan, also remained important. The prophets and Jesus had seen it as the land of eschatological fulfillment.[13] The Ebionites settled there to escape the consequences of the Jewish revolt of 65–70 and for ideological reasons. They interpreted the defeat of 70 C.E. as punishment of the Jews for having sanctioned the murder of James, the Jewish-Christian leader, by the Sanhedrin. His death was a major factor in the decline and dispersion of the Ebionites. James had not only been their leader, but was a link with Jesus and his authority. By 90 C.E. the Ebionites found themselves excluded from the synagogue and persecuted by Paul, who was vigorously condemned in the Ebionite "Acts."[14]

Schoeps outlines the beliefs of the Ebionites, showing that they considered Jesus to be the Messiah and the supreme prophet like Moses, but never deified him. The parallel between Moses and Jesus was worked out thoroughly: "They associated the teaching of Moses and the teaching of Jesus by means of the idea of a primordial religion. Both were sent by God to establish covenants with mankind. Just as Moses was the teacher of the Jews, so Jesus was the teacher of the Gentiles. Since the two kinds of teaching are identical, God accepts everyone who believes in either of them. Conversion to Jesus, therefore, is for them precisely the same thing as conversion to God and to the Jewish law. This Ebionite federal theology, apparently formulated in response to Paul's conception of the history of salvation, is a belief found only in Ebionitism."[15] This conception was the foundation of their mission and their opposition to Paul. For the Ebionites Judaism and Christianity coexisted with parallel covenants which finally were one covenant. They stressed the unity of Judaism and Christianity through the continuity of true prophecy, which was found in Moses and other early Israelite leaders and reached its climax in Jesus.[16] The Ebionites considered Jesus a purifying prophet. In his name they eliminated sacrificial cult, the monarch, female prophecy, false prophecies, the use of anthropomorphisms in Scripture, and reports of unworthy acts by Biblical figures.[17] The Ebionites also added laws and customs prohibiting the consumption of meat, encouraged poverty, and established the rite of purification through baptism.[18] Their intensification of good works led to praise by such acknowledged Jewish leaders as Resh Lakish.[19] "The Ebionite treatment of the Mosaic Law . . . is undoubtedly the most interesting and most original part of this religious system. It altered and narrowed the original teaching of Jesus concerning the law in a different way than Paul did; it de-eschatologized it, but not the way the early Catholic Church did."[20]

In later Church history, Schoeps found, the Ebionites "offered front-line opposition to the powerful movement of pagan Gnosticism."[21] Their earlier struggle against anthropomorphisms and their critique of false sections of the Bible made this task easier.

The Ebionites stood halfway between Judaism and Christianity and so suffered the hatred of both. Although they were the original Christians, they were destined to be considered heretics by those who shaped the Church in a different manner.[22] Their pattern of thought was not entirely lost in the history of religion, however, for, as Schoeps was able to demonstrate, they exercised a certain influence on Islam.[23]

Schoeps's reconstruction of Ebionite theology and history met a sharp critical reception. Smith felt his command of New Testament scholarship was insufficient for the conclusions reached.[24] Schneemelcher, Davies, Bream, and Barth judged inconclusive the evidence he took from the Pseudo-Clementine literature, claimed he had not given sufficient consideration to the divisions among the Judeo-Christians, and asserted that his position on Gnosticism, in which he opposed Bultmann, was overstated. Schoeps responded to these and other criticisms in various essays, modifying some of the conclusions reached in his earlier *Theologie und Geschichte des Judenchristentums.* [25] His work also met a good deal of scholarly approval, however, and he now has numerous Christian disciples.

Throughout these studies of the Ebionites, Schoeps is seeking to establish a link between early Christianity and Judaism as a possible basis for better understanding in our time. He maintains that Ebionite Christianity could have maintained a link to Judaism if it had become the mainstream of Christianity. However, Pauline Christianity, in a modified and reinterpreted form, became dominant. Schoeps has outlined its development and its divergence from Judaism, depicting Paul as a representative of Hellenistic

Judaism, which he considers to have been much more varied than it is usually described in scholarly literature, and disagreeing with Montefiore, whom he charges with replacing "one unknown quantity—the theology of Saul—by another unknown quantity, the theology of the Pharisaic Diaspora."[26] In order to establish Paul's position, Schoeps closely analyzed the Septuagint and Philo, the two chief sources on Hellenistic Judaism. Schoeps discounts the Hellenistic Gnostic influence on Paul; in his view Paul, as a citizen of Tarsus, must have known the Gnostic rites and doctrines, but they would not have influenced him because he was a Jew. All apparent Gnostic influences in Pauline Christianity are traced by Schoeps to occult Pharisaism.[27] Paul's entire development must be seen in the light of contemporary Judaism.

Schoeps considers Paul "a dynamic personality, on whom thoughts rained so that he was driven ceaselessly from the one to the other. Moreover his thought was penetrating, leading us to well-nigh unfathomable depths. Often he merely suggests and instead of a whole chain of thought will give us flashes of ideas. Further, he does not always discipline linguistically these thoughts which tumble over each other."[28]

Paul's ideas must have appeared fantastic to early Christians, who could hardly foresee their later dominance. Paul based his claim to authority on the vision on the road to Damascus; he considered himself the apostle of the "heavenly" Jesus, who superseded the "earthly" manifestation, the source authority for the other apostles. This struggle was the focus of all opposition to Paul.[29]

When we look at Schoeps's interpretation of Pauline eschatology, we find it set in the framework of first-century Judaism. It is a mixture of political Messianism as expressed by the prophets and Tannaim with the apocalyptic vision of transcendent Messianism. Both were combined by Jesus; Paul emphasized the latter, the Bar Enosh theme with all of its pessimism about early history.[30] His eschatology looked to the immediate future, perhaps forty years away rather than into the distance. This gave a sense of urgency to his missionary journeys, for he believed that the time for the completion of his task was limited.[31]

According to Paul, all who accepted the resurrected Jesus would be spiritually resurrected. With this doctrine, the earthly Jesus receded and the heavenly Jesus became predominant. For this development one need postulate no Hellenistic or Gnostic influence on Paul.[32] Paul remolded "the Jewish tradition of the Messianic feast . . . in such a way that it became a cultic feast in the style of the mystery religions. He exalted it to the status of a sacrament" and so established the foundation on which "the bread and wine become a means of extending the incarnation of the Christ."[33] His treatment of baptism was similar. In this way he made the *Parousia* bearable. As Schoeps points out, for the Jew nothing had changed, for the world remains the same despite the new faith—on these grounds Judaism continues to reject Christianity. Schoeps understands the debt of Judaism to Christianity. "Since Christ, the Gentiles too have gained access to the God of the fathers who revealed Himself on Sinai—and that without any violation of Jacob's rights as firstborn—for they have been called to tread their own Christian path."[34] Yet Judaism and Christianity differ, for Jews do not see a caesura in history with the coming of Jesus; "their gaze is focused inflexibly on a future which is yet to be, and they expect everything from an event which has not yet happened."[35]

Schoeps shows that Paul's Messianic theology is rooted in rabbinic and apocalyptic literature, where one finds the suffering Messiah, dying Messiah, warrior Messiah, and spiritual Messiah. Paul provided an original combination of elements already present, and added divinity. "Neither the Bible nor the rabbis know anything of a divine nature of the Messiah." The "expiatory death of the Son of God such as would benefit humanity as a whole" was also new with Paul. Furthermore, "Jewish Messianism has always expected salvation and redemption exclusively for Israel and those from the Gentile world who joined themselves to Israel,"[36] very different from Paul's emphasis on the Gentile world.

With Jesus' sacrificial death, Paul recalled the Akedath Isaac, but the Pauline concept was abhorrent to Judaism. In later rabbinic Judaism, the sacrifice of Isaac was developed to counter the claims of Jesus, as Schoeps and others have shown. Here, too, Paul's blending of Jewish elements was novel. "Paul's combination of these three Jewish faith motives, the atoning efficacy of the sufferings of the righteous, the suffering of the Messiah and the Akedath of Isaac, constituted an unheard-of novelty from the point of view of tradition."[37] These and other elements of Pauline thought "linked to the death of Jesus for the sins of mankind the necessity of His suffering and dying as a proof of His Messianic mission." Jesus' preexistence could be discussed within Judaism; Paul went beyond when "he combined these conceptions with the Messianically understood Akedath Isaac in such a way as to transfer the story from Abraham and Isaac to the eternal God Himself and His incarnate Son, and thus exalted the Messiah beyond all human proportions to the status of real divinity—this is the radically un-Jewish element in the thought of the apostle. For this there is no possibility of derivation from Jewish sources, but—if indeed it is a question of derivation—it is impossible to refute the idea of a link with heathen mythological conceptions, filtered through the Hellenistic syncretism of the time."[38] Any link with Jewish thought in this matter must be rejected; it can be "connected with Judaic-Hellenistic wisdom speculations only by ingenious contrivance."[39] These thoughts were vigorously opposed by Jews as well as by the Jewish Christians, who "always saw in Jesus no more than an exceptional prophetic figure like Moses, and accepted a two-fold parousia, one *in humilitate* and the other *in gloria* when He would return as Messiah-Son-of-Man."[40] Schoeps demonstrates that Biblical texts interpreted this way by Christians have never been so considered by Jewish tradition; the Christian interpretations were frequently based on mistranslations of the Hebrew text.

Like Benamozegh and Baeck before him, Schoeps understands Paul's view of the Law as akin to the halakhic presumptions of other Jewish Messianic groups like the Sabbatians. The Law is valid only in our age and not in the eon after resurrection. Anyone who claims further validity for the Law would reject Jesus as the Messiah. However, Paul went farther and combined Jewish elements in an unusual pattern, which was original, but not acceptable to Judaism. "The Pauline inference that the law, which could not prevent universal sinfulness, and on the basis of which no man could be justified by his works, is a law unto death, is one which no Jew could draw." It could only be based on "faith in

Jesus Christ, the Messiah who has come."[41] When Paul denied the saving character of the Law and its divine revelation, he moved beyond the confines of Judaism. His questions about the power of evil and sin, the fulfillability of the Law, and its sacred character had been raised by the rabbis, but were given a positive rather than negative response. "For Paul the Pharisee of Tarsus—as also for Philo of Alexandria—the law was no longer a living possession. And this for the obvious reason that he had ceased to understand the totality and continuity of the Berith-Torah. . . . Of all this there remained for Paul only the 'righteousness of the law' as a theologoumenon. The Torah Kedusha was reduced by him to the scope of the ethical law, which he understands as a law intended to make righteous, and which, he concludes, it is unable to do, since man is not righteous, but a sinner."[42]

Paul's most radical difference emerges in the arm of the Law. He "declared that a partial function of the law, which the rabbis used occasionally for homiletic purposes, was the very essence of the law. Thus he affirmed, on the one hand, that the law was intended to make manifest and increase sins, on the other, that it was intended to justify man and was unable to do so. This was already known to IV Ezra. But if this is intended as an essential answer by a Jew—even a sometime Jew—it is an impossibility. Every child of the Jews, whether the Diaspora or the Judaism of Palestine is in question, knows that the law had no other purpose than that of being given by God in order to be kept and not transgressed, in order to increase resistance to sin and not augment sin. And this applies equally to the twentieth century and the first."[43] Schoeps demonstrates through many illustrations that "every criterion suggesting that the law was inadequate for salvation was emphasized in order to dispense with the old covenant for intrinsic reasons, and to make the sun of the new covenant shine the more brightly."[44] When Paul's discussion of the Law is examined carefully, according to Schoeps, the "genesis of the whole structure is plain: the Messiah was Son of God—which is the sole un-Jewish point in Paul's thinking which explains all the other doctrines that have no parallel in Jewish writings; if we like, it is the Hellenistic premise of his thought, though there is not the smallest reason to explain its logical inference by referring specially to Hellenistic habits of thinking."[45]

Paul misunderstood the Law because of his Hellenistic Jewish background. "Paul succumbed to a characteristic distortion of vision which had its antecedents in the spiritual outlook of Judaic Hellenism. Paul did not perceive and for various reasons was perhaps unable to perceive, that in the Biblical view the law is integral to the covenant; in modern terms was the constitutive act by which the Sinai covenant was ratified, the basic ordinance which God laid down for His 'House of Israel.'"[46] This misconception began with the Septuagint and was carried further by Philo and other Hellenistic Jewish writers.

Following this, Schoeps explains the nature of Paul's mission to the Gentile world. Jewish missionary activity was at its height during the first century and met success with all levels of society. Its work was simplified through emphasis on the Noahide laws, which were an abridgement of the Torah for the Gentile world. "In the circles of Hellenistic Judaism from which Paul sprang, liberal-mindedness and large-heartedness toward the Gentiles must have been most marked."[47] Different classes of converts, the *ger toshav, yireh shamayim,* and *ger sedeq,* each a little closer to Judaism, were recognized by the rabbis and responded to Paul's missionary efforts. Like many Pharisees, Paul felt that proselytizing would bring the Messianic Age nearer; this thought became predominant after the vision on the road to Damascus. "The opinion current in liberal Jewish circles, that Paul conceived the idea of the mission to the Gentiles only after the failure of his synagogue preaching, only after the great majority of his own people had proved themselves unsuitable for Christian evangelization, completely misunderstands the real motives in the apostle's mind. With him it is not a question of sour grapes, but of the necessary consequences of his eschatological convictions."[48] In order to succeed with these groups and with the Jews whom he addressed, Paul reinterpreted the entire Jewish Bible typologically; every figure of the Bible in some way foreshadowed Christianity.

In his missionary efforts Paul was constantly embarrassed by Jews who did not accept Jesus as Messiah. He was forced to find a solution to this problem. God's election was now transferred to the

new Israel, a mixture of Jews and Gentiles. For the moment, the
other Jews had to be seen as enemies of God, but they remained
God's beloved and chosen, and at the proper time God's love
would be bestowed upon them. "The problem of the delay in the
parousia finds its ultimate and true explanation in the still
unconquered unbelief of Israel."[49]

Through Paul the distinctions between various groups of
converts to Judaism were eliminated and all converts were equated
with born Jews; this made his efforts more attractive than those of
Jewish missionaries, aside from his theology, which also aided his
missionary efforts. Jewish proselytizing continued, but with
diminishing success. "Insight into the facts of history on the
Jewish side—of course together with other causes—led to a
resigned self-limitation to the status quo, to the 'hedge about the
law.' The question as to the salvation of the nations now concerned
Judaism only in eschatology, for, as regards the present world, the
Christian church had taken over the missionary task."[50] Schoeps,
in this volume and other studies, shows that Jews have recognized
the improved status of the converted Gentile, who as a Christian
stands in a relationship to the God of Israel, something that is
impossible for a heathen. For Schoeps, the most appropriate
position for Judaism to maintain against Christianity is that of the
Ebionites, "which presupposes an undivided truth in God while
recognizing several covenants of God with man; such covenants as
those of the Torah and the Gospel, the Old and the New
Testaments taken together as the book giving an authoritative
account of God's dealings with mankind."[51]

Schoeps's work on Paul was vigorously criticized. Barth has
commented that "Schoeps seems to be saying: All that is good in
Paul is essentially present in Rabbinic Judaism, and all that is
Jewish, except where it is tinged by Hellenism, is good. . . . Paul
is presented and, as it were, pitied as a man subject to a grave
though somewhat excusable error." This judgment is too severe.
On the other hand, Barth agrees with many of Schoeps's
conclusions about the Law as well as his view of "Paul as the
theologian of the Messianic era."[52] Schoeps's views on Hellenism
and Gnosticism were accepted with reservations by Grant and
others,[53] and his volume on Paul, along with that of Samuel

Sandmel, remains a major Jewish contribution to New Testament studies.

Schoeps concludes in his study that Paul, who had frequently misunderstood Judaism, was in turn misunderstood by the early Church, which faced new problems. The Law was a problem for him, but not for Gentile proselytes, who needed guidance, not freedom. "Since the early Christian Fathers of the church were, to a large extent moralists, since they regarded faith as assent to the truth of propositions, and equated walking by faith with obedience to the commandments, they felt compelled to tone down the radical theses of the apostle."[54] The Catholic Church, therefore, amalgamated the thought of Paul and Peter; Paul's position was not recognized again until Luther "discovered it anew because he saw his own religious experience reflected in that of Paul, and first understood it against the Pauline background."[55] He then read his own doctrine into Paul's thought; when Protestantism was attacked by Nietzsche, Lagarde, and Rosenberg, they attacked Paul, not Jesus.[56]

Schoeps feels that Paul asked a decisive question about the nature of Judaism, one that was not raised again until the present century: Is the Law an exhaustive expression of the will of God and does its fulfillment completely realize the will of God? Several other thinkers, including Hermann Cohen and Martin Buber, have addressed themselves to this matter.[57] "Only modern Judaism can appreciate once again, like Christianity, Paul's concern and the tension which he felt between the works of the law and faith, and it can appreciate it all the more because it maintains that tension and refuses with Paul to dissolve the tension prematurely by the elimination of one of its poles."[58] Jewish faith rests as always on "fear of God," which is in the sphere of human free will in contrast to Christian faith, which is a gift of divine grace. Schoeps understands Paul's critique of the Law "as a possible means to the renewal of the classic Judaic fear of God and a new realization of the meaning of the covenant, even though this means, in fact, has never been adopted; this was done because the historian of religion is concerned to do justice to every aspect of a matter. The Jews might with some justice describe the venture as the rescue of the heretic."[59] Schoeps seeks to bring Paul closer to Judaism and stands with other modern Jewish thinkers who have admired him.

Schoeps concerned himself with some other aspects of Christianity in *Aus frühchristlicher Zeit, Theologie und Geschichte des Judenchristentums, Barocke Juden, Christen, Judenchristen, Philosemitismus im Barock, Vom Himmlischen Fleisch Christi,* and many essays. Such studies, conducted in a purely scholarly manner, must have been difficult to continue, for his parents were killed in the Nazi Holocaust while he was a refugee in Sweden.

His early attempt at dialogue[60]—published in that most inauspicious year, 1933—led nowhere. It can only be read as a final attempt to change the mood that had overwhelmed Germany. In it, Schoeps tried to prove that Jews can be part of the German people even though they are racially different. The tone of the entire argument on both sides sounds absurd to us and can only be understood as a prelude to the Holocaust. The publishers, well aware of the popular trend, affirmed their own belief in the nationalist point of view in the introduction; they had the courage, however, to print these essays, which express both viewpoints. This slender volume cannot be called a contribution to dialogue but is a continuation of medieval disputations.

Despite doubts about the future of Judeo-Christian relations, Schoeps returned to Germany as a professor and has won a notable place in the hearts of students and fellow scholars, who dedicated a *Festschrift* in honor of his fiftieth birthday.[61] Schoeps has stated that the time for dialogue may already be past;[62] yet his life and writings testify that this statement, made in 1949, was not intended to end his attempts at dialogue. He continues to follow the path of Steinheim and Rosenzweig and remains optimistic. Again and again Schoeps has stressed the difficulties that all religious groups face in our century, which is filled with doubt rather than belief.[63] He sees our world as a post-Christian world in which Christianity also finds itself in a Diaspora situation. This brings it closer to Judaism and makes a relationship with Judaism easier than during periods of Christian power.

In Europe Schoeps is the most important Jewish student of Christianity and the only one seriously pursuing the path of dialogue.

17

Samuel Sandmel

Liberal American Studies

Samuel Sandmel (b. 1911), provost of the Hebrew Union College, the center of Reform Jewish learning in America, has made valuable contributions to New Testament studies. He entered this field through his interest in Philo and Hellenistic literature, coming to it with a fine background in Judaism and the New Testament, and his works reflect the breadth of his knowledge. Throughout his books, Sandmel seeks to be objective, warning the reader of his preconceptions as a Reform rabbi. Unlike many Jews who have entered this field, he is aware that his own biases may unconsciously influence his judgment. Nonetheless, he has attempted to attain objectivity and has succeeded remarkably well.

Sandmel's books are intended as an introduction to Christianity for the Jew. In them he wishes to break through the "vestigial sense of taboo." All of us, he says, are "in constant contact with this great body of religious expression that has become a cultural force in our secular environment."[1] Despite this desire he also points to the reasons for the Jewish disdain of Jesus and the New Testament: long centuries of persecution made this field of study alien to most Jews; in addition, both Jews and Christians were kept apart by strong feelings of superiority.[2] In addition to his writings for general readers, Sandmel has also produced many scholarly essays for the New Testament specialist.

More than most Jewish scholars, Sandmel has overcome the hesitancy connected with writing about Christianity and the hostility that usually accompanies such works. He becomes angry only when he meets deliberate Christian misinterpretation: "the arrogant condescension, the pretentious superiority, and the self-congratulatory banalities which I encounter in some scholarly literature."[3] He remains well aware of the shortcomings of fellow Jewish scholars who often do not master New Testament studies or its higher criticism before entering the field. Still others assume that all good must come from Jewish sources and the rest is not worthwhile.[4]

In his latest book,[5] Sandmel stresses the basic problems of first-century studies, an area filled with uncertainties. He comments on Palestinian Judaism, Hellenistic Judaism, and Christianity, pointing to the innumerable gaps in knowledge and the broad areas open to speculation. Despite this, Sandmel indicates, the existing literature is so vast that no single person can hope to master it or to write a definitive study, although earlier he himself had hoped to do so.[6] Some of his other essays also touch on this theme.

Sandmel several times points to the danger in the uncritical use of rabbinic sources. He decries the feeling of superiority expressed by Strack and Billerbeck, who considered the statements of Jesus better than those of the rabbis, but he also points to the misuse of their work if the rabbinic and New Testament backgrounds of statements are not investigated. Some more recent Christian scholars feel this fault has been largely corrected; if this is so, then Samuel Sandmel can feel that his efforts have met success.

The haziness in which first-century scholarship is cloaked might lead to dissatisfaction, but Sandmel does not despair; he merely feels a necessity to define the limitations. Furthermore, he says, describing his own outlook: "Rationalist that I am, I still feel that that which is essentially religious in religions loses much of its significance when it is all too easily and too readily explicable. All too often there is a tendency in man to explain too much and, indeed, to explain away."[7]

Throughout his works, Sandmel uses an easy and at times journalistic style. Occasionally this has alienated scholarly reviewers who equate thoroughness with dense writing. However, his fine style, along with his excellent scholarship, has made his books attractive to both Jewish and Christian students.

Sandmel is not certain that the life of Jesus can ever be reconstructed, but he made an effort in that direction in a volume partially devoted to Jesus. In this volume, Sandmel discusses both the human and the divine aspects of Jesus. Reviewing the past century of Protestant scholarship directed toward recovering the historical Jesus, he presents a brief discussion of each point of view. In tracing the changing views several important Jewish scholars are mentioned at length and others in passing. Sandmel accepts the existence of Jesus, but feels the sources are insufficient for a real biography. He considers the entire scholarly effort of the past hundred years misplaced: "The Gospels so intertwine authentic material about Jesus with the pious meditation of the Church that I know of no way to separate the strands and end up with some secure and quantitatively adequate body of material. I simply do not know enough about him to have an opinion, and I surely do not have enough to set him, as it were, in some one single category. But beyond this, it is my conviction that the Gospels are not telling about the man that scholarship seeks, but about the human career of a divine being. To search the Gospels for the man seems to me to involve a distortion of what is in the Gospels."[8] The man is simply beyond recovery from the texts presently available; furthermore, they were written four decades after the death of Jesus and were composed to achieve a specific goal. This, rather than biographical considerations, led the authors to choose certain material about Jesus. Sandmel clearly points to the special place each Gospel had in the development of the early Church; he does so in his introduction to the New Testament and in his volume on Paul.[9] He feels that no single event of the Gospels can be accurately recovered; therefore, the events leading to the crucifixion also cannot be determined.[10] Despite these reservations in depicting the figure of Jesus, Sandmel feels that the literature emphasizes certain traits. Jesus was "someone who had gifts of leadership and who was something of a teacher. I believe, too that I discern in him a Jewish loyalty at variance with the views both of Christian and Jewish partisans." According to Sandmel, Jesus believed himself to be the Messiah and the end of the world to be at hand. There was little originality in the teachings of Jesus when taken individually. Therefore, "the uniqueness of Jesus would lie not in single particulars, but in the combination of facets, in the totality of what we may perhaps glimpse of him, and not in any one isolated way. Thus he was in part a teacher, a Jewish loyalist, a leader of men, with a personality unquestionably striking enough to be a leader, and his career must have been exceedingly singular for his followers to say that he had been resurrected. He was a martyr to his Jewish patriotism." As Judaism has had many martyrs, this did not especially impress Jews. "Yet the dominant note to me of his career is overwhelmingly one of pathos, of sympathy, that a man, with the normal frailties of men, aspired and labored and worked, and yet experienced defeat."[11] Sandmel here leans toward Montefiore, but without the latter's extreme praise, pointing out that "Jewish scholarly laudation of Jesus, however generous it may seem to Jews, is niggardly in comparison with Christian laudation of him for to Jews Jesus is never more than a mortal, fallible man."[12]

Throughout his works Sandmel has stressed the Jewish background necessary for a proper assessment of Jesus and the entire New Testament and its combination with liberal New Testament scholarship, which he follows. Geiger, Benamozegh, Salvador, Baeck, Montefiore, and others had sought to do this earlier, but they did not meet with Sandmel's success. He shows how Christian scholarship has slowly come to grips with rabbinic literature; this kept New Testament scholarship from becoming anti-Jewish during the rise of neo-orthodoxy in the 1920s.[13] There were pitfalls in such studies, and several times Sandmel has condemned the excessive and incorrect application of parallels discovered in rabbinic literature. Equally dangerous is quoting out of context, of which Jews and Christians have been equally guilty. Although the individual statements of the Gospels may often not be original, their use and placement are often unique and give them a special flavor not found in related Jewish sources.[14]

When Sandmel turned to the divine Jesus he could do little more than trace this concept as depicted by modern scholarship, for this aspect of Jesus can have no meaning for a Jew.[15] Throughout the book Sandmel draws a clear distinction between his opinion as a NewTestament scholar and his feelings as a Jew. In some ways, the title of his book is misleading, for he states: "I discern no possible religious assessment of Jesus, either by me or by other Jews. I cannot share in the sentiments of Montefiore which seems to me to fly in the face of prudent scholarship, nor in Klausner's distant dream of a reclaimed Jesus. I must say most plainly that Jesus has no bearing on me in a religious way." For Sandmel as a Jew, Jesus occupies a place in Western culture akin to Plato and should be studied similarly. No one need fear conversion from such studies, for the words of Jesus so read would be a part of Western culture and not of Christianity.[16] Sandmel views Jesus objectively; he does not attempt to reclaim him for Judaism nor does he denounce him for misunderstanding Judaism. His work has met critical acclaim, although in matters of dating sources and determining the dependence of one document on another, there has been scholarly debate.

Just as Sandmel differs from his predecessors in the treatment of Jesus, so he approaches Paul differently. He sees Paul as a purely Hellenistic Jew and feels that this explains Paul's discontent with Judaism. Sandmel's studies of Philo have enabled him to find many parallels to Paul, although Philo sought to solve the religious problems of the Hellenistic community in a different manner. He also sees similarities between Philo and the Gospels.[17] In assessing Paul as a Hellenistic Jew, Sandmel does not wish to indicate an inferior form of Judaism, but a different kind of Judaism from that of Jesus and his contemporaries; Paul's Hellenistic Judaism represented the overwhelming majority of Jews in the first century.[18] According to Sandmel, Paul's background, his education, and the problems he saw can be explained only in terms of Hellenistic Judaism. "For Paul, as for other Greek Jews whom history records, Judaism in its usual form had become inadequate. . . . The need of the imperiled individual was not for the symbol representing God, not for His codified word, but for direct communion with God Himself. We can understand the Greek Jew Philo who lived in Alexandria about the same time. . . . For Philo and for Paul, who were Jews inclined by the Greek atmosphere towards the goal of transcending physical nature, salvation from the material world was the very focus of religious aspiration. Philo paved his road to salvation with an allegorical midrash on the meaning of Jewish law. Paul found salvation in his interpretation of the meaning of the career of Jesus."[19] The Greek background of Paul and his contemporary coreligionists gave them a different view of Judaism. They accepted the pessimism of Greek thought, which regarded the material world as evil and emphasized individual paths to salvation. This thought was foreign to Palestinian Judaism.

Paul's search for an answer was ended by the revelation in which Jesus appeared to him; this brought him a new path to salvation through Jesus, who represents an aspect of God similar to Philo's Logos. The Law had been God's way for Israel in the past, but now "God has revealed Himself in Jesus Christ. Here is at once the continuity with Judaism and the difference."[20] Paul always considered this way to represent the logical continuity of Judaism. "To Paul, the newer convictions are the essence of true Judaism, and Christ is not a nullification of Judaism or of the Old Testament, but actually crowns them."[21] Paul felt the need for a contemporary answer to religious problems; no ancient document could suffice, for only a new revelation would bring a solution. "To Paul the Law of Moses was a revelation which came at one particular time in history—that is, there was a period of time in history before it was given—and it could therefore be supplanted by a revelation more recent in history." Furthermore, Paul felt it had been only indirectly revealed by God and so was the product of a "second-rate revelation"; in his own search for God he could supplant it and could see its defects.[22] This was diametrically opposed to rabbinic doctrine. The rabbinic tradition considered Sinai the pinnacle of revelation, while Paul felt that revelation had continued and reached its culmination in himself.[23] That revelation was "in Jesus, but it is to Paul," and there attains its noblest height according to Paul's thought.[24] According to Sandmel's presentation, the attitude of Paul toward the Law can be understood as grudging praise for its role in the past. It offered nothing for his time because one who had not been "transformed into a spiritual being . . . struggled vainly in his effort to observe the Law of Moses." Later Paul became bitter about the Law, but this was a response to Jewish opposition, which brought about his unjust condemnation of the Law.[25] Certainly he was not an opportunist who made this basic change to attract converts, as has sometimes been charged.[26]

In Sandmel's view, Paul considered Jesus divine, and therefore, unlike later Christian writers, he had no need to deify Jesus. Paul did precisely the opposite: "he humanized the divine Christ."[27] Sandmel clearly demonstrates the relationship between Philo's Logos and Paul's Christ. To Paul Christ remained the vessel through which he attained the "fullest communion in the world with God who is remote and outside the world."[28] The death of Jesus in addition represented atonement; "a man could become 'spirit' like the Christ, by 'dying' in respect to his body, just as Paul had done." This was to be done by all his followers in the interval between the first and second coming of the Christ.[29] Paul did not emphasize the second coming and stressed the actions of Jesus in the past.

Sandmel sees Paul as an emissary of the new revelation to the Gentile world; the revelation placed him at the pinnacle of all revelation and made him the chief apostle. He came to the Gentiles with a unique mixture; "the three strands—Hellenism, Judaism, Christianity—are blended in Paul, [along with] a resounding echo of popular philosophy, popular religion, and both the attitudes and the sense of arrival which characterized the Greek mysteries."[30] With this combination Christianity succeeded in spreading itself through the Hellenistic world. This new religion appealed as a universal faith, but in reality it was as particularistic as Judaism; its particularism centered about the Church rather than the nation.[31] Sandmel is not only concerned with the enormous influence of Paul, but also with the problem he created for the early Church. He had rejected all law, but a stable institution needed law and could not establish itself upon personal inspiration. In short, "when one canonizes a rebel, one enshrines rebellion. . . . It is a truly wonderful church which shapes itself solely after Paul's prescription in I Corinthians 13 of faith, hope and love as sufficient 'rules.' However, a more realistic church, if it is to be organized, systematized and regulated requires more humanly feasible vehicles, such as a constitution, regulations and persons with authority."[32] For this reason the Church had to neutralize Paul; it did so first in the Acts of the Apostles, which places him in a Palestinian setting with Gamaliel as his teacher, made him one among many apostles, and allowed the acceptance of "Pauline doctrine as a correct basic doctrine of Christianity, and at the same time denies the clear corollaries and implications of that doctrine."[33] The same process was followed by all the other New Testament writings; each author or editor sought to harmonize the thought of Paul with the needs of the growing Church. This trend was essential for the development of the Church. "Without Paul, the Church would scarcely have swept the Hellenistic world; without neutralizing Paul, it would in all likelihood have had the same fate as the cult of Isis or of Mithraism."[34]

The very title of Sandmel's book shows that he considers Paul a man of outstanding stature. "When Paul joined the movement, it received no ordinary man, but a highly individualistic genius. Almost half of the writings in the New Testament came from his hand. . . . There is a fascination about him for any reader who is challenged by a vigorous, original, and creative mind."[35] Paul's critique of Judaism was an internal matter, so far as Sandmel is concerned, for he was speaking about his inherited Judaism. One had to understand his background and his limitations. "The allegations which Paul makes about the Law are subjective and one-sided; thus, the picture of Judaism evolved from the New Testament is a grotesque caricature. Paul's is the characteristic criticism which emanates in an established religion from the individual who makes the claim of immediate divine revelation." When one views these criticisms a little more broadly, Sandmel points out, they really are not only directed against Judaism, but are "a protest against all institutionalized religion."[36] Paul shifted his religious emphasis from national Judaism to an individual and a universal sphere, but this was not unique, it was the path of many Greek Jews.[37] In other matters he left Judaism for the new Christianity. Sandmel interprets Paul's thought in an objective and scholarly fashion. Not following the pattern of the nineteenth century, which sought to emphasize the historical Jesus at the expense of Paul, he sees him as a historian. "The historian sees in Paul one of history's paramount religious geniuses. A modern Jew can certainly not follow Paul. But he can try to assess him more justly than Paul assessed Judaism."[38]

Sandmel deals with all the books of the New Testament in a similarly sympathetic and scholarly manner. He has been able to do so because "the New Testament, although it is not ours, is closer to us than any other sacred literature which is not our own." His work follows liberal Protestant scholarship, to which he has made special contributions that do not lie within the purview of this chapter.[39]

Sandmel has not concerned himself with the later development of Christianity. Luther and the Protestant Reformation are mentioned in his books, but primarily to show the later influence of Pauline doctrine.[40] However, he has concerned himself with the evolution of New Testament studies among Protestants during the last two centuries.[41]

Sandmel continues to feel hopeful for the future and believes the present mood of cooperation and mutual understanding to be a lasting element in American life. "I do not regard Judaism as objectively superior to Christianity, nor Christianity to Judaism. Rather, Judaism is mine, and I consider it good, and I am at home in it, and I love it, and want it. That is how I want Christians to feel about their Christianity."[42] This is the mood of late-twentieth-century dialogue.

18

Richard L. Rubenstein and Emil Fackenheim

After the Holocaust

The Holocaust of European Jewry totally changed the Judeo-Christian relationship. The failure of German Christianity to prevent the slaughter of six million Jews made dialogue impossible. The well-documented failure of Pope Pius XII to take strong action on behalf of the Jews, as well as the moral collapse of German Protestantism, with a few individual exceptions, ended the optimism of earlier days, which had dominated even in the darkest days of the previous century. The earlier Jewish advocates of better understanding had seen only temporary setbacks, not permanent defeat.

The major Jewish effort to understand Christianity and to develop a relationship with it had been made in Germany, the land in which the emancipation began. With bitter irony, it was also the land of the Holocaust.

Some Jewish thinkers since World War II have reflected on the tragedy and its effect on Jewish-Christian relationships, but many have avoided this area. Among the American-Jewish theologians, Richard L. Rubenstein and Emil Fackenheim have made outstanding contributions.

Richard L. Rubenstein (b. 1924), currently professor of religion at Florida State University in Tallahassee, has taken a new approach to the Judeo-Christian dialogue. In the early 1960s he became one of the first since Baeck and Schoeps to undertake serious discussion in Germany itself, expressing his feeling that "we have been too directly and too violently involved in each other's destiny for either side to permit murder to be the last word, if we can help it."[1] The discussion must continue by looking at the basic claims of Judaism and Christianity. We Jews must recognize that there is no solution in the major area of conflict, for Christianity has tied itself to the Jewish idea of being a people chosen by God, whose "relationship to the world is primarily historical."[2] Israel, as God's chosen people, occupies a special place in world history. On the other hand, Christianity feels that this choice has been superceded by "Christ as the fulfillment and climax of that revelation."[3]

Each religion has also interpreted Jewish history in a special manner. The Jew sees his sufferings as punishment for impiety; the Christian sees them as a punishment inflicted on the Jew because of his unwillingness to accept the Christ. Since the Jew must remain a part of the Christian myth, it is impossible for the Christian to demythologize his conceptions of Israel and the Jew. Whatever Israel may do with the doctrine of its election, which Rubenstein believes must be rejected as a consequence of Auschwitz, for Christianity it remains indispensable. "Unless Israel is the vessel of God's revelation to mankind, it makes no sense to proclaim Christ as the fulfillment and climax of that revelation."[4]

Christianity is not only intimately tied to the myth, but also to a mythological way of seeing the Jew as a saint (Jesus) or a sinner (Judas); it cannot see him as an ordinary person. In time of crisis the Jew is Judas, and since the Jewish people has its share of sinners, such accusations will always be partially true.

Therefore, the problem of Judeo-Christian relations cannot be solved as long as the myth of the election of Israel is held by Christians, no matter what the Jewish attitude toward it might be. "For the Jew who holds firmly to the doctrine of the election of Israel and the Torah as the sole content of God's revelation to mankind, the Christian insistence upon the decisive character of the Christ-event in human history must be at best error, and at worst blasphemy. For the Christian who is convinced that the Divine-human encounters recorded in Scripture find their true meaning and fulfillment in the Cross, Jews are at best the blind who cannot see; at worst, they are the demonic perverters, destroyers, and betrayers of mankind's true hope for salvation."[5] The persecution of the Jew, according to Rubenstein, is also intimately connected with the most sacred ancient religious act, the sacrifice of the King-Priest-Savior. This sacrifice is kept alive for each Christian in the story of Jesus. Since it may be reenacted through the murder of a contemporary Jew, the "ritual-murder aspect of sacrifice predominates. . . . The death camps were one huge act of ritual murder."[6]

The situation would be hopeless but for America, where the religious factor is not dominant in society, and ideology plays a minor role. Only in a land of theological ambiguity can there develop the kind of a person-to-person relationship that may be able to overcome the old hatred. Another possibility is the secular society. This has diminished anti-Semitism, but it is distasteful to Rubenstein because in it the "society of myth is replaced by a society of calculation and contrast. What is needed, however, is a society of persons."[7] The secular society does not fulfill the needs of modern man and cannot lead to the community of persons which is necessary for mankind's future. "If we concentrate less on what our religious inheritance promise and threaten and more on the human existence which we share through these traditions, we will achieve the superlative yet simple knowledge of who we truly are."[8]

Rubenstein points to yet another possibility for understanding. "The myth separates me from my brother. What the myth points to unites me with him. This is even true of the person of the Christ. I cannot accept the historicity of the tradition. The historical Jesus remains for me just another Jew. I can, however, share with my brother the complex intersection of promethean self-assertion and pious submission which all men feel before the incarnational reality of the Divine."[9] A statement like this may be helpful to Jews, but it can bring little satisfaction to a believing Christian. The essay concludes with a plea for union through guilt, if unity in innocence is impossible; in this way we will at least sense the potential for murder that exists in all of us.

The solutions suggested by Rubenstein are novel but represent only an alternative for a post-Christian society. Similar conclusions are repeated in other essays in the same volume. Although Rubenstein can no longer believe in the myth of the chosen people, he sees no way in which "Jews can be entirely quit of this myth."[10] In his contribution to a symposium on Jewish belief, he does not find it necessary to claim a superior truth for Judaism over Christianity; yet he must "regard the claim of the Church vis-à-vis Judaism as inherently mistaken. . . . I find myself in the paradoxical position of asserting that Christianity is as true psychologically for Christians as Judaism is for Jews, while maintaining that the manifest claims of the Church concerning Israel and Israel's Messiah are without foundation."[11] Rubenstein views Judaism and Christianity again in his *Religious Imagination*, in which he seeks a psychoanalytic understanding of both religions. He shows a strong admiration for Paul in that volume, stating that "he [Paul] understood the inability of the Jewish religious system to overcome the anxiety and guilt it engendered. Luther made a somewhat similar discovery about Catholicism. Today another path is available when sublimation fails, psychoanalytic insight."[12] In his next book Rubenstein went much farther than any other Jewish figure in his assessment of Paul: his open approach was indicated by the title of his psychoanalytical study, *My Brother Paul*. In the opening sentences he calls Paul "one of the most influential Jews of all time."[13] He says that modern Jewish scholarship, which has revised its negative evaluation of Jesus, has done so largely at the expense of Paul. It was Jesus' Messianic claim, not Paul's proclamation of it, which divided the Judeo-Christians from the Pharisees and other Jewish sects of the time. Paul did not cease to be a faithful Jew according to Rubenstein; he sought to prove his point within the framework of Judaism. Paul understood the need for the Jerusalem Judeo-Christian community, which lived within a Jewish environment, to observe the Law; however, he and the early Jewish Christians felt the Law was no longer needed as the path to salvation because the Age of the Messiah had dawned.[14] Rubenstein several times points out that Paul's radical interpretation of the Law used the methodology of the Pharisees, who interpreted it in the "light of their own experience." Paul did so in the light of his vision of the Risen Christ. Paul did not think of himself as the founder of a new religion, but as the harmonizer of the new and old traditions.[15] Throughout Rubenstein's book Paul is depicted as viewing Christ as the older brother, a different Christology than is usually provided,[16] and, of course, more congenial to a Jewish interpreter.

Perhaps most significant for the dialogue is Rubenstein's view of Paul's harsh statements about the Pharisees. Though frequently used by anti-Semites, they must be viewed as part of a family quarrel. When seen in this way, they are no harsher than the statements of the prophets or of Paul's contemporaries, the Qumran community. Paul saw Church and Synagogue in terms of fraternal strife—as Rubenstein recognizes, this could and did lead to fratricide, and thus the title of his book was chosen "with considerable sadness." He recognizes further that the emotional power of Paul's message aroused bitter anti-Semitism and led to a continual misunderstanding of the role of Israel by well-meaning Christian Biblical interpreters. "What is so sad about this point of view is that even the more liberal Christian commentators seem unable to regard Judaism as a distinctive religion with its own autonomous integrity; instead, they look at it as an apostate form of Christianity."[17]

So far as Hellenistic influences are concerned, Rubenstein feels that Paul's "religious life was far more Jewish than Greek";[18] however, his mystical experience separated him from contemporary religious figures.

Rubenstein, from the outset stating that all attempts to understand Paul are subjective, proceeds in the book with a frankly personal appraisal of Paul. He provides us with a view of Paul as understood through the "work of the twentieth century's most important secularized Jewish mystic, Sigmund Freud," finding Paul's fear of death and his search for redemption illuminated by Freud, as well as by his own personal experiences. Paul was convinced by his conversion that Christ had defeated death. This solution, of course, is not acceptable to Rubenstein, but his path was clarified through the application of depth psychology, and Paul's conversion experience is divided into three elements: "(1) his loss of normal ego functions; (2) his vision of the Risen Christ; and (3) his recovery of his capacities."[19]

According to Rubenstein, Paul's theology also gave vent to feelings normally supressed by Judaism. Men fear death; they also yearn for a new beginning. This was provided by the rite of baptism, with which Paul replaced circumcision—he did so, not because it was an easier rite, as often stated by commentators, nor for its outward purifying effect, but because it was "the womb and the tomb" and so reflects mankind's universal yearning for a new beginning.[20] Rubenstein interprets the Lord's Supper in the Freudian manner as totemic atonement for the "primal crime of humanity, the cannibalistic devouring of the father by the sons, so that they might become like him and take secular possession of his females."[21] This is done "without harming either himself or others. On the contrary, he does much good, for he achieves a solidarity of shared complicity, aspiration, and hope that is the basis of any viable human community. Sacrificial worship is the most perfect form of human worship. It effects a convergence of the destructive and the loving, the sinful and the hopeful, the latent and the manifest in human consciousness and experience." He comments further that "it terminates to some extent the need to handle archaic cravings by sublimation or repression, which had been characteristic of Judaism."[22]

In the concluding chapter of the book, Rubenstein demonstrates that Paul regarded humanity as existing in an exile that cannot end until the Messiah, the Last Adam, restores mankind to Eden and to the original position of the First Adam. Instinctively, according to Freud, all men yearn for a return to the fetal condition, which is also a return to the "maternal matrix"; all progress, therefore, is disguised regression. This thought is combined with the end of man's rebellion against the Father, so that the Last Adam becomes "the cosmic agent through whom the eschatological return of the cosmos to its originating Sacred Womb is finally attained."[23]

Rubenstein's work is a highly original interpretation of Paul, as well as of other aspects of Christianity, providing numerous insights through the application of Freudian psychology. Many of these will seem strange and unacceptable to both Jew and Christian, but Rubenstein's frank approach, as well as his willingness to speak in highly personal terms, brings a new level of understanding to the dialogue.

Emil Fackenheim (b. 1915), of the University of Toronto,

introduces another facet to the interreligious dialogue, which has changed radically since Auschwitz. His approach is entirely different from Rubenstein's and is philosophical in character. In the 1930s, when it was necessary for Jews and Christians to unite against Hitler, he saw no need for dialogue. He felt that modern Judaism owes a debt to Christian theologians and wondered "whether, had there not been a Christian renewal initiated by such men as Barth, Tillich and Niebuhr, the Jewish renewal initiated by Buber and Rosenzweig would have been possible."[24]

Long afterward, just before the Six-Day War, when Fackenheim looked back upon the years of the Second World War and the problems of Israel, his attitude toward Christianity changed. "I am thus left with no doctrine, but only with openness to Jewish-Christian dialogue. But what is a religious recognition which does not recognize the other terms of his own self-understanding? The heart of dialogue, it seems to me, is to refuse to give an abstract answer to this question, and instead risk self-exposure. If Jew and Christian are both witnesses, they must speak from where they are. But unless they presume to be on the throne of divine judgment, they must listen as well as speak, risking self-exposure just because they are witnesses. For many years I believed that the long ago of Christian triumphalism over Judaism had ended and the age of Jewish-Christian dialogue had arrived. Today I am less sanguine."[25]

The Christian, according to Fackenheim, has been unwilling to understand Jewish survival and existence; he sees only a fossil, not a living religion. With some notable exceptions, Christians find it even more difficult to recognize Israel as a living state. These factors, as well as the inability of Christians to face up to their responsibility for the Holocaust, constitute the obstacles to a modern Judeo-Christian dialogue. Christians could not defend Israel in 1967 because Christianity "failed to recognize the danger of the second holocaust, for it still cannot face the fact of the first."[26]

Thus Hitler succeeded in widening the gap between Jews and Christians, yet both must unite to face the challenge of the modern secular society. Jews may be able to teach Christians the danger of the "secular city" as we have celebrated it since the French

Revolution.[27] We have been committed to modern secularism because it gave us freedom. The traditionalists among us welcomed the emancipation after centuries of Christian oppression. Yet we could not identify ourselves completely with liberal secularism. "Throughout the ages, the choice to remain Israel has been based on a commitment to the God of Israel; and even today a Jew cannot persist in his Jewishness without hanging on to some remnants at least of his religious past. The God of Israel, however, is rejected by the secularist liberal. Moreover, he is the God shared by Jew and Christian. In the modern West, therefore, the Jew has existed and still exists between secularist liberalism and Christianity."[28] Although most Christians refuse to recognize the Jew as a full member of mankind, we must learn to unite our efforts in order to struggle together for the God of all mankind in a secular world. "One of the major charges a religious Jew must make against modern Christendom is that it has tempted Jews to throw in their lot with secularism, thereby turning their back on Him Who is the God of both Israel and the Church."[29] We have seen secular freedom and its ideal of a universal man lead to "the man of modern nationalism. And this man had religious, or rather, pseudo-religious, pretensions. His voice (especially, but not exclusively, in Germany) became ever more strident, and the realm reserved for private conscience ever more precarious."[30] This led to Nazism, which found the path well prepared by the easy adjustment of German Christianity to secularism in the nineteenth century. These views led Fackenheim to a vigorous attack on all forms of Christian surrender to secularism, especially as expressed by the "Secular City" and the "Comfortable Pew."[31] In his thorough analysis of secularism, which may also lead to a virulent new anti-Semitism, Fackenheim states the challenge presented to modern Jew and Christian alike.[32] Both Judaism and Christianity must expose themselves to the secular world, for that is "where the action is." We must struggle against it together. This is a bond uniting both religions, although we have only recently begun to understand this.[33]

Fackenheim entirely avoids the usual categories of discussion. Secularism threatens Judaism and Christianity with destruction, even as German-Christian anti-Semitism brought the Holocaust.

Judeo-Christian understanding will only come if we unite to face secularism. This necessity makes all other discussions superfluous.

Rubenstein and Fackenheim demonstrate clearly the latest concern with dialogue. Unlike many others, they do not wish to give up, but rather search for totally new ways to approach the problems that divide Jew and Christian. The gulf separating them clearly indicates how varied future discussions may be.

19

Other Studies

Jewish interest in Christianity has continued to develop in the United States, Europe, and Israel. Most recent studies have been devoted to an objective view of early Christianity and avoid the critical and polemical path of their predecessors. This chapter will summarize some important, but less extensive, bodies of writing on the subject.

Solomon Zeitlin (b. 1892) has devoted himself to the history of the Second Jewish Commonwealth for many decades. The center of controversy over the Dead Sea Scrolls, which he dates later than most scholars, he has polemicized on this subject and many others throughout his life and seems to enjoy scholarly battles.

Zeitlin generally concentrates on specific questions within early Christianity. Sometimes his ideas have been expressed in long book reviews rather than formal essays.

The Second Jewish Commonwealth, which has been Zeitlin's lifelong interest, led him to study the Jewish sects of the period. Zeitlin explains the appeal of Bar Kokhba, in contrast to the minor influence of Jesus, on the rise of Messianic hopes after the destruction of the Second Temple. Earlier, he says, only small bands of apocalyptics expressed this thought. John the Baptist was an apocalyptic, not an Essene; there was no connection between early Christianity and the Essenes.[1] Zeitlin believes that many widely held opinions on the Pharisees are wrong, holding that the animosity between the Pharisees and the disciples of Jesus described in the Gospels existed, but that specific controversies were later inventions. He has sought to prove that much Pharisaic legislation was not fixed until the destruction of the Temple.[2] In the heated controversy described in the Gospels the Pharisees are called hypocrites, which is totally unjustified.[3] The basic disagreement between Jesus and the Pharisees centered around the different tasks which each set for themselves. The Pharisees were interested in the welfare of society and reinterpreted the old laws accordingly. Statements like "An eye for an eye" (lex talionis) were interpreted to require an eye of similar size, color, and so forth; consequently, the law became a dead letter. This was a realistic approach to a society ruled by law. Jesus, however, was utopian: "As a moralist he appealed to the people that they should not only not demand satisfaction by talio, but that they should not resist evil at all. . . . This may be a great moral teaching but could a society really function on such principles? Have the followers of Jesus ever practiced this way of life? . . . The literal words an eye for an eye . . . were followed more among the Christians than the teachings of the Sermon on the Mount."[4] Zeitlin analyzes the Sermon on the Mount in a similar fashion, and he shows that controversies over healing on the Sabbath were the Pharisees' way of denying Jesus' Messianic claims.[5] Jesus always emphasized the ideal rather than a realistic approach. He remained a Pharisee. "The Pharisees with their teachings were in a great measure responsible for the ideas which brought about Christianity. The Pharisees with their ideas about the Future World and reward and punishment and Providence made possible the teachings of Jesus and his disciples." The resentment between Jesus and the Pharisees arose because they shared a basic philosophy; there was little animosity between Jesus and the Sadducees because they had nothing in common.[6] Jesus wished to interpret the Law differently than the Pharisees, but he never intended to abolish the Law.[7]

For a time Zeitlin doubted the existence of Jesus and the authenticity of the Gospels on the grounds that they often reflected later halakhic developments.[8] In later essays Zeitlin changed his mind, although the sources remain confused. "The history of the beginnings of Christianity is shrouded in confusion. The archaeologists and the theologians have made confusion worse confounded."[9]

Zeitlin feels that the disciples of John the Baptist and Jesus were enemies; later Christian theology created a tie which had actually not existed.[10]

Zeitlin's best-known work deals with the trial and crucifixion of Jesus. This book provides also a historical account of the period and a critical analysis of the sources. Zeitlin was troubled by the differences between the Mishnaic trial procedure and the Gospel account, and he concluded that the second-century Mishnah describes a Pharisaic court, while Jesus was tried by a Sadducean tribunal, which disappeared with the Temple. Zeitlin shows that the charges against Jesus were not punishable under Jewish law. Moreover, he rejects the theory of a special court summoned for this emergency; Jesus was not popular enough to create a crisis.[11] Zeitlin concluded that the Romans considered Jesus a rebel, while the High Priest disliked Jesus' interference in Temple affairs and summoned a political Sanhedrin to begin his removal. The High Priest phrased his questions so that the Sanhedrin would judge Jesus guilty of blasphemy. They could then hand him over to the Romans without qualms. The Romans felt endangered by his claim to be "King of the Jews"; in their eyes he was guilty of a political offense, and for this he was tried and executed. The High Priest was a quisling who betrayed others to save himself.[12] He and a small clique were responsible for delivering Jesus to Pilate, but later editors of the Gospels, who disliked the Jews, blamed them rather than Pilate. Zeitlin shows that the Apostolic Fathers, who polemicized at length against Judaism, never used this accusation.[13]

Zeitlin's views have not been widely accepted, although they have aroused considerable interest. He disagrees strongly with Klausner's evaluation of Jesus as an ethical man par excellence. "I beg leave to enter an emphatic denial. No, this conclusion cannot be accepted nor the ethical pre-eminence of a man admitted, whose acts were at times inconsistent with his moral teachings; who, even according to many modern Christian scholars, has contributed nothing new or original that was not already known to the Jews of that period, and whose very existence is denied by many Gentile scholars."[14]

In a number of reviews Zeitlin has touched on the life of Paul. He feels that "Paul wanted Judaism superseded by his new religion and the Jewish people assimilated with the Gentiles"; this led to animosity between Jew and Gentile.

Zeitlin sees little possibility of a genuine relationship between

Judaism and Christianity, for he considers dialogue "contrary to the history of true Judaism." Jews should acknowledge the influence of Christianity, which "brought monotheism to the pagan world." The primary need for a better relationship between the two religions is "the enlightenment of Christians about the true spirit of Judaism."[15] Zeitlin is not concerned with any grand distant goal, but with the building of a foundation on which later generations can progress.

The modern Israeli scholar David Flusser (b. 1915), who is professor of comparative religion at the Hebrew University in Jerusalem, has concerned himself primarily with the relationship of Jesus to various strands of the Jewish tradition. His works have been influenced by Winter and Daube, as well as others. His views have been set forth in essays, as well as in a volume on Jesus. In the spirit of ecumenism, this book was published by Herder and Herder, a Catholic firm. Flusser feels that a life of Jesus is easily possible since we have more information about him than most ancient figures. In his critical approach he agrees with R. Lindsey, seeking to base himself on an old account of Mark which was known to both Luke and Matthew.

Flusser feels that "the present age seems specially well disposed to understand him [Jesus] and his interests. A new sensitivity has been awakened in us by profound fear of the future, and of the present, to understand him and his interests. Today we are receptive to Jesus' reappraisal of all our usual values, and many of us have become aware of the questioning of the moral norm, which is his starting point too. . . . If we free ourselves from the chains of dead prejudice, we are able to appreciate his demand for undivided love, not as philanthropic weakness, but as a true psychological consequence."[16]

According to Flusser's biography of Jesus, many details of the life of Jesus, though questioned by other scholars, are appropriate to the first and second centuries. The Davidic ancestry provided for Jesus was also arranged for Bar Kokhba in order to legitimize his Messianic claim. Even the Virgin Birth and the miracles of Jesus have parallels in contemporary literature. Jesus' education, his precociousness shown while lost in the Temple, the tension within his family, need not be questioned.

Flusser also discusses the relationship of Jesus to John the Baptist, showing that the latter had a profound influence upon the former. "In Jesus' view, John was a prophet, if you like, the one who was preparing the way of God at the end of time, the Elijah who was to return."[17] Because Jesus felt compelled to go farther than John, he could not become a disciple.

Flusser sees Christianity's relationship to the Law differently from most scholars. The Law presented no problem to Jesus, but it was a problem for Paul in his effort to spread Christianity into Europe. "Had Christianity spread first to the eastern Asiatic regions, it would have had to develop a ritual and ceremonial law based on the Jewish law in order to become a genuine religion in that part of the world."[18] Paul wished to spread the religion westward. "The Graeco-Roman civilization was not based upon a ritualistic system of precepts and prohibitions. Thus the conquest of the Western world by Christianity was only possible if the new religion abandoned the ritualistic way of life."[19] Flusser proves that later misunderstanding of contemporary Jewish law shows Jesus to be opposed to the Law (Luke 6:1–5, Mark 7:5). When Jesus criticized Pharisaic practices and Sadducean ritual, he was echoing sentiments expressed by many first-century Jews who opposed hypocrisy in all forms.

Flusser emphasizes the distinctions between the Scribes and various groups of Pharisees who were not as united as it sometimes appears to modern scholars. The anti-Pharisaic polemic in rabbinic literature must not be overlooked.

The anti-Gentile nature of Jesus' statements is stressed. "The picture preserved for us by the first three gospels is clear: Jesus, the Jew, worked among Jews and wanted to work only among them."[20] This created difficulties for the Jewish-Christian sects. Though history soon by-passed them, they remained loyal to their traditions until the tenth century.

Flusser's most interesting contribution comes in a lengthy discussion of Jesus' ethic and his special emphasis on love. Flusser clearly shows that these statements of Jesus fit into the developments of the first century. "The black and white morality of the old covenant was clearly inadequate for the new sensitivity of the Jews of classical times."[21] Because all men are a mixture of good and evil, one should recognize these qualities in every man and see the capacity for repentance. You should therefore love your neighbor as though he were yourself. A Pharisaic tradition combined this with the injunction not to hate your evil neighbor. Thus we come very close to the "Love your enemy" of Jesus. The Essene influence on Jesus can also be traced, mainly through the pietistic approach to the neighbor demonstrated by the semi-Essene Testament of the Patriarchs, which went farther than the Essene "peaceful coexistence" with evil. The first-century emphasis on love of neighbor paralleled the teaching of love of God rather than awe of Him. The combination of love of God and of one's fellow man in a single statement was presented only by Jesus, but Flusser feels this was an accident.[22] His long discussion shows that Jesus' ethic may be understood in an uneschatological setting, although he does not underestimate Jesus' emphasis on the coming of the kingdom. Its imminence removed any necessity to resist evil; in this Jesus agreed with the Essenes.

Flusser stresses that Jesus and later Christianity went farther than Judaism through the demand to love one's enemy. Judaism limited itself to proscribing hatred of the enemy. "As has already been said, Christianity surpasses Judaism, at least theoretically, in its approach of love to all men, but its only genuine answer to the powerful wicked forces of this world is, as it seems, martyrdom. There is both human greatness and human weakness in our religions, but there is also the common hope for the kingdom of heaven."[23]

Although Jesus had premonitions of his death, he did not actively seek martyrdom, although that idea was also found in contemporary Jewish sources. Nor did he unequivocally declare himself to be the Messiah. At the end he was condemned by a group of Sadducees, not a regular court. The Pharisees were not connected with the trial, nor were the important men of the city, as we can see by the support provided by Nicodemus and Joseph of Arimathea.[24] Pilate's actions demonstrated his cruelty and weakness, which may also be seen from other sources.

Flusser's discussion of Paul is brief. Paul's Jewish and Greek learning are both regarded as limited. Paul's rejection of the Law was due to his preaching to the Gentiles of Europe, to whom the ritual would not be meaningful; this has already been discussed.

For Jewish-Christians, however, Paul considered the Law essential. In all other ways Paul had a positive attitude toward Judaism.

In other writings Flusser has extensively treated the Dead Sea Scrolls and their meaning for the period of the Second Commonwealth.

His approach to Christianity is sympathetic without condescension. His insights into the earliest period of Christianity have gained recognition by Christian scholars.

The noted French historian Jules Isaac (1877–1963) spent the last fifteen years of his life analyzing the Christian roots of anti-Semitism. This great scholar had shown little interest in Judaism before Nazi anti-Semitism killed members of his family and friends. In his subsequent studies of Christianity, he concentrated on the elements of the New Testament and the Church Fathers that contributed to the catastrophe suffered by the Jews in the twentieth century. Isaac sought to disprove seven commonly held Christian contentions which he felt provided the theoretical basis for this hatred; they were: the degenerate nature of Judaism at the time of Jesus, the sensuality of first-century Jews, the deliberate rejection of Jesus by the Jews, the rejection of the Jewish people by God, the charge of deicide, the Diaspora as punishment for the crucifixion, and the satanic nature of later Judaism.[25] Isaac tried to trace each idea from the New Testament and its commentaries to the present day.[26] He countered each charge with carefully assembled historical arguments. In the long sections devoted to deicide he stressed the human nature of Jesus and emphasized the Roman part in the crucifixion, which has often been neglected by later Christian writers.[27] Isaac was primarily concerned with changing current Christian teachings about Judaism. "The Christian religion does not require for her own glorification a corresponding disparagement of ancient Israel."[28] Isaac was a fine apologist, and he succeeded in changing French Catholic teachings.

Paul Winter (1904–1969), a Czech lawyer who survived the European Holocaust and settled in England, devoted himself to a systematic study of the trial of Jesus.[29] He concluded that the Romans granted local jurisdiction in nonpolitical matters and that the Sanhedrin possessed the power to try and execute within this limited jurisdiction. The High Priest was justified in his trial of Jesus because he sought thereby to avoid violence and to preserve a semblance of Jewish independence. Subsequent abortive revolts proved him correct. Loyalty to Rome was not altruistic since it served Sadducean interests. Winter judged Pilate to have been a good governor, as is shown by the length of his tenure in office and by the fact that Philo and Josephus describe him as a harsh, resolute figure, not the weakling of the Gospels.

Winter pointed to the numerous sects in first-century Judaism. "Many divisions among the Jewish people existed in the time of Jesus, but no religious party denied another the right to propagate their teaching."[30] Jesus faced no organized opposition during his lifetime—certainly not from the Pharisees, whose ethics were so akin to his own.

Another analysis of the trial of Jesus has been undertaken by an associate justice of Israel's Supreme Court, Haim Cohn (b. 1911).[31] He agrees with Winter that the Sanhedrin still exercised jurisdiction in capital cases but feels it did not try Jesus. He proves that Pilate, who was known for his merciless and despotic ways, had to try and sentence Jesus as soon as he claimed to be king of the Jews; he could not delegate this authority. Thus the entire section of the Gospels dealing with Barabbas, the people's clamor, and the High Priest's interference is unhistorical, for Pilate would have acted far more directly.

As Cohn moves from the Roman trial to that of the Sanhedrin, he shows that the New Testament account is inconsistent with our knowledge of this tribunal in matters of time, place, and procedure. Passover would have been a most inconvenient time for such a trial for a High Priest busy with Temple ritual. Had the High Priest been afraid that Jesus would rouse the people to rebellion, he or the Romans could have arrested him. Cohn comes to the original conclusion that the High Priest assembled a council, not a tribunal, in his chambers in an attempt to save Jesus and to prevent his execution by the Romans; by doing so he would have saved a popular figure and prevented a rebellion. The High Priest did not succeed; as a sign of failure he rent his clothes to mourn Jesus' forthcoming death.

Cohn marshals a mass of evidence from Jewish, Christian, and Roman sources for his lengthy reconstruction of the trial. However, his novel approach to the crucifixion is unlikely to gain much acceptance.

The English classics scholar David Daube (b. 1909) has undertaken a new approach to the New Testament literature and rabbinic Judaism in various monographs and essays.[32] He emphasizes the variety within first-century Judaism, pointing out that it was far less unified than is generally suspected. Some New Testament ideas, which appear strange to us, fit into first-century Judaism, even doctrines as foreign as Virgin Birth. Throughout his careful study Daube shows that the distinction between Hellenistic and rabbinic Judaism has been exaggerated; there was much interplay, and some forms of expression considered purely rabbinic contain Hellenistic roots. Daube does not concentrate on demonstrating the existence of verse-by-verse parallels in the New Testament and rabbinic literature; rather, he seeks to show how rabbinic ideas, legends, and forms of expression influenced the Gospels. Some New Testament pericopes reveal the influence of haggadic material; similarities in the construction of halakhic sections may be as important as verbal kinship. Many original ideas are presented in his studies, which represent modern objective scholarship and are not concerned with developing a Jewish attitude toward Christianity.

20

Some Conclusions

The last century and a half have seen the world change enormously; almost every field has been marked by progress. When one studies the Jewish-Christian dialogue against this background, however, change has been slow. Surprisingly little has happened, and in many ways we are not far removed from the days of Mendelssohn and his first approaches to this complex matter. We must now seek the reason for this limited progress, which has taken four avenues, all of which continue to be followed.

We have linked the beginning of a modern Jewish concern with Christianity to Moses Mendelssohn in the eighteenth century, but the conditions of Jewish life did not make dialogue possible until well into the next century. The poverty and exploitation of the ghetto demanded immediate attention; political and economic emancipation had to be achieved. The nineteenth century in Western Europe saw progress interspersed with periods of repression. In the Eastern lands nothing changed till the twentieth century. Moreover, because most Jews continued to live under vigorous persecution in Eastern Europe, the shadow of persecution remained ominously visible in the progressive states of the West. Even where direct manifestations of persecution had receded, the West European Jew was not secure; he never knew when a change in national policy might remove the rights he had so laboriously won.

The churches did nothing to alleviate anti-Semitic outbursts, and Christianity remained a source of hatred. In addition, its missionary efforts continued to be strong throughout the nineteenth century and Jewish converts were won, albeit more through social or economic pressure than religious conviction. Even if a West European Jew managed to overlook these matters, the pogroms in Russia and Poland could only embitter him. Often his coreligionists fled to Central Europe or passed through its ports on the way to America. He knew that the Eastern Church and Roman Catholicism in that area remained powerful agents of persecution. At every level, hatred of the Jews was encouraged. It was public policy in Russia to force a third of the Jews to emigrate, another third to convert, and let the remaining third be wiped out. Few churchmen spoke against such policies. Under these conditions statements of friendship toward Christianity by Jews would have been utter folly; even a scholar in the rarefied realm of books could not overlook such conditions.

Toward the end of the nineteenth century matters began to look more hopeful. The industrial revolution and the age of science had led to changes in policy, and the condition of the Jew improved. The churches also changed their attitude—but slowly. The best witness to the pace of change within Christianity is Vatican II, which considered some aspects of the Jewish-Christian relationship only after six million Jews had been killed. Even the much lauded statement on the Jews and the crucifixion remains mild and came only after much argument.

Against this gloomy background we are better able to understand the position taken by various Jewish scholars. Mendelssohn wished to avoid the entire area of discussion, fearing that such matters would hinder the emancipation of his coreligionists. Until faced with a personal challenge he avoided all involvement. Such reluctance still characterizes Jewish leaders in lands where Jewish communities are in a precarious position. The million Jews of South America have shown no interest in dialogue; Jewish communities in other lands have also assumed this stance whenever their position has been endangered. Real dialogue is obviously impossible under conditions of uncertain friendship. During periods of crisis the Jewish community still usually finds itself alone or with only the wavering support of the organized Christian community. Mendelssohn's position may not be our ideal, but it remains a realistic alternative.

The various positions reflected by nineteenth-century Jewish students of Christianity find strong echoes among American and European Jews today. Our position is akin to theirs; most of them were only a generation removed from persecution. Benamozegh, Salvador, Hirsch, Steinheim, Formstecher, and others felt reasonably secure in their respective lands. They were not subject to persecution, but its memory remained vivid. They were sufficiently at ease to defend their religion without hesitation, as is reflected in their vigorous critiques of Christianity. In short, this was a generation engaged in combat rather than dialogue. Its spokesmen wished to struggle directly against anti-Semitism and to destroy any new intellectual foundations it might develop in the philosophies of Hegel and Schelling. Their aggressive apologetical works may appear crude to us, and they obviously failed to understand another religious viewpoint or to appreciate the emotional feelings of members of another religious community. Nonetheless, their writings have positive value for us as a prolegomenon to dialogue, for they made the serious study of Christianity an area of legitimate Jewish concern. Jews slowly became accustomed to Jewish scholars writing about the religion of their neighbors. These writings also reminded Christian scholars that Jewish sources can make a contribution to the knowledge of early Christianity, though few Christians bothered to acknowledge this fact. The Jewish scholars of the mid-nineteenth century realized that the Church could now be attacked without fear of retaliation. Its power had faded, and its influence was constantly diminishing. The decline of Christianity was a hopeful sign. Jewish scholars saw it as beneficial for Judaism and mankind, for they believed that Judaism or a new religion akin to it would eventually become dominant. Although this optimism is gone, the weakening of Christianity is still welcomed by many contemporary Jews.

As Jews in many Western lands still find themselves in a position of doubtful security, the mid-nineteenth-century approach to Christianity continues. The destruction of European Jewry in the Holocaust cannot be forgotten. The Christian religious community did not arise to halt mass death. The churches were at best passive and occasionally encouraged the destruction of local Jewish communities. Apologetics and polemics continue, therefore, as an expression of Jewish thought. The path of Hermann Cohen, Max Brod, and Leo Baeck is still necessary in an indifferent world. We Jews need no longer guard ourselves against missionary efforts, although they have not ceased, but we must defend ourselves against mass destruction of political origin, which can sometimes count upon the churches as its ally. This point of view was reinforced by Christian indifference to Israel's plight during the Six-Day War of 1967. A new Holocaust was threatened by the Arab states, but the churches, with a few exceptions, remained silent. A large portion of the Jewish community justifiably remains very suspicious; it will take more than a few statements by individual members of the Christian community to change this attitude. Some crises must be weathered together; till then, apologetics and polemic will play a leading role in the Judeo-Christian relationship.

Perhaps the best basis for dialogue is the one built by the Jewish scholars who sought to reclaim Jesus, Paul, and early Christian literature for Judaism. Montefiore, Baeck, and Klausner were pioneers in this endeavor. Their efforts must be somewhat shocking to Christians, for the resulting pictures of Jesus and Paul are obviously distorted, and the Christian writings, when rewritten, may be only vaguely recognizable. Such ventures are always speculative, and the biases of the authors may leave them open to question. The significance of such efforts is not primarily in their scholarly accuracy, but in the desire to build bridges. How bold and original an approach to understanding! By seeking to discover some kinship with ancient figures as the basis of a relationship with modern Christianity, each of these scholars was able to treat Jesus in a sympathetic manner and to write of him with considerable respect. The suggested solutions to the problem of Paul may be somewhat ingenious, but they deflect much of the anti-Semitic bias of the New Testament and enable Jews to study it.

A great obstacle to interreligious discussion is the distaste of many Jews for Christian literature. Any effort which enables Jews to read the Gospels with less discomfort is a step in the proper direction. This generation led by Sandmel, Schoeps, and others has made serious contributions to New Testament studies, winning acknowledgment from both Jews and Christians.

Rosenzweig and Buber were able to begin dialogue itself, the first on a private basis through a long exchange of letters that were later published, and the second through public statements. Both men looked at the divisive issues more philosophically; they sought to understand the full depth of religious feeling and also understood their own limitations as sympathetic outsiders. The friendship expressed, the sincerity of the effort, should have resulted in a fruitful exchange, but both men were largely ignored. No earlier Jewish scholars, aside from Hermann Cohen, had viewed Christianity with such genuine understanding of the basic problems. These men were ready for dialogue, but the Christian community was not.

In America, Jewish concern with Christianity began a century ago, but it has developed more slowly than in Europe. The Central European Jews who came to this country in the early and middle 1800s eventually began to think about their relationship to the majority religion as shown by Wise, but the East European Jews, who began arriving at the turn of the century, considered such discussion taboo. Those who dealt with Christianity were condemned as disloyal to Judaism; the long tradition of persecution and numerous attempts at forced conversion made such efforts contemptible. This may account for the strong popular reaction against Joseph Klausner. The new immigrants faced more pressing problems than developing a contemplative approach to Christianity. They had to establish themselves in a new land, and, since the environment was not hostile, the problem of religious differences could be postponed.

The current American scene and the last two centuries in Europe point to the conditions necessary for dialogue. Enlightenment, freedom, and personal security are required before Jews can be interested in Christianity. These conditions have at least partially existed in Western Europe for two centuries, but they have never been attained in the Slavic lands, and as a result Jews there do not discuss Christianity. Continual contact with Christians is also needed to stimulate such discussion, so it is unlikely that Israeli Jewry will ever show great interest in this problem. On the other hand, the West European communities, although decimated, may continue to play some role in the development of new Jewish attitudes toward Christianity.

The various stages of the past cannot yet be discarded. Only a handful of Jews and Christians are ready for the level of Buber and

Rosenzweig; the remainder will follow other paths. Serious dialogue may continue if Christianity intends to engage in it. The statements of the various churches indicate a willingness to do so, but the actions of many churchmen bespeak a desire to refrain from deeper involvement.[1]

21

The Future

We must inquire about the future of the interreligious relationship and the direction it might take.

Among Liberal Jews, the discussion of Christianity has been carried on intermittently and as a peripheral area of scholarship. The most important factor leading to dialogue has been the decline of religious belief during the last two centuries. A growing number of Christians and Jews no longer consider religion a dominant element of their lives. Enlightenment, political and industrial revolutions, and the rise of scientific thought have created a powerful secular society. Superficially this society remains Christian, but religion is not taken seriously by large portions of the population. This makes dialogue easy, but irrelevant. Many Jews have welcomed secularization as a solution to thousands of years of religious persecution, but others, like Fackenheim, consider it the most important threat to Judaism. They feel that Judaism and Christianity can no longer afford to expend energy on mutual hostility. Rather, the two faiths must learn to understand each other in order to join together in the struggle against the secularism that threatens them both. In addition, some Jews feel that much more thought and energy should now be devoted to developing Jewish-Islamic understanding as well as a closer relationship with the other great world religions.

Dialogue may develop in the public arena, where it has usually been attempted, but it might be far more successful in the private realm. Perhaps meaningful encounters at this stage of history can only develop in the manner of Franz Rosenzweig and his friends—in close, intimate discussions. Rosenzweig's correspondence with Christians was characterized by frankness and deep friendship. The discussion developed easily because it was not intended for publication; it was allowed to ripen through the years and did not conclude with a single encounter, so characteristic of our impatient modern mood.

Our conversations with Christianity should be an avenue of mutual understanding. They must be founded upon a strong sense of security and mutual trust. Christians must be sensitive to our concern for Israel and to the Jewish plight in other lands, such as the Soviet Union.

In a pluralistic society, a well-defined relationship toward other religions must be developed, but it need not take the path of dialogue, popular though that be at the moment. Dialogue has definite limitations. It must take much for granted. It requires a level of understanding at which no subject is considered too sacred for study and discussion. As in the past, it will be necessary to continue to defend ourselves and to reevaluate Christianity. A critical understanding of Christianity is also desirable for the constantly changing pattern of Judaism.

Jewish studies of Christianity have been the exclusive province of Liberal Jews. Few Orthodox thinkers—excepting Emden, Mendelssohn, Kook, and Benamozegh—have written on this subject. Orthodoxy has considered the traditional position of Judaism adequate; it recognizes Christianity as a monotheistic religion but gives it a status below Judaism—Christianity is to prepare the world for Judaism; all further discussion is superfluous. Thus Orthodoxy has not entered the interreligious dialogue, and it has defined specific areas of contact between individual Jews and Christians with great precision in its vast legal literature, which forms the basis for personal and business relationships.

Some of the poverty of results from the dialogue is due to the limited range of the studies that have been undertaken. I do not only refer to the concentration on the early Christian tradition to the exclusion of most later developments in Christianity, but also to the framework within which these studies were undertaken. Almost all of them have been conducted in the realm of theology, philosophy, or history. It is possible and relatively easy to approach Christianity through these disciplines, and one finds the

Christian material readily available when studied from these perspectives. Yet theology lies outside the mainstream of Jewish tradition.

There has always been Jewish theology, but through most of the centuries it was developed in the form of the Midrash, the homily, rather than in systematic fashion. One might almost say that there is no Jewish systematic theology. Thus, the vast Christian theological literature may be studied in great detail, but the area remains alien to the Jewish mind, and as a result such efforts will be viewed only with mild interest.

One must express similar reservations about Jewish philosophy. There is a long tradition of the development of philosophical thought in Judaism. The tradition is old and is studded with great names, but except for the Spanish-Jewish community, philosophy was never the central concern of Judaism. Jewish philosophers are remembered primarily because of their work in other areas; their contributions to philosophy have been almost incidental. Maimonides, the greatest Jewish philosopher of the Middle Ages, is remembered by the tradition for his legal compendium, the *Mishneh Torah*, not for the *Guide to the Perplexed*, his philosophical masterpiece. Philosophy has never been central to Jewish life.

As Protestant and Catholic scholarly bias decreases, Jewish scholars have found it possible to become completely objective. The high standards of much modern scholarship make it almost impossible to distinguish the work of Christian and Jewish New Testament specialists. This development has led to the writing of better history, but it leaves the task of defining the relationship between Judaism and Christianity to someone else. This has now become the work of the theologian, not of the historian, who so often undertook it in the past.

Jews have made significant contributions to New Testament studies, but to the exclusion of most other periods of Christian history. Few Jews have concerned themselves with the later development of Christianity and later Jewish-Christian relations. There are some notable books in this area by Blumencranz, Simon, Katz, Hailperin, Werner, Sholem, and others, but the number remains small. The Christian study of Judaism has often ended with the New Testament; we should not make the same mistake in our study of Christianity.

If Christianity is to be understood by Jews, and if we are to participate in dialogue with Christians, it will have to be approached in ways normative to Judaism in addition to the paths of history, Biblical studies, and philosophy. A study of the legal tradition and the mystical literature of Christianity may bring us closer together.

Mysticism is only slowly regaining popularity in our age, but it was very important for the religious life of Judaism throughout the Middle Ages. The mystical literature was immensely popular. Considerable common ground can surely be found with Christianity.

The approach of Christianity through law might be fruitful; Judaism has always been a religion of law. Liberal Judaism, which discarded law in its initial revolt, is again adopting Jewish legal forms. All of Judaism has consistently been expressed through legal statements. The literature is vast; responsa, novellae, commentaries, compendia, and various ancillary works have always stood at the center of our tradition. A study of the legal tradition in Judaism and Christianity would lead to a better relationship.

Much work in common has been done by Jewish and Protestant Biblical scholars in the realm of texts, dealing primarily with the original meaning of Biblical statements. Such work is good, but largely irrelevant to the modern person, for it strips the texts of the overtones accrued during several millennia. A religion develops from interpretations, which are quite independent of the original meaning or slight corruptions in ancient records. Very few comparative studies of Biblical commentators and their exegesis have been undertaken. This would approach theology, but without the disadvantages of systematic theology. These and other routes might be profitably explored if we are to understand each other better.

It is tempting for Jews to assert that the declining power of Christianity makes dialogue unimportant. The churches have suffered enormous attrition in almost every land, but this does not mark the end of Christianity. Modern secular philosophies have failed to satisfy the religious yearnings of man, and so he will seek new strength from the religion of his fathers. Christianity is seeking ways of adapting itself to this challenge. During this period of adjustment there is a unique opportunity for a permanent better understanding between Judaism and Christianity—whether we decide to struggle against secularism side by side or each alone.

Christianity remains a force in the modern world. It has changed and will continue to change in its effort to survive and adapt itself to the twentieth century. It cannot be ignored—it must be understood. The Jewish study of Christianity is especially important for us in the United States because our contacts with Christians play a major part in our lives. In practical matters Jews and Christians have been able to work together; there are no theological differences in dealing with the poverty-stricken peoples of the world. It is possible to go farther and necessary to strive toward dialogue, but it would be folly to expect results soon.

Bibliography

Agus, J. B. *The Evolution of Jewish Thought from Biblical Times to the Opening of the Modern Era*. London, 1959.

——. *Modern Philosophies of Judaism*. New York, 1941.

——. "Claude Montefiore and Liberal Judaism" *Conservative Judaism* 13 (1959): 1-20.

Ahad Ha-Am. "Al sh'teh ha-s'ifim." *Al Parashat Derakhim*. Berlin, 1925, 4:38–58.

Badt-Strauss, B. *Moses Mendelssohn: Der Mensch und das Werk.*, Berlin, 1929.

Baeck, L. *Aus Drei Jahrtausenden*. Tübingen, 1948.

——. *Das Evangelium Als Urkunde der Jüdischen Glaubensgeschichte*. Berlin, 1938.

——. *Dieses Volk, Jüdische Existenz*. Frankfurt, 1957.

——. *The Essence of Judaism*. Trans. V. Grubenwieser and L. Pearl. 1936. Reprint. New York, 1948.

——. "Harnack's Vorlesung über das Wesen des Christentums." *Monatsschrift für die Geschichte und Wissenschaft des Judentums* 45 (1901).

——. *Judaism and Christianity*. Trans. W. Kaufmann. Philadelphia, 1958.

——. "Judaism in the Church." *Hebrew Union College Annual* 2 (1925): 125–144.

——. *The Pharisees and Other Essays*. New York, 1947.

——. "Romantische Religion." In *Festschrift zur 50 Jährigen Bestehung der Hochschule für die Wissenschaft des Judentums*. Berlin, 1922.

——. "Some Questions to the Christian Church from the Jewish Point of View." In *The Church and the Jewish People*. Ed. G. Hendenquist. London, 1954.

———. *Von Moses Mendelssohn zu Franz Rosenzweig*. Stuttgart, 1948.

———. *Wege im Judentum* Berlin, 1933.

Balthaser, H. U. von. *Martin Buber and Christianity*. Trans. A. Dru. New York, 1960.

Baron, S. W. *A Social and Religious History of the Jews*. 10 vols. New York, 1965–1972.

Barth, M. "Paul: Apostate or Apostle." *Judaism* 12 (1963): 370–375.

Bauer, B. *Die Judenfrage*. Brunswick, 1843.

Benamozegh, E. *Israël et l'Humanité*. Paris, 1914.

———. *Morale Juive et Morale Chrétienne*. Paris, 1914.

Bergmann, J. *Jüdische Apologetik im neutestamentlichen Zeitalter*. Berlin, 1908.

———. "Paulus." In *Jüdisches Lexikon*. Berlin, 1929.

Berkovits, E. *A Jewish Critique of the Philosophy of Martin Buber*. New York, 1962.

Bloch, J. S. *Israel und die Völker*. Berlin, 1922.

Blüher, H., and Schoeps, H. J. *Streit um Israel: Ein jüdisch-christliches Gespräch*. Hamburg, 1933.

Blumenkranz, B. *Juifs et Chrétiens dans les Monde Occidental (430–1096)*. Paris, 1960.

Bonsirven, L., *Les Juifs et Jésus*. Paris, n.d.

Borowitz, E. B. *A New Jewish Theology in the Making*. Philadelphia, 1968.

Brod, M. *Der Meister*. Gütersloh, 1952.

———. *Heidentum, Christentum, Judentum, ein Bekenntnisbuch*. Munich, 1922.

———. *Tycho Brahe's Weg zu Gott*. Berlin, 1915.

Buber, M. *Der Jude und Sein Judentum*. Cologne, 1963.

———. *For the Sake of Heaven: A Chronicle*. Trans. L. Lewisohn. Philadelphia, 1953.

———. *Israel and the World: Essays in a Time of Crisis*. New York, 1948.

———. *Nachlese*. Heidelberg, 1966.

———. *The Origin and Meaning of Hasidism*. Trans. M. Friedman. New York, 1960.

———. *Two Types of Faith: The Interpretation of Judaism and Christianity*. Trans. N. Goldhawk. New York, 1951.

———. *Werke*. Munich, 1962.

———, and Rosenzweig, F. *Die Schrift und ihre Verdeutschung*. Berlin, 1936.

Cohen, A. A. *The Myth of the Judeo-Christian Tradition*. New York, 1957.

———. *The Natural and the Supernatural Jew*. New York, 1964.

Cohen, H. *Die Religion der Vernunft aus den Quellen des Judentums*. Berlin, 1911.

———. *Jüdische Schriften*. Ed. F. Rosenzweig. Berlin, 1924.

Cohn, H. *The Trial and Death of Jesus*. New York, 1971.

Daube, D. *Concerning the Reconstruction of the Aramaic Gospels*. Manchester, 1945.

———. *He That Cometh*. London, 1966.

———. *The New Testament and Rabbinic Judaism*. Oxford, 1956.

———. *The Sudden in the Scriptures*. London, 1964.

Delitzsch, F. *Jesus und Hillel: Mit Rücksicht auf Renan und Geiger*. Erlangen, 1879.

Diamond, M. L. *Martin Buber: Jewish Existentialist*. New York, 1960.

Diwalt, H., ed. *Lebendiger Geist*. Leiden, 1959.

Dubnow, S. *Weltgeschichte des Jüdischen Volkes*. Trans. A. Steinfeld. Berlin, 1925.

Edelman, L., ed. *Face to Face: A Primer in Dialogue*. Washington, 1967.

Elbogen, I. *A Century of Jewish Life*. Philadelphia, 1944.

———. *Geschichte der Juden in Deutschland*. Berlin, 1935.

Elk, M. "Neues Testament." In *Jüdisches Lexikon*. Berlin, 1929.

Eloesser, A. *Vom Ghetto Nach Europa: Das Judentum im geistigen Leben des 19. Jahrhunderts*. Berlin, 1936.

Enelow, H. *Jewish Views of Jesus*. New York, 1920.

Eschelbacher, J. *Das Judentum und das Wesen des Christentums*. Berlin, 1905.

Fackenheim, E. *God's Presence in History*. New York, 1970.

———. "Jewish Values in the Post-Holocaust Future." *Judaism* 16 (1967): 269–273.

———. *Quest for Past and Future*. London, 1968.

Finkel, A. *The Pharisees and the Teacher of Nazareth*. Leiden, 1964.

Flusser, D. "Blessed Are the Poor in Spirit." *Israel Exploration Journal* 10 (1960).

————. *Dead Sea Sect and Pre-Pauline Christianity.* Scripta Hierosolyitana IV. Jerusalem, 1958.

————. *Jesus.* Trans. R. Walls. New York, 1969.

————. "Jesus." In *Encyclopedia Judaica.* Jerusalem, 1971.

————. "Jesus in the Context of History." In *The Crucible of Christianity.* Ed. A. Toynbee. London, 1969.

————. "A Literary Approach to the Trial of Jesus." *Judaism* 20 (1971): 32–36.

————. "Melchizedek and the Son of Man." *Christian News from Israel,* 1966.

————. "A New Sensitivity in Judaism and the Christian Message." *Harvard Theological Review* 61 (1968): 107–127.

————. "New Evidence on Jesus." *New York Times,* Feb. 13, 1972.

————. "Paul of Tarsus." In *Encyclopedia Judaica.* Jerusalem, 1971.

————. "Qumram und die Zwölf. In *Initation.* Leiden, 1965.

Formstecher, S. *Die Religion des Geistes.* Frankfurt, 1841.

Freehof, S. B. *Reform Jewish Practice and Its Rabbinic Background.* New York, 1963.

Friedlander, A. H. *Leo Baeck: Teacher of Theresienstadt.* New York, 1968.

Friedländer, G. *Sources of the Sermon on the Mount.* London, 1911.

Friedländer, M. *Synagogue und Kirche in Ihren Anfängen.* Berlin, 1908.

Friedman, M. S. *Martin Buber: The Life of Dialogue.* New York, 1955.

Geiger, A. "Bruno Bauer und die Juden." *Wissenschaftliche Zeitschrift für jüdische Theologie* 5 (1844): 199–234, 325–371.

————. "Entstehung des Christenthums." *Jüdische Zeitschrift für Wissenschaft und Leben* 11 (1874): 8–17.

————. *Das Judenthum und seine Geschichte.* Breslau, 1864.

————. "Das Judenthum unserer Zeit und die Bestrebung in Ihm." *Wissenschaftliche Zeitschrift für jüdische Theologie* 1 (1835): 1–2.

————. "Jüdische Philosophie." *Jüdische Zeitschrift für Wissenschaft und Leben* 1 (1862): 276–282.

————. *Ueber den Austritt aus dem Judenthume. Ein Aufgefundener Briefwechsel.* Leipzig, 1858.

————. *Urschrift und Übersetzung der Bibel.* Breslau, 1857.

Geiger, L. *Abraham Geiger: Leben und Lebenswerk.* Berlin, 1910.

————, ed. *Abraham Geiger's Leben in Briefen.* Breslau, 1885.

———, ed. *Nachgelassene Schriften, A. Geiger*. Berlin, 1875.

Glatzer, N. N., *Franz Rosenzweig: His Life and Thought*. New York, 1953.

Goldschmidt, H. L. *Die Botschaft Des Judentums*. Frankfurt, 1960.

Goldschmidt, J. *Das Wesen des Judentums 1907*.

Goldstein, M. *Jesus in the Jewish Tradition*. New York, 1950.

Graetz, H. *Geschichte der Juden. 11 vols. Leipzig, 1853–76*.

———. *Sinai et Golgotha*. Paris, 1867.

Güdemann, M. *Geschichte des Erziehungswesens und der Cultur der Abendländischen Juden*. Amsterdam, 1966.

———. *Jüdisches im Christentum des Reformationszeitalter*. Vienna, 1870.

Guillon, N. S. *Examen critiques des doctrines de Gibbon, due docteur Strauss et de M. Salvador sur Jésus-Christ, son Evangile et son Eglise*. Paris, 1840.

Gutmann, J. "Jesus in jüdischen Quellen." In *Encyclopaedia Judaica*. Berlin, 1932.

Gutmann, J. *Die Philosophie Des Judentums*. Munich, 1933.

Gutmann, M. *Das Judentum und seine Umwelt*. Berlin, 1927.

Hailperin, H. *Rashi and the Christian Scholars*. Pittsburgh, 1963.

Halevi, J. *Kuzari*. Trans. Ibn Tibbon. Jerusalem, 1950.

Hammerstein, F. von. *Das Messiasproblem bei Martin Buber*. Stuttgart, 1958.

Harnack, A. *Christianity and History*. London, 1907.

———. *Das Wesen des Christentums*. Berlin, 1900.

Heller, J. G. *Issaac M. Wise: Life, Work and Thought*, New York, 1965.

Hensel, S. *Die Familie Mendelssohn*. Leipzig, 1929.

Herberg, W. *Protestant–Catholic—Jew*. New York, 1956.

———, ed. *The Writings of Martin Buber*. New York, 1956.

Herford, R. T. "Jesus in Rabbinical Literature." In *Universal Jewish Encyclopedia*. New York, 1941.

Hirsch, E. G. *The Crucifixion, Viewed from a Jewish Standpoint*. New York, 1908.

Hirsch, S. *Das Judentum, der christliche Staat und die moderne wissenschaftliche Kritik. 1843*.

———. *Die Humanität als Religion*. Trier, 1854.

———. *Die Religionsphilosophie der Juden*. Leipzig, 1842.

Isaac, J. *Has Anti-Semitism Roots in Christianity?* Trans. J. Parkes. New York, 1961

——. *Jésus et Israël.* Paris, 1947.

——. *The Teaching of Contempt: Christian Roots of Anti-Semitism.* Trans. H. Weaver. New York, 1964.

Jacob, B., *Auge um Auge.* Berlin, 1929.

——. *Im Namen Gottes.* Berlin, 1903.

——. *Die Stellung Jesu zum mosaischen Gesetz.* 1893.

Jacob, E. I. "Christianity." In *Universal Jewish Encyclopedia.* New York, 1948.

——. "Christentum." In *Encyclopaedia Judaica.* Berlin, 1932.

——. "Jesus of Nazareth." In *Universal Jewish Ecnyclopedia.* New York, 1941.

——. "New Testament." In *Universal Jewish Encyclopedia.* New York, 1941.

——. "Paul." In *Universal Jewish Encyclopedia.* New York, 1941.

Jacob, W. "The Inter-religious Dialogue." *Jewish Heritage,* 6 (1963): 31–35.

——. "The Inter-religious Dialogue: Three Jewish Pioneers." In *Face to Face,* ed. L. Edelman. Washington, 1967.

——. "Kaufmann Kohler on Christianity." *Central Conference of American Rabbis Journal* 21 (1974): 47–54.

——. "To Rome with Cardinal Wright." In Selection of Sermons. 4 (1970): 3–13.

Jacobs, J. *Jesus as Others Saw Him.* New York, 1925.

Jelski, J. *Das Wesen des Judentums.* Berlin, 1902.

Joseph, M. "Apostel." In *Jüdisches Lexikon.* Berlin, 1929.

——. "Jesus von Nazarüt." In *Jüdisches Lexikon.* Berlin, 1929.

Jost, J. M. *Geschichte Des Judenthums und Seiner Sekten.* Leipzig, 1859.

Journal of Ecumenical Studies 1–12 (1958–1972.)

Kaminka, A. "Torat Hakhmey Yisrael ve-ha-agadah ha-Notzrit." *Hator* 3 (1922): 59–77.

Kaplan, M. *The Purpose and Meaning of Jewish Existence.* Philadelphia, 1964.

Karo, J. *Shulchan Arukh.* New York, 1953.

Karpeles, V. G. *Geschichte der Jüdischen Literatur.* Berlin, 1909.

Katz, J. *Exclusiveness and Tolerance.* Oxford, 1961.

———. "To Whom Was Mendelssohn Replying in *Jerusalem?*" *Zion* 29 (1964): 112–132.

Kayserling, M. "Moses Mendelssohn." *Jeshurun* 4 (1858): 132–140.

———. *Moses Mendelssohn.* Leipzig, 1862.

Klatzkin, J. *Hermann Cohen.* Berlin, 1921.

Klausner, J. *From Jesus to Paul* Trans. W. Stinespring. 1943. Reprint. Boston, 1961.

———. *Jesus.* Berlin, 1934.

———. *Jesus of Nazareth: His Life, Times, and Teachings.* Trans. H. Danby. 1925. Reprint. Boston, 1964.

———. "Jesus von Nazareth." In *Encyclopaedia Judaica.* Berlin, 1932.

Kohler, K. "Christianity." In *Jewish Encyclopedia.* New York, 1903.

———. "Didache." In *Jewish Encyclopedia.* New York, 1903.

———. *Jewish Theology.* New York, 1928.

———. "New Testament." In Jewish Encyclopedia. New York, 1903.

———. *The Origins of the Synagogue and the Church.* New York, 1929.

———. "Saul of Tarsus." In *Jewish Encyclopedia.* New York, 1903.

Kohn, H. *Martin Buber: Sein Werk und Seine Zeit.* Cologne, 1961.

Krauss, S. "Apostel." In *Encyclopaedia Judaica.* Berlin, 1932.

———. "Jesus." In *Jewish Encyclopedia.* New York, 1903.

———. "The Jews in the Works of the Church Fathers." *Jewish Quarterly Review,* o.s. 5 (1893): 122–157; 6 (1894): 82–99, 225–261.

———. *Das Leben Jesu nach jüdischen Quellen.* Breslau, 1902.

Landman, I. "Judaism's Attitude Toward Christians." In *Universal Jewish Encyclopedia,* New York, 1941.

Lewkowitz, A. *Das Judentum und die geistigen Strömungen des 19. Jahrhunderts.* Breslau, 1935.

Loewenberg, J. *Aus jüdischer Seele.* Hamburg, 1900.

———. *Kämpfen und Bauen.* Hamburg, 1925.

Lindeskog, G. *Die Jesusfrage im Neuzeitlichen Judentum.* Uppsala, 1938.

Macquarrie, J. *Twentieth Century Religious Thought.* New York, 1963.

Maimonides, M. Mishneh Torah. New York, 1960.

———. *Moreh Nevukhim.* New York, 1952.

Marcus, J. R. *The Americanization of I. M. Wise.* Cincinnati, 1931.

May, M. B. *Isaac Mayer Wise, The Founder of American Judaism: A Biography.* New York, 1916.

Mayer, R. *Christentum und Judentum in der Schau Leo Baecks.* Stuttgart, 1961.

Melber, J. *Hermann Cohen's Philosophy of Judaism.* New York, 1968.

Mendelssohn, M. *Gesammelte Schriften.* Leipzig, 1844.

———. *Gessammelte Schriften.* Ed. F. Bamberger. Berlin, 1929.

———. *Jerusalem.* Trans. M. Samuels. London, 1838.

Mevorah, B. "The Background of Lavater's Appeal ot Mendelsohn." *Zion* 30 (1965): 158–170.

Meyer, M. A. *The Origins of the Modern Jew.* Detroit, 1967.

Montefiore, C. *The Bible for Home Reading.* London, 1899.

———. *Liberal Judaism: An Essay.* London, 1903.

———. *Liberal Judaism and Hellenism and Other Essays.* London, 1918.

———. *The Old Testament and After.* London, 1923.

———. *Outlines of Liberal Judaism.* London, 1923.

———. *Rabbinic Literature and Gospel Teachings.* London, 1930.

———. *Some Elements of the Religious Teaching of Jesus According to the Synoptic Gospels.* London, 1910.

———. *The Synoptic Gospels.* London, 1927.

———. *Truth in Religion and Other Sermons.* London, 1906.

———. "Unitarianism and Judaism in Their Relationship to Each Other." *Jewish Quarterly Review,* o.s. 9 (1897): 240–253.

Parkes, J. *The Conflict of the Church and the Synagogue.* 1934. Reprint. Cleveland, 1961.

Petuchowski, J. J. *Heirs of the Pharisees.* New York, 1970.

Pfeiffer, R. H. *History of New Testament Times: With an Introduction to the Apocrypha.* New York, 1949.

Philippson, L. *Haben die Juden wirklich Jesum gekreuzigt.* Berlin, 1901.

Philippson, M. *Neueste Geschichte des jüdischen Volkes.* Leipzig, 1907.

Philipson, D. *The Reform Movement in Judaism.* New York, 1931.

Plaut, W. G. *The Growth of Reform Judaism: American and European Sources until 1948.* New York, 1965.

———. *The Rise of Reform Judaism: A Source Book of its European Origins.* New York, 1963.

Raisin, J. S. *Gentile Reactions to Jewish Ideals.* New York, 1953.

Renan, E. *La vie de Jésus.* Paris, 1863.

Rieger, P. "Christentum." In *Jüdisches Lexikon. Berlin, 1929.*

Rivkin, E. *Judaism and Christianity.* New York, 1969.

————. *The Shaping of Jewish History: A Radical New Interpretation*. New York, 1971.

Rosenbluth, P. E., et al. "Tradition in Judentum, Franz Rosenzweig —Martin Buber." *Emuna Horizonte* 5 (1970).

Rosenzweig, F. *Briefe*. Berlin, 1925.

————. *Kleinere Schriften*. Berlin, 1937.

————. *Der Stern der Erlösung*. Heidelberg, 1930.

Rotenstreich, N. *Jewish Philosophy in Modern Times: From Mendelssohn to Rosenzweig*. San Francisco, 1968.

Rubenstein, R. L. *After Auschwitz*. New York, 1966.

————. *My Brother Paul*. New York, 1972.

————. *The Religious Imagination*. New York, 1968.

Sachar, H. M. *The Course of Modern Jewish History*. Cleveland, 1958.

Salvador, G. *Joseph Salvador, sa Vie, ses oeuvres, et ses critiques*. Paris, 1881.

Salvador, J. *Geschichte der Mosaischen Institutionen und des jüdischen Volkes*. Trans. G. Essenna. Hamburg, 1856.

————. *Historie des institutions de Moise et due peuple he'breux*. Paris, 1828.

————. *Histoire de la Domination Romaine en Judee et de la Ruine de Jerusalem*. Brussels, 1847.

————. *Das Leben Jesu und seine Lehre*. Trans. H. Jacobson. Dresden, 1841.

————. *La Loi de Moise*. Paris, 1822.

————. *Paris, Rome, Jerusalem, ou la question religieuse au XIXe siecle*. Paris, 1860.

Sandmel, S. "Apostle." In *Encyclopedia Judaica*. Jerusalem, 1971.

————. *The First Christian Century in Judaism and Christianity*. New York, 1960.

————. *The Genius of Paul*. New York, 1958.

————. "Isaac Mayer Wise's 'Jesus Himself.'" In *Essays in American Jewish History*. Cincinnati, 1948.

————. "Jewish Scholars and Early Christianity." In *Seventy-fifth Anniversary Volume of Jewish Quarterly Review*. Philadelphia, 1967.

————. *A Jewish Understanding of the New Testament*. Cincinnati, 1956.

————. "Judaism, Jesus, and Paul." *Vanderbilt Studies in the Humanities* I (1951): 220–250.

————. "Myths, Genealogies, Jewish Myth and the Development of the Gospels." *Hebrew Union College Annual* 27 (1956): 201–212.

————. "Parallelomania." *Journal of Biblical Literature* 81 (1962): 1–13.

————. *We Jews and Jesus.* New York, 1965.

Schneelmelcher, W. *Verkündigung und Forschung.* Berlin, n.d.

Schoeps, H. J. *Barocke Juden, Christen, und Judenchristen.* Munich, 1965.

————. *Geschichte der jüdischen Religionsphilosophie in der Neuzeit.* Berlin, 1953.

————. *The Jewish Christian Argument.* New York, 1963 (*Israel und Christenheit*, Berlin, 1937)

————. *Jewish Christianity: Factional Disputes in the Early Church.* Philadelphia, 1969.

————. *Das Judenchristentum.* Bern, 1964.

————. *Jüdischer Glaube in dieser Zeit.* Berlin, 1932.

————. *Der Moderne Mensch und die Verkündigung der Religionen.* Antwerp, 1939.

————. *Paul: The Theology of the Apostle in the Light of Jewish Religious History.* Philadelphia, 1961.

————. *Philosemitismus im Barock.* Tübingen, 1952.

————. *Salomon Ludwig Steinheim zum Gedenken.* Leiden, 1966.

————. *Studien zur unbekannten Religions und Geistesgeschichte.* Göttingen, 1963.

————. *Theologie und Geschichte des Judenchristentums.* Tübingen, 1949.

————. *Was ist der Mensch? Philosophische Anthropologie als Geistesgeschichte.* Berlin, 1960.

————. *Was-ist und was will die Geistesgeschichte?* Göttingen, 1959.

Schwartz, F. C. "Claude Montefiore on Law and Tradition." *Jewish Quarterly Review* 55 (1964–65): 23–52.

Schweitzer, A. *Paul and His Interpreters: A Critical History.* Trans. W. Montgomery. 1912. Reprint. New York, 1964.

————. *The Quest of the Historical Jesus.* Trans. W. Montogomery. New York, 1910.

Seltzer, S. "Reactions to Jesus in the Reform Rabbinate." Unpublished thesis, Hebrew Union College, 1959.

Simon, A. *Verus Israel: Etudes sur les relations entre Chretiens et Juifs dans l'Empire romain (135–425).* Paris, 1947.

Simon, E., et al. *Al Franz Rosenzweig.* Jerusalem, 1956.

Smith, M. "Das Judenchristentum, A Review." *Journal of Biblical Literature* 84.

Smith, R. *Martin Buber*. Richmond, 1967.

Steinheim, S. L. *Die Offenbarungs lehre nach dem Lehrbegriff der Synagogue*. Leipzig, 1863.

Strack, H. L., and Billerbeck, P. *Kommentar zum Neuen Testament aus Talmud und Midrasch*. Berlin, 1929.

Tradition und Erneuerung. Zeitschrift der Vereinigung Für Religios-Liberales Judentum in der Schweiz, 1957-1973.

Trattner, E. R. *As a Jew Sees Jesus*. London, 1931.

Troki, I. *Faith Strengthened*. Trans. M. Mocatta. New York, 1970.

Vogel, M. "The Jewish-Christian Argument—A Review Essay." *Journal of Bible and Religion* 33 (1965): 131-136.

Walker, T. *Jewish Views on Jesus*. London, 1931.

Wallach, L. *Liberty and Letters: The Thoughts of Leopold Zunz*. London, 1959.

Walter, H. *Moses Mendelssohn: Critic and Philosopher*. New York, 1930.

Weltsch, R. "Jesus in jüdischen Darstellungen der jüngsten Zeit." In *Jüdisches Lexikon*, Berlin, 1929.

Werblowsky, Z. "Christianity." In *Encyclopedia Judaica*. Jerusalem, 1971.

Wiener, M., ed. *Abraham Geiger and Liberal Judaism*. Philadelphia, 1962.

Winter, P. *On the Trial of Jesus*. Berlin, 1961.

Wise, I. M. *A Defense of Judaism versus Proselytizing Christianity*. Cincinnati, 1889.

———. *Judaism and Christianity*. Cincinnati, 1883.

———. *Martyrdom of Jesus of Nazareth*. Cincinnati, 1888.

———. *Origin of Christianity*. Cincinnati, 1868.

———. "Paul and the Mystics." In *Selected Writings of I. M. Wise*, ed. Philipson and Grossman. Cincinnati, 1900.

———. *Reminscences*. Cincinnati, 1901.

Wolf, A. J. "The Dilemma of Claude Montefiore" *Conservative Judaism* 13 (1959): 22-25.

Wünsche, A. *Neue Beiträge zur Erläuterung der Evangelien aus Talmud Midrasch*. Göttingen, 1878.

Zeitlin, S. "The Crucifixion of Jesus Re-Examined." *Jewish Quarterly Review* 31 (1940-1941): 327-369; 32 (1941-1942): 175-189, 279-301.

———. "The Dates of the Birth and the Crucifixion of Jewus." *Jewish Quarterly Review* 55 (1964–1965): 1–22.

———. "The Duration of Jesus' Ministry." *Jewish Quarterly Review* 55 (1964–1965): 181–200.

———. "The Halaka in the Gospels and Its Relation to the Jewish Law in the Time of Jesus." *Hebrew Union College Annual* 1 (1924): 357–373.

———. "The Ecumenical Council." *Jewish Quarterly Review* 56 (1965–1966): 93–111.

———. "Essenes and Messianic Expectations." *Jewish Quarterly Review* 45 (1954–1955): 83–119.

———. "From Jesus to Paul." *Jewish Quarterly Review* 31 (1940–1941): 309–321.

———. *Josephus on Jesus.* New York 1931.

———. "The Pharisees." *Jewish Quarterly Review* 16 (1925–1926): 383–394.

———. "The Pharisees: A Historical Study." *Jewish Quarterly Review* 52 (1961–1962):

———. "The Pharisees and the Gospels." In *Essays and Studies in Memory of Linda R. Miller.* New York, 1938.

———. "The Prophet of Nazareth." *Jewish Quarterly Review* 52 (1961–1962): 187–189.

———. "Studies in the Beginnings of Christianity." *Jewish Quarterly Review* 14 (1923–1924): 111–139.

———. *Who Crucified Jesus?* New York, 1964.

Notes

Notes to Chapter 1

1. A. Simon, *Verus Israel, Etudes sur les relations entre Christiens et Juifs dans l'Empire romain (135–425)* (Paris, 1947); Berhnard Blumenkranz, *Juifs et Chrétiens dans le Monde Occidental (430–1096)*, (Paris, 1960); Jacob Katz, *Exclusiveness and Tolerance* (Oxford, 1961); S. W. Baron, *A Social and Religious History of the Jews* (New York, 1965), vol. 9, chaps. 28, 29, and especially notes to pp. 266 ff.

Notes to Chapter 2

1. Ernest I. Jacob, "Christianity," *Universal Jewish Encyclopedia*, 3:181.
2. Jacob Katz, *Exclusiveness and Tolerance* (Oxford, 1961), p. 121.
3. *Ibid.*, 167.

Notes to Chapter 3

1. Brief an Homburg, *Gesammelte Schriften* (Leipzig, 1844), 5:668.
2. Lavater an Mendelssohn, *Gesammelte Schriften* (Berlin, 1930), 7:3.
3. Schreiben an Lavater, *Gesammelte Schriften*, 7:7 f.
4. *Jerusalem*, trans. M. Samuels (London, 1838), 2:87 f.
5. Mendelssohn an Lavater, *Gesammelte Schriften*, 7:362.
6. Gegenbetrachtungen, *Gesammelte Schriften*, 7:93.
7. *Ibid.*, 7:lxxxi f.
8. *Ibid.*, 7:101.
9. *Ibid.*, 91.
10. Mendelssohn an Lavater, *Gesammelte Schriften*, 7:362.
11. Reply to Charles Bonnet, *Jerusalem*, 1:171 f.
12. *Jerusalem*, 1:167 f.
13. *Ibid.*, 2:89.
14. *Ibid.*, 2:96 f.
15. Mendelssohn an den Erbprinzen, *Gesammelte Schriften*, 7:304.
16. *Ibid.*, 305.
17. Gegenbetrachtungen, *Gesammelte Schriften*, 7:73.
18. "Was ihn zu diesen Schritte bewogen?" *Gesammelte Schriften*, 7:63
19. *Jerusalem*, 2:85.

20. Reply to Charles Bonnet, *Jerusalem*, 1:160 f.
21. Reply to Lavater, *Jerusalem*, 1:154.
22. *Jerusalem*, 1:151 ff.
23. J. Katz, "To Whom Was Mendelssohn Replying in *Jerusalem*?" *Zion* 29, no. 1–2 (1964): 113 ff.

Notes to Chapter 4

1. *La loi de Moise* (Paris, 1822) and *Histoire des institutions de Moise et du peuple hebreux* (Paris, 1828).
2. *Das Leben Jesu und seine Lehre*, trans. H. Jacobson (Dresden, 1841), p. viii.
3. Gabriel Salvador, *Joseph Salvador, sa vie, ses oeuvres, et ses critiques* (Paris, 1881), pp. 127 ff., 256 ff., 266 ff.
4. *Ibid.*, 304 ff., 364 ff.
5. *Das Leben Jesu*, pp. 5 ff.
6. *Joseph Salvador*, pp. 76 ff., 93 ff., etc.
7. *Ibid.*, 106 ff., 181 ff., etc.
8. *Das Leben Jesu*, p. 92.
9. *Ibid.*, 87 ff. and 94.
10. *Joseph Salvador*, pp. 124 ff.
11. *Ibid.*, 95.
12. *Ibid.*, 106 f.
13. *Das Leben Jesu*, p. 120.
14. *Ibid.*, 121.
15. *Ibid.*, 127.
16. *Ibid.*, 128.
17. *Ibid.*, 329.
18. *Ibid.*, 314 f.
19. J. Salvador, *Geschichte der Mosaischen Institutionen und des jüdischen Volkes*, trans. Dr. Essenna (Hamburg, 1856), 2:77.
20. *Das Leben Jesu*, p. 354.
21. J. Salvador, *Histoire de la Domination Romaine en Judée et de la Ruine de Jerusalem* (Brussels, 1847), 2:38 ff.
22. *Das Leben Jesu*, p. 368.
23. *Ibid.*, 273.
24. *Ibid.*, 296.
25. *Ibid.*, 301.
26. *Ibid.*, 191.
27. *Ibid.*, 218, also 189 f.
28. *Ibid.*, 219 f., also J. Salvador, *Paris, Rome, Jerusalem, ou la question religieuse au XIXe siècle* (Paris, 1860), 1:300 ff., 474 ff.
29. *Das Leben Jesu*, 266 ff., 394.
30. *Ibid.*, 374.
31. *Ibid.*, 157 and 427 f.
32. *Ibid.*, 480.
33. *Ibid.*, 342, and *Paris, Rome Jerusalem*, 1:305 ff, 2:45 ff.
34. *Paris, Rome, Jerusalem*, 2:473 ff., 484 f.
35. *Joseph Salvador*, pp. 146 ff., pp. 332 ff.

36. Nicholas-Sylvestre Guillon, *Examen critique des doctrines de Gibbon, du docteur Strauss et de M. Salvador sur Jesus-Christ, son Evangile et son Eglise* (Paris, 1840).

37. Schweitzer, *The Quest of the Historical Jesus* (New York, 1910), p. 162.

Notes to Chapter 5

1. Benamozegh, *Morale Juive et Morale Chrétienne* (Florence, 1925), p. 1.
2. *Ibid.*, 5.
3. *Ibid.*, 8.
4. *Ibid.*, 10.
5. *Ibid.*, 8 ff.
6. *Ibid.*, 11.
7. *Ibid.*, 14.
8. *Ibid.*, 17, 166.
9. *Ibid.*, 16.
10. *Ibid.*, 21.
11. *Ibid.*, 22.
12. *Ibid.*, 31, 36 f., 40, 95 f.
13. *Ibid.*, 35, 53 ff.
14. *Ibid.*, 27 ff., 63 ff., 72 ff.
15. *Ibid.*, 139 f., 143.
16. *Ibid.*, 219 ff.
17. *Ibid.*, 193 ff.
18. *Ibid.*, 74 f.
19. *Ibid.*, 261 ff.
20. *Ibid.*, 4 f.

Notes to Chapter 6

1. Geiger, An Jakob Auerbach (January, 1837), in *Abraham Geiger's Leben in Briefen*, ed. Ludwig Geiger (Breslau, 1885), p. 96. See also An M. A. Stern (March, 1836).

2. Geiger, "Ein Blick auf die neuren Bearbeitungen des Lebens Jesu," *Anhang. Das Judenthum und seine Geschichte* (Breslau, 1864), pp. 164 ff.

3. Geiger, *Das Judenthum und seine Geschichte* (Breslau, 1910), pp. 118 f.

4. *Ibid.*, 121.

5. Geiger, "Einleitung in das Studium der jüdische Theologie," *Nachgelassene Schriften*, ed. Ludwig Geiger (Berlin, 1875), 2:116 f.

6. *Ibid.*, 113 f.

7. Geiger, "Ein Blick aud die neueren Bearbeitungen des Lebens Jesu," pp. 175 f.

8. Geiger, "Entstehung des Christenthums," *Jüdische Zeitschrift fur Wissenschaft und Leben* 11 (1874): 15 ff. Also "Einleitung in das Studium der jüdischen Theologie," 117 f.

9. *Das Judenthum und seine Geschichte*, p. 130 ff.

10. "Einleitung in das Studium der jüdischen Theologie," p. 116.

11. *Das Judenthum und seine Geschichte*, p. 120.

12. *Ibid.*, 130. Also "Entstehung des Christenthums," p. 17.

13. "Einleitung in das Studium der jüdischen Theologie," pp. 8, 24, 39, 110, etc.

14. *Das Judenthum und seine Geschichte*, p. 143.

15. "Ueber den Austritt aus dem Judenthume—Offenes Sendschreiben an Herrn M. Maass," *Nachgelassene Schriften* 1:281.

16. *Das Judenthum und seine Geschichte*, p. 144.

17. "Einleitung in das Studium der jüdischen Theologie," p. 172.

18. *Das Judenthum und seine Geschichte*, pp. 145 ff.

19. An Emilie Geiger (May, 1858), *Abraham Geiger's Leben in Briefen*, p. 226.

20. An D. Honigman (March, 1845), *Abraham Geiger's Leben in Briefen*, p. 178.

21. An M. A. Stern (January, 1855), *Abraham Geiger's Leben in Briefen*, p. 292.

22. *Das Judenthum und seine Geschichte*, p. 145.

23. An L. R. Bischoffsheim (October, 1872), *Briefe*, p. 347.

24. Geiger, "Jüdische Philosophie," *Jüdische Zeitschrift für Wissenschaft und Leben* 1(1862):278.

25. Geiger, "Zweiter Literatur Brief," *Nachgelassene Schriften* (July, 1853), 2:296 f; "Ueber den Austritt aus dem Judenthume—Offenes Sendschreiben an Herrn M. Maass," 1:262.

26. Geiger, Dritter Literatur Brief (July, 1853), *Abraham Geiger's Leben in Briefen*, p. 308; also, *idem*, Vierter Literatur Brief (August, 1853), *ibid.*, p. 338.

27. *Das Judenthum und seine Geschichte*, p. 147.

28. "Einleitung in das Studium der judischen Theologie," p. 39.

29. *Ibid.*, 8.

30. "Ueber den Austritt aus dem Judenthume—Offenes Sendschreiben an Herrn M. Maass," p. 263.

31. Geiger, Introduction to *Nachgelassene Schriften*, vol. 2.

32. Geiger, Dritter Literatur Brief (August, 1853), p. 309.

33. Geiger, *Ueber den Austritt aus dem Judenthume. Ein aufgefundener Briefwechsel* (Leipzig, 1858) and "Ueber den Austritt aus dem Judenthume—Offenes Sendschreiben an Herrn M. Maass, pp. 252 ff.

34. *Ibid.*, 278.

35. Geiger, "Das Judenthum unserer Zeit und die Bestrebungin ihm," *Wissenschaftliche Zeitschrift fur jüdische Theologie* 1 (1835):12; also "Die letzten zwei Jahre—Sendschreiben ben an einen befreundeten Rabbiner," *Nachgelassene Schriften*, 1:27.

36. Geiger, "Isaak Troki Ein Apologet des Judenthums am Ende des des sechszehnten Jahrhunderts," *Nachgelassene Schriften*, 3:208 ff.

37. Geiger, An M. A. Stern (September, 1861), *Briefe*, p. 252.

38. Geiger, "Ein Blick auf die neueren Bearbeitungen des Leben Jesu," p. 176.

39. *Ibid.*, 181 and "Ein Blick auf die neuren Bearbeitungen des Leben Jesus," p. 177; also, An Th. Nöldede (July, 1872), *Briefe*, p. 343.

40. Geiger, An M. A. Stern (December, 1872), *Briefe*, p. 357, also An M. A. Levy (November, 1865), *Briefe*, p. 299. Ernest Renan, *The Life of Jesus* (London, 1864), pp. 6 f.; Franz Delitzsch, *Jesus und Hillel, Mit Rücksicht auf Renan und Geiger* (Erlangen, 1879).

41. Geiger, An Wechsler (January, 1873), *Briefe*, p. 359.

42. Geiger, "Einleitung in das Studium der jüdischen Theologie," p. 118, and Geiger, "Bruno Bauer und die Juden," *Wissenschaftliche Zeitschrift für jüdische Theologie* 5 (1844):109 ff.

43. Geiger, An Th. Noldeke (June, 1868), *Briefe*, p. 320.

Notes to Chapter 7

1. Hirsch, *Die Religionsphilosophie der Juden* (Leipzig, 1842), pp. 820 ff.
2. *Ibid.*, 624.
3. Bruno Bauer, *Die Judenfrage* (Brunswick, 1843), p. 6.
4. Hirsch, *Das Judentum, der christliche Staat und die moderne wissenschaftliche Kritik* (1843), pp. 97 ff.
5. *Die Religionsphilosophie der Juden*, p. 626.
6. *Ibid.*, 688.
7. *Ibid.*, 728.
8. *Ibid.*, 653; also Hirsch, *Die Humänitat als Religion* (Trier, 1854), p. 225, and *Das Judentum*, pp. 88, 101.
9. *Die Religionsphilosophie der Juden*, p. 688.
10. *Die Humänitat als Religion*, p. 224.
11. *Die Religionsphilosophie der Juden*, pp. 672 f., 745 f.
12. *Ibid.*, 689.
13. *Ibid.*, 680, and Hirsch, *Die Humanität als Religion*, p. 226.
14. *Die Religionsphilosophie der Juden*, p. 686.
15. *Ibid.*, 688.
16. *Ibid.*, 720 f.
17. *Ibid.*, 726, 754.
18. *Ibid.*, 726 f.
19. *Ibid.*, 726, 751, 775, 862.
20. *Ibid.*, 658, 754, 765.
21. *Ibid.*, 787, 789, and *Die Humänitat als Religion*, p. 244.
22. *Die Humänitat als Religion*, 243, and Hirsch, *Die Religionsphilosophie der Juden*, pp. 832 f.
23. *Ibid.*, 761.
24. *Ibid.*, pp. 794, 835 ff.
25. *Die Humänitat als Religion*, p. 248.
26. Formstecher, *Die Religion des Geistes* (Frankfurt, 1841), pp. 18 ff.
27. *Ibid.*, 70.
28. *Ibid.*, 71 f.
29. *Ibid.*, 411.
30. *Ibid.*, 365 f.
31. *Ibid.*, 364.
32. *Ibid.*, 369 f.
33. *Ibid.*, 374.
34. *Ibid.*, 372.
35. *Ibid.*, 378.
36. *Ibid.*, 385.
37. *Ibid.*, 389 f.
38. *Ibid.*, 398 (113).
39. *Ibid.*, 393, 427.
40. *Ibid.*, 422, 429, 435 f.
41. *Ibid.*, 394 f. (114)

42. *Ibid.*, 447.

43. Letter of Steinheim to Zunz in Hans Joachim Schoeps, *Salomon Ludwig Steinheim zum Gedenken* (Leiden, 1966), p. 284.

44. Steinheim, *Die Offenbarung nach dem Lehrbegriff der Synagogue Dritter Theil, Die Polemik. Der Kampf der Offenbarung mit dem Heidenthume, ihr Synthese und Analyse* (Leipzig, 1863), p. 319. Also, Letter to Zunz (1843) in Schoeps, *Salomon Ludwig Steinheim*, p. 284.

45. Schoeps, *Salomon Ludwig Steinheim*, pp. 10 f.

46. *Die Offenbarung nach dem Lehrbegriff der Synagoge* (Leipzig, 1863) 2:xii f.

47. *Die Offenbarung nach dem Lehrbegriff der Synagoge*, 3:53.

48. *Ibid.*, 66.

49. *Ibid.*, 72 ff.

50. *Ibid.*, 72 ff.

51. *Ibid.*, 76 f.

52. *Ibid.*, 96, 183, 192 f., 199 ff., 220.

53. *Ibid.*, 167.

54. *Ibid.*, 179 f.

55. *Ibid.*, 246, 197, 222 ff.

56. *Ibid.*, 265.

57. *Ibid.*, 228.

58. *Ibid.*, 244.

59. *Ibid.*, 283.

60. *Ibid.*, 301, 277 ff.

61. *Ibid.*, 335 f.

62. *Ibid.*, Introduction to Vol. 2.

63. Schoeps, *Salomon Ludwig Steinheim*, pp. 5, 223 ff., 314 ff. Heinrich Graetz, *Geschichte der Juden* (Leipzig, 1875), 2:475 ff.

64. *Ibid.*, 3:332.

Notes to Chapter 8

1. Wise, *Reminiscences* (Cincinnati, 1901), p. 122 ff.

2. *Ibid.*, 63.

3. Wise, Preface to *A Defense of Judaism versus Proselytizing Christianity* (Chicago and Cincinnati, 1889).

4. *Reminiscences*, p. 229.

5. Wise, *Judaism and Christianity* (Cincinnati, 1883), p. 117.

6. *Ibid.*, 4 ff.

7. *Ibid.*, 5.

8. Wise, Preface to *Martyrdom of Jesus of Nazareth* (Cincinnati, 1888).

9. Sandmel, "Isaac Mayer Wise's 'Jesus Himself'," *Essays in American Jewish History* (Cincinnati, 1958), pp. 325 ff.

10. *Martyrdom of Jesus of Nazareth*, p. 11.

11. *Ibid.*, 12.

12. *Ibid.*, 131 ff.

13. J. Marcus, *The Americanization of I. M. Wise* (Cincinnati, 1931), p. 19.

14. *Martyrdom of Jesus of Nazareth*, p. 132.

15. *Ibid.*, 134.

16. *Ibid.*
17. *Ibid.*, 132.
18. *Ibid.*, 45.
19. *Judaism and Christianity*, p. 24.
20. Wise, *Origin of Christianity* (Cincinnati, 1868), p. 49.
21. *Ibid.*, 126.
22. *Judaism and Christianity*, p. 15.
23. *Judaism versus Proselytizing Christianity*, p. 26.
24. *Ibid.*, 28.
25. *Ibid.*, 87.
26. *Ibid.*, 106.
27. *Ibid.*, 21.
28. *Judaism and Christianity*, p. 102.
29. *Judaism versus Proselytizing Christianity*, p. 48.
30. *Judaism and Christianity*, p. 43.
31. *Ibid.*, 46.
32. Preface to *The Origin of Christianity and a Commentary to the Acts of the Apostles.*
33. *Judaism and Christianity*, p. 118.
34. *Origin of Christianity*, p. 15.
35. *Ibid.*, 311 ff. Also "Paul and the Mystics," in *Selected Writings*, ed. Philipson and Grossman (Cincinnati, 1900), p. 354.
36. *Origin of Christianity*, p. 396.
37. *Ibid.*, 412.
38. *Ibid.*, 414 ff.
39. "Paul and the Mystics," p. 352.
40. *Origin of Christianity*, p. 425.
41. *Ibid.*, 388.
42. *Ibid.*, 520.
43. *Ibid.*, 118.
44. *Ibid.*, 121 ff.
45. *Origin of Christianity*, pp. 533 ff.
46. *Judaism versus Proselytizing Christianity*, p. 61.
47. *Ibid.*, 127 ff.
48. *Origin of Christianity*, p. 523.
49. *A Defense of Judaism versus Proselytizing Christianity*, p. 6.
50. "Paul and the Mystics," p. 375.

Notes to Chapter 9

1. "Der Jude in der christlichen Kultur," in Cohen, *Jüdische Schriften*, ed. Franz Rosenzweig (Berlin, 1924), 2:200.
2. "Der Heilige Geist," *Jüdische Schriften*, 3:192.
3. *Ibid.*, 193.
4. Cohen, *Die Religion der Vernunft aus den Quellen des Jüdentums* (Berlin, 1911), p. 493.
5. "Die Bedeutung des Judentums für den religiosen Forschritt der Menscheit," *Jüdische Schriften*, 1:21.
6. *Die Religion der Vernunft*, p. 377.
7. "Gedanken uber Jugendlekture," *Jüdische Schriften*, 2:128.

8. *Ibid.*, 129 ff.
9. *Ibid.*, 128.
10. "Der Jude in der christlichen Kultur," 2:208.
11. "Religion und Sittlichkeit," *Jüdische Schriften*, 3:157.
12. *Die Religion der Vernunft*, p. 518.
13. "Der Juden in der christlichen Kultur," 2:197 ff.
14. "Religion und Sittlichkeit," 3:135.
15. *Die Religion der Vernunft*, p. 476.
16. "Religion und Sittlichkeit," 3:142 f.
17. *Die Religion der Vernunft*, p. 142.
18. *Ibid.*, 275.
19. *Ibid.*, 200.
20. *Ibid.*, 404 f.
21. *Ibid.*, 292.
22. *Ibid.*, 181 and 482.
23. *Ibid.*, 461.
24. "Liebe und Gerechtigkeit in den Begriffen Gott und Mensche," *Jüdische Schriften*, 3:62 ff.
25. *Die Religion der Vernunft*, p. 463.
26. "Ein Bekentniss in der Judenfrage," *Jüdische Schriften*, 2:93.
27. *Die Religion der Vernunft*, p. 63.
28. *Ibid.*, 389 f.
29. "Die religose Bewegungen der Gegenwart," *Jüdische Schriften*, 1:47.
30. "Die Jude in der christlichen Kulture," 2:205 f.
31. "Ein Bekentniss in der Judenfrage," 2:93.
32. "Die religöse Bewegungen der Gegenwart," 1:63 f.
33. "Deutschtum und Judentum," *Jüdische Schriften*, 2:305 f.
34. *Ibid.*, 308 f.
35. "Die religose Bewegungen der Gegenwart," 1:64.
36. "Gedanken uber Jugendlektüre," 2:131.
37. "Der Jude in der christlichen Kulture," 2:193 ff.

Notes to Chapter 10

1. Montefiore, *The Synoptic Gospels* (London, 1927), 1:xxi.
2. *Ibid.*, xx.
3. Montefiore, *Outlines of Liberal Judaism* (London, 1923), p. 313.
4. Montefiore, *Liberal Judaism and Hellenism and Other Essays* (London, 1918), p. 78. Also, *The Synoptic Gospels*, p. cxxxvii.
5. Montefiore, *Some Elements of the Religious Teaching of Jesus According to the Synoptic Gospels* (London, 1910), p. 5.
6. Montefiore, *Liberal Judaism* (London 1903), p. 2.
7. *Liberal Judaism and Hellenism*, p. 80.
8. *The Synoptic Gospels*, p. cxliii.
9. *Liberal Judaism and Hellenism*, p. 113; *Outlines of Liberal Judaism*, p. 333.
10. Montefiore, *The Bible for Home Reading* (London, 1899), 2:779.
11. Montefiore, *Some Elements of the Religious Teaching of Jesus*, p. 110 f.
12. *Liberal Judaism and Hellenism*, p. 93.

13. *Ibid.*, 86.

14. Montefiore, *The Old Testament and After* (London, 1923), P. 283.

15. *Liberal Judaism and Hellenism*, p. 84; *Outlines of Liberal Judaism*, p. 334.

16. *Some Elements of the Religious Teachings of Jesus*, p. 7.

17. *Liberal Judaism and Hellenism*, p. 114.

18. *The Synoptic Gospels*, cxxxvii.

19. *Liberal Judaism and Hellenism*, p. 127 f.

20. *Ibid.*, 90.

21. *Ibid.*, 83; and Montefiore, "Unitarianism and Judaism in Their Relations to Each Other," *Jewish Quarterly Review*, O.S. 9:251.

22. *Some Elements of the Religious Teaching of Jesus*, p. 19.

23. *Ibid.*, 115.

24. *Ibid.*, 39; *Liberal Judaism and Hellenism*, p. 97 f; also *The Old Testament and After*, p. 230.

25. *Ibid.*, 42.

26. *Ibid.*, 157, and *The Synoptic Gospels*, cxxxv.

27. *Ibid.*, 80.

28. *The Synoptic Gospels*, cxxxiv.

29. *Outlines of Liberal Judaism*, p. 357.

30. *Liberal Judaism and Hellenism*, p. 105.

31. *Some Elements of the Religious Teachings of Jesus*, p. 70 f., 144.

32. *Ibid.*, 119.

33. *Ibid.*, 87 f.; *Liberal Judaism and Hellenism*, p. 107.

34. *Ibid.*, 132; also 81 f.

35. *Ibid.*, 135.

36. *Ibid.*, 151 f., 159.

37. *Ibid.*, 108, 103.

38. *Ibid.*, 103.

39. *Ibid.*, 116.

40. *Ibid.*, 117 f., also *Liberal Judaism and Hellenism*, p. 126 f.

41. *Ibid.*, 141.

42. *Ibid.*, 146.

43. *Outlines of Liberal Judaism*, p. 316.

44. *The Synoptic Gospels*, 1:xxiv.

45. *Ibid.*, cxxxvi.

46. *Some Elements of the Religious Teaching of Jesus*, p. 9; *Outlines of Liberal Judaism*, p. 330 f.

47. *Ibid.*, 336.

48. *Liberal Judaism*, p. 174.

49. *Liberal Judaism and Hellenism*, p. 116.

50. *Outlines of Liberal Judaism*, pp. 319, 331 f.

51. *Ibid.*, 332.

52. *Liberal Judaism and Hellenism*, p. 119 f.

53. *Outlines of Liberal Judaism*, p. 332.

54. Montefiore, *Judaism and St. Paul* (London, 1914), p. 93.

55. *Ibid.*, 101.

56. *Ibid.*, 59.

57. *Ibid.*, 87.

58. *Ibid.*, 81 f.

59. *Ibid.*, 95 f.

60. *Ibid.*, 141; also *The Old Testament and After*, p. 208.
61. *Judaism and St. Paul*, p. 159; also *Outlines of Liberal Judaism*, p. 321.
62. *Judaism and St. Paul*, p. 179.
63. *Ibid.*, 201.
64. *Ibid.*, 203.
65. Ahad Ha-Am, "Al sh'teh ha-s'ifim," *Al Parashat Derakim* (Berlin, 1925), 4:38 ff.

Notes to Chapter 11

1. *Heidentum, Christentum, Judentum, ein Bekenntnisbuch* (Munich, 1922), 1:28 ff.
2. *Ibid.*, 1:58 ff.
3. *Ibid.*, 1, 9.
4. *Ibid.*, 1:11 ff.
5. *Ibid.*, 220 ff.
6. *Ibid.*, 228.
7. *Ibid.*, 228.
8. *Der Meister* (Gütersloh, 1952), pp. 458 ff.
9. *Ibid.*, 82, 99.
10. *Ibid.*, 2:97 ff.
11. *Ibid.*, 2:88 f., 1:16 ff., 217 f.
12. *Ibid.*, 2:102, 108 ff.
13. Buber, *Israel and the World*, p. 40.
14. *Ibid.*, 2:160 f., 200.
15. *Ibid.*, 164.
16. *Ibid.*, 199 f.
17. *Ibid.*, 176 f.
18. *Ibid.*, 186, 183, 225.
19. *Ibid.*, 203 ff., 307 ff.,
20. *Ibid.*, 165.
21. *Ibid.*, 210.
22. *Ibid.*, 214, 227.
23. *Ibid.*, 229 f.
24. *Ibid.*, 235.
25. *Ibid.*, 259, 261.
26. *Ibid.*, 280.
27. *Ibid.*, 285 f.
28. *Ibid.*, 285, 289 ff.
29. *Ibid.*, 236 f., 239 ff.
30. *Ibid.*, 236 f., 239 ff.
31. *Ibid.*, 236.

Notes to Chapter 12

1. Rosenzweig, *Briefe* (Berlin, 1935), pp. 328 ff.
2. *Ibid.*, 279.
3. *Ibid.*, 688.

4. Rosenzweig, *Der Stern der Erlösung* (Heidelberg, 1930), 2:39 f., 100 f., 179 ff.
5. "Das neue Denken," in Rosenzweig, *Kleinere Schriften* (Berlin, 1937), p. 382; also, *Briefe*, p. 512 f.
6. "Das neue Denken," p. 381.
7. *Der Stern der Erlösung*, 3:200 ff.
8. *Briefe*, pp. 315 f., 331, 347.
9. *Der Stern der Erlösung*, 3:127.
10. *Ibid.*, 109.
11. *Ibid.*, 111.
12. *Briefe*, 688 f.
13. *Ibid.*, 356.
14. *Ibid.*, 672.
15. *Ibid.*, 69 f.
16. *Der Stern der Erlösung*, 3:190 f.
17. *Ibid.*, 104 f.
18. *Briefe*, p. 302.
19. *Der Stern der Erlösung*, 3:114 ff.
20. *Briefe*, p. 73.
21. *Ibid.*, 74 f.
22. *Ibid.*, 77 f.
23. *Ibid.*, 668.
24. *Der Stern der Erlösung*, 3:117, 119.
25. *Briefe*, p. 315.
26. *Der Stern der Erlösung*, 3:87 f.
27. *Briefe*, p. 667.
28. *Ibid.*, 356.
29. *Briefe*, pp. 706 ff., 310.
30. *Ibid.*, 310 f.

Notes to Chapter 13

1. Abraham Klausner, *Jesus of Nazareth* (London, 1925), p. 96.
2. "Harnack's Vorlesung über das Wesen des Christentums," *Monatsschrift für die Geschichte und Wissenschaft des Judentums* 45 (1901): 97–120.
3. A number of works under the same title appeared as replies to Harnack, but they were soon forgotten; cf. J. Jelski, *Das Wesen des Judentums* (Berlin, 1902) and J. Goldschmidt, *Das Wesen des Judentums* (1907).
4. Baeck, *Dieses Volk, Jüdische Existenz* (Frankfurt, 1957), 2:145.
5. *Ibid.*, 145.
6. Baeck, "Some Questions to the Christian Church from the Jewish Point of View," in *The Church and the Jewish People*, ed. Göte Hedenquist (London, 1954), p. 102 f.
7. Baeck, *Von Moses Mendelssohn zu Franz Rosenzweig* (Stuttgart, 1958), p. 22.
8. Reinhart Mayer, *Christentum und Judentum in der Schau Leo Baecks* (Stuttgart, 1961), p. 90.
9. "Some Questions to the Christian Church from the Jewish Point of View," p. 104.
10. *Ibid.*, 105.
11. *Ibid.*, 106.
12. *Ibid.*, 106.

13. *Ibid.*, 107.

14. "Romantic Religion," in Baeck, *Judaism and Christianity*, trans. Walter Kaufmann (Philadelphia, 1958), p. 290.

15. Baeck, *The Essence of Judaism*, trans. V. Grubenwieser and L. Pearl (reprint ed., New York, 1948), p. 13.

16. "Geheimniss und Gebot," in Baeck, *Wege im Judentum* (Berlin, 1933), pp. 38 f.

17. "Romantic Religion," p. 197.

18. *Ibid.*, 198 f.

19. *Ibid.*, 202 f.

20. *Ibid.*, 205.

21. *Ibid.*, 205.

22. *Ibid.*, 206.

23. "Helfer und Lehrer," *Wege im Judentum*, p. 403.

24. "Vollendung und Spannung," *Wege im Judentum*, p. 18.

25. *Ibid.*, 18.

26. *Ibid.*, 32.

27. *Dieses Volk, Jüdische Existenz*, p. 92.

28. "Romantic Religion," pp. 210–11.

29. *Ibid.*, 217.

30. *Ibid.*, 219.

31. *Ibid.*, 222.

32. *Ibid.*, 227.

33. *Ibid.*, 235.

34. *Ibid.*, 238.

35. *Ibid.*, 238.

36. *Ibid.*, 233.

37. *Ibid.*, 214.

38. *Ibid.*, 245.

39. *Ibid.*, 249.

40. *Ibid.*, 258.

41. *Ibid.*, 269.

42. *Ibid.*, 275.

43. *Ibid.*, 289.

44. *Ibid.*, 229.

45. *Ibid.*, 291 f.

46. Mayer, *Christentum und Judentum in der Schau Leo Baecks*.

47. "The Gospel as a Document of the History of the Jewish Faith" *Judaism and Christianity*, p. 42.

48. *Ibid.*, 48.

49. *Ibid.*, 63.

50. *Ibid.*, 99 f.

51. *Ibid.*, 100 f.

52. *Ibid.*, 102.

53. Mayer, *Christentum und Judentum*, pp. 52 ff.

54. *The Essence of Judaism*, p. 73.

55. "The Gospel as a Document of History," pp. 100 f.

56. *Christentum und Judentum*, p. 57.

57. "The Gospel as a Document of History," p. 71.

58. *Ibid.*, 72.

59. "Romantic Religion," p. 200.

60. Baeck, "The Faith of Paul," *Judaism and Christianity*, p. 140.

61. *Ibid.*, 147.

62. *Ibid.*, 156.

63. *Ibid.*, 160.

64. *Ibid.*, 161.

65. *Ibid.*, 163; also Baeck, "Judaism in the Church," *Hebrew Union College Annual.* 2 (1925):127, 134 ff.

66. Baeck, "The Faith of Paul," p. 166.

67. "Judaism in the Church," p. 127.

68. *Ibid.*, 128.

69. *Ibid.*, 134.

70. *Ibid.*, 136.

71. "Romantic Religion," p. 203.

72. *Dieses Volk, Jüdische Existenz*, 2:190.

73. "The Faith of Paul," *Op. Cit.*, 167.

74. "Mystery and Commandment," *Judaism and Christianity*, p. 177.

75. Mayer, *Christentum und Judentum*, p. 64.

76. "Romantic Religion," p. 225.

77. *Ibid.*, 226.

78. Baeck, "Heimgegangene des Krieges," *Wege im Judentum*, p. 385.

79. *Ibid.*, 386 f.

80. "Judaism in the Church," p. 140.

81. "Romantic Religion," p. 211.

82. *Ibid.*, p. 252 f.

83. *Ibid.*, 254.

84. *Ibid.*, 289.

85. "Some Questions to the Christian Church from the Jewish Point of View," p. 111.

86. *Ibid.*, 112.

87. *Ibid.*, 113.

88. *Ibid.*, 108.

89. *Ibid.*, 109.

90. *Ibid.*, 110.

91. *Ibid.*, 114.

92. *Ibid.*, 115.

93. *Ibid.*, 115.

94. *Ibid.*, 116.

Notes to Chapter 14

1. *Jesus of Nazareth: His Life, Times, and Teaching*, trans. Herbert Danby (1925; reprint ed., Boston, 1964), p. 10.

2. *Ibid.*, 371 f., 390, and *From Jesus to Paul*, trans. William F. Stinespring (1943; reprint ed., Boston, 1961), pp. 465, 528 ff.

3. *From Jesus to Paul*, p. 485; see also pp. 495, 515, 527, 536.

4. Armand Kaminka, "Torat Hakhmey Yisrael ve-ha-agadah ha-Notzrit," *Hator* 3 (1922): 59–77.

5. Samuel Sandmel, *We Jews and Jesus* (New York, 1965), p. 92; *idem, The First Christian Century in Judaism and Christianity* (New York, 1969), p. 197; *idem,* "Jewish Scholars and Early Christianity," *Seventy-fifth Anniversary Volume of Jewish Quarterly Review* (Philadelphia, 1967), p. 478.

6. *Jesus of Nazareth*, p. 239.

7. *Ibid.*, 245.

8. *Ibid.*, 248.

9. *Ibid.*, 235.

10. *Ibid.*, 259.

11. *Ibid.*, 254.

12. *Ibid.*, 255.

13. *Ibid.*, 265.

14. *Ibid.*, 267 ff.

15. *Ibid.*, 276.

16. *Ibid.*, 279.

17. *Ibid.*, 293.

18. *Ibid.*, 322.

19. *Ibid.*, 334 ff.

20. *Ibid.*, 348; see also Solomon Zeitlin, *Who Crucified Jesus?* (New York, 1964).

21. *Jesus of Nazareth*, p. 359.

22. *Ibid.*, 361.

23. Kaminka, "Torah Hakhmey Yisrael ve-ha-agadah ha-Notzrit," p. 68; Sandmel, *The First Christian Century*, p. 197.

24. Klausner, *Jesus of Nazareth*, p. 368.

25. *Ibid.*, 371 ff.

26. *Ibid.*, 381.

27. *Ibid.*, 397.

28. *Ibid.*, 374, 405 f.

29. *Ibid.*, 371 f., 390.

30. *Ibid.*, 406.

31. *Ibid.*, 411.

32. *Ibid.*, 413 f.

33. *From Jesus to Paul*, pp. 423 f.

34. *Ibid.*, 425 ff.

35. *Ibid.*, 297.

36. *Ibid.*, 300.

37. *Ibid.*, 441 ff.

38. *Ibid.*, 444 ff.

39. *Ibid.*, 452 f.

40. *Ibid.*, 465 f.

41. *Ibid.*, 477 ff.

42. *Ibid.*, 485.

43. *Ibid.*, 494.

44. *Ibid.*, 496 ff., 606.

45. *Ibid.*, 516 ff.

46. *Ibid.*, 548 ff.

47. *Ibid.*, 465 ff.

48. *Ibid.*, 579.

49. *Ibid.*, 588.

50. *Ibid.*, 591.

51. *Ibid.*, 599.

52. *Ibid.*, 603 ff.

53. *Ibid.*, 608.

54. *Ibid.*, 609.

Notes to Chapter 15

1. Martin Buber, *Die Stunde und die Erkenntnis* (Berlin, 1936), p. 152.

2. *Ibid.*, 154.

3. *Ibid.*, 162 f.

4. *Ibid.*, 155 f.

5. Buber, *Two Types of Faith*, trans. Norman P. Goldhawk (1951; reprinted., New York, 1961), pp. 12 f.

6. *Ibid.*, 107 f.

7. Buber, *The Origin and Meaning of Hasidism*, trans. Maurice Friedman (New York, 1960), p. 110; and *idem, For the Sake of Heaven*, trans. Ludwig Lewisohn (Philadelphia, 1953), p. xii.

8. *The Origin and Meaning of Hasidism*, p. 109.

9. *Two Types of Faith*, p. 29.

10. *Ibid.*, 25 and 27.

11. *Ibid.*, 96 f.

12. "Zwiesprache," in Buber. *Werke, vol. 1 Schriften zur Philosophie* (Munich, 1962), p. 178.

13. *Two Types of Faith*, p. 62.

14. *Ibid.*, 114 f.

15. *Ibid.*, 63.

16. *Ibid.*, 65–68.

17. *Ibid.*, 79.

18. *Ibid.*, 91.

19. *Ibid.*, 75.

20. *Ibid.*, 89 f.

21. *Ibid.*, 34.

22. Franz von Hammerstein, *Das Messiasproblem bei Martin Buber* (Stuttgart, 1958), p. 54.

23. *Ibid.*, 59.

24. *Two Types of Faith*, p. 44.

25. *Ibid.*, 47.

26. *Ibid.*, 86.

27. *Ibid.*, 149 f.

28. Buber, *Israel and the World* (New York, 1948), pp. 178 f.

29. *Two Types of Faith*, p. 172.

30. *Israel and the World*, p. 202.

31. *Ibid.*, 192 f, 25 f.

32. Hammerstein, *Das Messias Problem bei Martin Buber*, pp. 61 ff.
33. *Two Types of Faith*, p. 162.
34. *Ibid.*, 173 f.
35. *Israel and the World*, p. 177.
36. *The Origin and Meaning of Hasidism*, p. 242.
37. Hans Urs von Balthasar, *Martin Buber and Christianity* (New York, 1960), p. 51.
38. *Ibid.*, 106.
39. *Ibid.*, 110.
40. *Ibid.*, 77 ff.
41. *Israel and the World*, p. 40.

Notes to Chapter 16

1. "Person and Myth in the Judaeo-Christian Encounter, in Rubenstein, *After Auschwitz* (New York, 1966), p. 61.
2. *Ibid.*, 64.
3. *Ibid.*, 71.
4. *Ibid.*,
5. *Ibid.*, 75.
6. *Ibid.*, 74.
7. *Ibid.*, 77.
8. *Ibid.*, 78.
9. *Ibid.*, 79.
10. Rubenstein, "Symposium on Jewish Belief," *After Auschwitz*, p. 147.
11. *Ibid.*, 149.
12. Rubenstein, *The Religious Imagination* (New York, 1968), p. 165.
13. Rubenstein, *My Brother Paul* (New York, 1972), p. 1.
14. *Ibid.*, 126.
15. *Ibid.*, 118.
16. *Ibid.*, 51.
17. *Ibid.*, 137.
18. *Ibid.*, 19.
19. *Ibid.*, 46.
20. *Ibid.*, 61.
21. *Ibid.*, 79.
22. *Ibid.*, 112 f.
23. *Ibid.*, 170.
24. "These Twenty Years," in Fackenheim, *Quest for Past and Future* (London, 1968), p. 21.
25. *Ibid.*, 22.
26. *Ibid.*, 25.
27. Fackenheim et al., "Jewish Values in the Post-Holocaust Future," *Judaism* 15 (1966): 270.
28. Fackenheim, "A Jew Looks at Christianity and Secularist Liberalism," *Quest for Past and Future*, p. 264.
29. *Ibid.*, 267.
30. *Ibid.*, 273; also "On the Self-Exposure of Faith to the Modern Secular World," *Quest for Past and Future*, p. 299; also *God's Presence in History* (New York, 1970), p. 61.

31. "On the Self-Exposure of Faith to the Modern Secular World," pp. 278 ff.

32. Fackenheim, *God's Presence in History* (New York, 1970), p. 45.

33. "On the Self-Exposure of Faith to the Modern Secular World," p. 285.

Notes to Chapter 17 16

1. Schoeps, *The Jewish Christian Argument* (New York, 1963), p. vii; Hans Bluher and Schoeps, *Streit um Israel, ein jüdischchristliches Gespräch* (Hamburg, 1933).

2. *The Jewish Christian Argument*, p. xi.

3. Schoeps, *Philosemitismus im Barock* (Tubingen, 1952); *idem, Barocke Juden, Christen, und Judenchristen* (Munich, 1965).

4. Schoeps, *Jüdischer Glaube in dieser Zeit* (Berlin, 1932); *idem, Geschichte der jüdischen Religionsphilosöphie in der Neuzeit* (Berlin, 1953); *idem, Was-ist und was will die Geistesgeschichte?* (Göttingen, 1959); *idem, Was ist der Mensch? Philosophische Anthropologie als Geistesgeschichte* (Göttingen, 1960); also numerous essays.

5. *The Jewish-Christian Argument*, p. 4.

6. *Ibid.*, 4.

7. *Ibid.*, 8; *Was ist Der Mensch?* pp. 323 ff. Also, Schoeps, *Der Moderne Mensch und die Verkundigung der Religionen* (Antwerp, 1939), pp. 9 ff, 42 ff.

8. *The Jewish Christian Argument*, p. 170. (Also, Schoeps, *Baroke Juden, Christen, Judenchristen*, pp. 114 ff., is the German original of the final chapter in the book cited above.)

9. *Ibid.*, 172.

10. Vogel, "The Jewish-Christian Argument—A Review Essay," *Journal of Bible and Religion* 33 (1965): 131 ff.

11. *The Jewish-Christian Dialogue*, pp. 165 ff.

12. *Theologie und Geschichte des Judenchristentums* (Tubingen, 1949), pp. 247 ff.

13. Schoeps, *Studien zur unbekannten Religions—und Geistesgeschichte* (Göttingen, 1963), pp. 77 f.

14. Schoeps, *Jewish Christianity: Factional Disputes in the Early Church* (Philadelphia, 1969), pp. 45 f.

15. *Ibid.*, 67.

16. *Ibid.*, 71 f.; Schoeps, *Paul: The Theology of the Apostle in the Light of Jewish Religious History* (Philadelphia, 1961), p. 248.

17. *Theologie und Geschichte*, pp. 155 ff.

18. *Ibid.*, 188 ff.

19. *Jewish Christianity*, p. 106.

20. *Ibid.*, 108.

21. *Ibid.*, 121.

22. *Ibid.*, 134.

23. *Theologie und Geschichte*, pp. 334 ff.

24. Morton Smith, "Das Judenchristentum, A Review," *Journal of Biblical Literature* 84 (1965): 176 ff.

25. W. Schneemelcher, *Verkundigung und Forschung* (Berlin, n.d.) pp. 229 ff; W. D. Davies, Urgemeinde, "Judenchristentum, Gnosis: A Review," *Journal of Biblical Literature* 76 (1957): 66 ff.; Markus Barth, "Paul: Apostate or Apostle," *Judaism* 12 (1963): 370 ff.; Howard Bream, "Theologie und Geschichte des Judenchristentums: A Review,"

Journal of Religion 32 (1952): 57 ff.; Schoeps, *Das Judenchristentum* (Bern, 1964), and elsewhere.

26. *Paul*, p. 26.
27. *Ibid.*, 47 ff.
28. *Ibid.*, 49.
29. *Ibid.*, 85 f.
30. *Ibid.*, 96.
31. *Ibid.*, 101 ff., 107 ff.
32. *Ibid.*, 108.
33. *Ibid.*, 118.
34. *Ibid.*, 125.
35. *Ibid.*, 120.
36. *Ibid.*, 141.
37. *Ibid.*, 149.
38. *Ibid.*, 149, 158.
39. *Ibid.*, 153.
40. *Ibid.*, 154, 164 ff.
41. *Ibid.*, 175.
42. *Ibid.*, 198.
43. *Ibid.*, 194 f.
44. *Ibid.*, 201, 260 f.
45. *Ibid.*, 209.
46. *Ibid.*, 213.
47. *Ibid.*, 225.
48. *Ibid.*, 230.
49. *Ibid.*, 243.
50. *Ibid.*, 251.
51. *Ibid.*, 257.
52. Barth, "Paul: Apostate or Apostle," 372 ff.
53. Robert Grant, "Paulus: A Review," *Journal of Religion* 40 (1960): 215 f.
54. *Paul*, p. 272.
55. *Ibid.*, 274.
56. *Ibid.*, 278.
57. *Ibid.*, 283.
58. *Ibid.*, 284.
59. *Ibid.*, 293.
60. Bluher and Schoeps, *Streit um Israel, Ein jüdischchristliches Gespräch*.
61. Hellmut Diwald, ed., *Lebendiger Geist* (Leiden, 1959).
62. *The Jewish-Christian Argument*, p. xi.
63. *Was ist der Mensch?* p. 299; also, *Barocke Juden, Christen, Judenchristen*, p. 114.

Notes to Chapter 18

1. Sandmel, *Jewish Understanding of the New Testament* (Cincinnati, 1956), p. xi.
2. Sandmel, *We Jews and Jesus* (New York, 1965), pp. 7 ff.

3. Sandmel, "The Jewish Scholar and Early Christianity" *Seventy-fifth Anniversary Volume of the Jewish Quarterly Review* (Philadelphia, 1967), p. 475.

4. Sandmel, "Parallelomania," *Journal of Biblical Literature* 81 (1962): 9.

5. Sandmel, *The First Christian Century in Judaism and Christianity: Certainties and Uncertainties* (New York, 1969).

6. Sandmel, "Judaism, Jesus, and Paul," *Vanderbilt Studies in the Humanities* 1 (1951): 249.

7. *The First Christian Century*, p. 196.

8. *Ibid.*, 108.

9. *A Jewish Understanding of the New Testament*, pp. 107 ff.; *The Genius of Paul* (New York, 1958), pp. 163 ff.

10. *A Jewish Understanding of the New Testament*, pp. 203 f.; *We Jews and Jesus*, pp. 122, 139.

11. *We Jews and Jesus*, pp. 109 f.

12. "Jewish Scholarship and Early Christianity," p. 480.

13. *Ibid.*, 98 ff.; *A Jewish Understanding of the New Testament*, pp. 199 ff.; "Parallelomania," p. 9.

14. "Parallelomania," p. 4.

15. *We Jews and Jesus*, p. 48.

16. *Ibid.*, 110 f.

17. *The Genius of Paul*, pp. 17 ff., 53 ff.; and Sandmel "Myths, Genealogies, Jewish Myth and the Development of the Gospels," *Hebrew Union College Annual* 27 (1956): 201 ff.

18. *Ibid.*, 10.

19. *A Jewish Understanding of the New Testament*, pp. 49 and 51.

20. *Ibid.*, 52.

21. *Ibid.*, 57.

22. *The Genius of Paul*, pp. 55 f.

23. *Ibid.*, 59.

24. *Ibid.*, 106, 118.

25. *Ibid.*, 56 f.

26. *Ibid.*, 28.

27. *Ibid.*, 69.

28. *Ibid.*, 72.

29. *Ibid.*, 88.

30. *Ibid.*, 114.

31. *Ibid.*, 21.

32. *Ibid.*, 159 f.

33. *Ibid.*, 157.

34. *Ibid.*, 217.

35. *Ibid.*, 35; also *The First Christian Century*, pp. 161 ff.

36. *Ibid.*, 218.

37. *Ibid.*, 19.

38. *Ibid.*, 220.

39. See Bibliography to *The First Christian Century*, pp. 231–32.

40. *Ibid.*, 117, 218; *A Jewish Understanding of the New Testament*, pp. 316 f.

41. *We Jews and Jesus*, pp. 51 ff.

42. *Ibid.*, 151.

Notes to Chapter 19

1. Zeitlin, "Essenes and Messianic Expectations," *Jewish Quarterly Review* 45 (1954–1955): 106, 114, 119.

2. Zeitlin, "The Halaka in the Gospels and Its Relation to the Jewish Law at the Time of Jesus," *Hebrew Union College Annual* 1 (1924): 364; *idem*, "The Pharisees," *Jewish Quarterly Review* 16 (1925–1926): 393; *idem*, "The Duration of Jesus' Ministry," *Jewish Quarterly Review* 55 (1964–1965): 199.

3. Zeitlin, "The Pharisees: A Historical Study," *Jewish Quarterly Review* 52 (1961–1962): 119 ff.

4. *Ibid.*, 120 f.; Zeitlin, "The Prophet of Nazareth," *Jewish Quarterly Review* 52 (1962–1962): 187 f.; B. Jacob, *Auge Um Auge* (Berlin, 1929), pp. 121–43.

5. Zeitlin, "The Pharisees and the Gospels," in *Essays and Studies in Memory of Linda R. Miller* (New York, 1938), pp. 255 ff.

6. "The Pharisees and the Gospels," p. 269.

7. *Ibid.*, 240; Zeitlin, *Who Crucified Jesus?* (New York, 1964), pp. 114 f.

8. "The Halaka in the Gospels and Its Relation to the Jewish Law at the Time of Jesus," p. 373.

9. "The Duration of Jesus' Ministry," p. 197.

10. *Ibid.*, 187 ff.

11. *Who Crucified Jesus?* pp. 152 ff.

12. *Ibid.*, 162 ff., 172.

13. *Ibid.*, 173 ff., *Ibid.*, 179, "The Ecumenical Council," *Jewish Quarterly Review* 56 (1965–1966): 105.

14. Zeitlin, "Studies in the Beginnings of Christianity," *Jewish Quarterly Review* 14 (1923–1924): 139, 111 ff.; *idem*, "From Jesus to Paul," *Jewish Quarterly Review* 31 (1940–1941): 309 ff.

15. "The Ecumenical Council," pp. 106 ff.

16. Flusser, *Jesus* (New York, 1969), p. 12. See also *idem*, "Jesus in the Context of History," in *The Crucible of Christianity*, ed. A. Toynbee (London, 1969), pp. 216 ff.; *idem*, "Melchizedek and the Son of Man," *Christian News from Israel*, 1966, pp. 23 ff.; and *idem*, "New Evidence on Jesus," *New York Times*, February 13, 1972, pp. 1 and 24.

17. *Jesus*, p. 40.

18. *Ibid.*, 44.

19. "Jesus in the Context of History," p. 226.

20. *Jesus*, p. 64.

21. *Ibid.*, 66; also Flusser, "A New Sensitivity in Judaism and the Christian Message," *Harvard Theological Review* 61 (1968): 107–127; *idem*, "Blessed Are the Poor in Spirit," *Israel Exploration Journal* 10 (1960): 1 ff.; *idem*, "Qumram und die Zwölf," *Initation*, Leiden, 1965, pp. 134 ff.; *idem*, *Dead Sea Sect and Pre-Pauline Christianity*, Scripta Hierosolymitana IV (Jerusalem, 1958), pp. 215 ff.

22. *Jesus*, p. 71.

23. "A New Sensitivity in Judaism and the Christian Message," p. 227.

24. *Jesus*, pp. 116 ff.; Flusser, "A Literary Approach to the Trial of Jesus," *Judaism* 20: no. 1 (1971): 32–36.

25. Isaac, *Has Anti-Semitism Roots in Christianity?* (New York, 1961), pp. 58 ff.

26. Isaac, *Jésus et Israël* (Paris, 1947).

27. *Ibid.*, 351 ff.; and Isaac, *The Teaching of Contempt: Christian Roots of Anti-Semitism*, trans. Helen Weaver, (New York, 1964), p. 132.

28. *Ibid.*, 146.

29. *On the Trial of Jesus* (Berlin, 1961).

30. *Ibid.*, 132.

31. *The Trial and Death of Jesus* (New York, 1971).

32. *The New Testament and Rabbinic Judaism* (Oxford, 1956); *Concerning the Reconstruction of the Aramaic Gospels* (Manchester, 1945); *He That Cometh* (London, 1966); *The Sudden in the Scriptures* (London, 1964).

Note to Chapter 20

1. A number of genuine efforts at dialogue during the last decade led to the following writings: *The Jews, Views and Counterviews: A Dialogue between Jean Danielou and André Chouraqui* (New York, 1966), *Torah and Gospel: Jewish and Catholic Theology in Dialogué* (New York, 1966), "The Jewish-Lutheran Dialogue," *Lutheran Quarterly* (November, 1969). Other publications will be found in the *Journal of Bible and Religion* and the *Journal of Ecumenical Studies*, which present a complete record of interreligious books, essays, and encounters.

Index

Abraham, 127, 195

Abrahams, Israel, 93

Agamemnon, 127–28

Ahad HaAm, 109

Akedath Isaac, 127–28, 194–95

Albo, Joseph, 11

Anti-Semitism, 5, 24, 64, 68–69, 92, 211–12, 214, 217, 225, 228. *See also* Holocaust; Nazism

Aus frühchristlicher Zeit (Schoeps), 200

Bacharach, Ya'ir Hayyim, 13

Baeck, Leo, 5, 7, 115, 121, 136, 204, 210, 230; life and career, 136; major exponent of Liberal Judaism, 136; analyzed Judaism as "classic," Christianity as "romantic," 26, 47, 96, 135, 141–47, 153; response to Harnack's *Essence of Christianity*, 137–38, 152; eagerness for dialogue and "polemic of silence," 138–39, 140, 148; emphasized Jewish background of Jesus and Jewish elements in Christianity, 6, 116, 146, 148–49; 150–52, 160, 175; on Paul and Paulinism, 142, 143, 152–56, 195; on medieval Christianity and the Reformation, 146, 148–49; his evaluation of Luther, 157–59. Works: *The Essence of Judaism*, 137, 138, 139, 148, 151, 156; "The Faith of Paul," 156; *The Gospel as a Document in the History of the Jewish Faith*, 26, 148; "Romantic Religion," 26, 96, 116, 140, 141, 142, 156

Balthasar, Hans Urs von, 185

Barabbas, 26

Bar Kokhba, 44, 219, 222

Barock Juden, Christen, and Judenchristen (Schoeps), 200